THE FIGHTING KINGS OF WESSEX

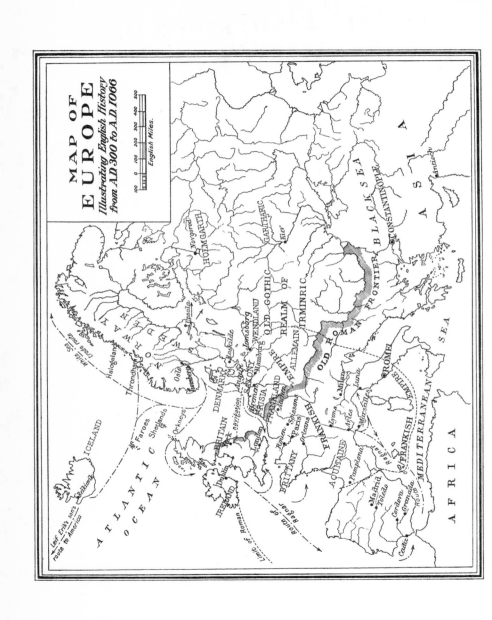

THE FIGHTING KINGS OF WESSEX

A Gallery of Portraits

G. P. Baker

COMBINED BOOKS
Pennsylvania

Originally published by G. Bell and Sons, Ltd., London in 1931.

Combined Books edition, 1996.

For information, address:
Combined Books, Inc.
151 East 10th Avenue
Conshohocken, PA 19428

Library of Congress Cataloging-in-Publication Data

Baker, G.P. (George Philip), 1879-1951.
    The fighting kings of Wessex / G.P. Baker.
        p.   cm.
    ISBN 0-938289-63-2 (hc : alk. paper). -- ISBN 0-938289-64-0 (pb.)
    1. Great Britain--History--Anglo-Saxon period, 449-1066. 2. Anglo-
-Saxons--England--Wessex--Kings and rulers--Biography. 3. Danes-
-England--Wessex--Kings and rulers--Biography. 4. Wessex (England)-
-Kings and rulers--Biography. 5. Great Britain--History, Military-
-449-1066. 6. Wessex (England)--History, Military. I. Title.
DA135.B24 1996   96-7109
942.01'6--dc20   CIP

Printed in the United States of America.

PREFACE

SINCE the outbreak of the Great War of 1914 the modern civilized man has seen a terrifying possibility before him, such as his father and grandfather never dreamed of—the possibility of the collapse of civilization. The most brilliant success of the war was not won on the battlefield. It was won in the counting-houses and exchanges of the world ; and it consisted in the skill and address with which civilization was steered through the dangers of economic collapse. Nothing at one time seemed likelier than that all our currencies might grow meaningless, all our credit begin to vanish and all our commercial relations become impossible. Civilized man flattered himself that the slaughter of millions of men was the really serious feature of the war. But civilization can survive far greater slaughters. What civilization cannot survive is economic disaster. Financial and commercial organization is the rainbow spell which holds together the irridescent enchantment of the civilized life. Once it fails—the whole thing has gone like a dream. And we were face to face with a possibility that this might happen.

It has, of course, happened in the past, as every student of history knows. The gulf which cuts us off from Roman civilization was just such a failure of economic function as this. The reader who blenches at the thought of reading a history of the Dark Ages may be reassured. He is not going to read of any " battle of kites and crows." He is going to survey the last occasion on which civilization actually did break down. There are two interesting features in such a survey. One is the way in which an old and powerful civilization can vanish ; the other is the method by which a new civilization begins.

It is the latter process which possesses the more serious and permanent interest for us : for this beginning of a new civilization is the perfect moment when we can see the absolutely fundamental principles at work. In every later stage of growth they are hidden ; at the present day they are lost amid the tremendous complexity which baffles all direct analysis. But in their beginning, there they are, isolated and visible.

The principles which govern the formation and evolution of civilization are not to be found by abstract theorizing. There is no Euclid of politics. They are to be found by examining the actual processes by which our world began and grew. History, not philosophy, is the original source from which correct political ideas may be derived. The apparatus of the philosophical sciences is only the means by which we test and verify our knowledge. And a clear acquaintance with these principles would save many men from disastrous errors, from disappointed hope and unnecessary frustration.

A full discussion of such things would mean not one, but a hundred volumes. The object of the present book is more modest. It is to illustrate a limited thesis : namely, that the kingship of England is not an organ of the State, created by a pre-existent body-politic to fulfil diverse functions of government, but is the original force which created the body-politic. The history of kingship in England consists of the actions by which successive kings first of all created the human community known as the English nation, and then, in the face of continually increasing difficulty, moulded it step by step until the nation which they had thus created took over the work of its own government and became, as we say, " self-determining " or self-governed'; though it only determined itself to be what they had made it.

There are other examples of the same process ; for

instance, the Athenian and the Roman states, and the
French nation. Kingship is the origin of every political
state ; and the most interesting political problem which
awaits solution is whether the process by which a state
repudiates its kings and takes charge of its own destiny
is an advance towards a higher political condition or is
a sign of decay and death. Hitherto the advocates of
the former opinion have had the advantage of numbers
and skill in stating their case. And yet one of the most
successful states in the world's history—the Roman—
actually went back to a modified form of kingship ; and
in every case in which special creative work has been
imperative, men have resorted to improvised varieties
of the personal rule of which kingship is the supreme
type : that is, to dictatorship.

The English kingship has special interest on several
grounds. It is almost the only surviving kingship whose
representative can trace his descent clearly back to the
ancient beginnings. King George V descends not merely
from a god, but from three gods : Woden, Geat, and
Sceaf. It is also the only one which has repeatedly and
successfully adapted itself to the crises and problems
which have been caused by the political evolution of a
great and growing state. The English kingship has,
moreover, from its earliest origins down to the present
day, been in the main singularly humane, enlightened
and careful of the welfare of its people. In days when
crowns have fallen more through neglect of certain
obvious human considerations than for any other reason,
it is worth while to remind ourselves that good feeling
is a good investment in the world of statesmanship.

It is to the English kings, rather than to any other,
that we must look for a solution of the problem, what is
to become of kingship. An institution that loses its
usefulness is little likely to survive ; but the English

kings have demonstrated so acute a perception as to where their function should lie at any given time, and so sound an instinct in seizing positions which they alone could fill, that we may perhaps look forward to a future in which they will once more prove themselves indispensable. And the more we suspect them of a future, the more carefully we ought to study their past to find the secret of it.

One rule prevails throughout all human society. The human community is a creation which is constructed from above. The idea that it is constructed from below, and receives its power by delegation, is a rare, an abnormal, and probably a transitional view, owing its existence now, as on former occasions, to an unusual combination of circumstances. It is an excellent doctrine that men at large should completely possess and fully enjoy all that the austere men of creative power have made for them. Democracy is sound, as a doctrine of enjoyment. It is not true, as a doctrine of creation. The people at large never invented all the modes of life which now feed them, guard them, and teach them. Nothing can ever belong to the community which was not first created by individuals. A republic is organized for the administration of an existent state rather than for the quality of design, invention, or creation which is necessary to advance. All creation is the work of an individual.

The history of early England has taken a new form of recent years, thanks to the patient and skilful work of a number of scholars who have combined the virtues of Porson with those of Sherlock Holmes. Perhaps the most acceptable of the improvements they have introduced is a more enlightened view of their material. Anyone who wishes to believe in the historicity of Ragnar Lothbrok can do so in good company. Scholars no

longer dismiss King Arthur as altogether a myth—least
of all as a sun-myth. Such genealogical descents as those
of the English kings from Woden are no longer regarded
as the amusing freaks of an ignorant age. Sir James
Frazer has taught us that they enshrine a sober meaning.
Perhaps few modern historians would now look upon
the imperial titles of the early English kings as mere
bombast and vanity. They seem, to a modern eye,
rather more like prophecy.

But there still remains ground to be won. A very
eminent scholar, in the course of a dissertation upon a
subject in which he is an expert, remarked that the
attribution of a conscious political tendency to early
Saxon annals verged, and perhaps more than verged,
upon anachronism. To which it must be answered that
all the living and progressive institutions of early English
society were political. All its living ideas were political.
Men who could speak such a language as Anglo-Saxon
were capable not only of political jealousy, but of hatred,
of intrigue, and of principle. And if we may judge by
their actions, men like the early Franks were capable
of anything.

Historians have frequently made demands upon our
incredulity which must be rejected. Men are to be
known by their deeds far more than by their words.
Words may be false : but actions—if persistent—tell a
true tale of the intentions of those who performed them.
And when we see these early statesmen, who left no
memoirs and very few personal records, carrying out,
over long stretches of time, stolidly and persistently,
great, systematic and logical schemes of action, then our
verdict must be that they intended them. A man does
not compose the Moonlight Sonata by accident.

Our remote ancestors, although they were frequently
guilty of murder, and sometimes of theft, do not seem to

have cared for adultery to an extent which would secure them a really wide reading public to-day. But this book, nevertheless, is no despicable raree-show. A book that includes, in one sweep, such tremendous personalities as Hengist, " King Arthur," Charlemagne, Ragnar Lothbrok, King Alfred, Archbishop Alphege, Olaf the Holy and Knut the Great, has respectable claims to call itself interesting, even if it confines itself to the more sober of the facts concerning them. In the year 1930 is the nine-hundredth anniversary of the death of King Olaf the Holy at Sticklestead. Perhaps the description in this book of his early career in England may be accepted as the writer's tribute to a very great man who profoundly influenced the history of both Norway and England.

G. P. B.

Elmer, Sussex
1930

CONTENTS

CONTENTS

CONTENTS

CONTENTS

MAPS AND PLANS

GENEALOGICAL TABLES

THE FIGHTING
KINGS OF WESSEX

CHAPTER I

THE POLITICAL PROPAGANDA
OF ALFRED THE GREAT

I

THE history of the English kingship begins suddenly,
amid a great confusion of battles, presided over by
one great dominating figure, the most dramatic, as he
was perhaps the most successful, of all the English kings—
Alfred the Great. We have not very much more than his
word for what had happened immediately before him,
or how he came to be the centre of the play. He edited
most of the previous history—such as it was—and coloured
it to suit his own policy. But during and after his reign
the tale becomes coherent and continuous. After gigantic
and heroic shadows have flitted obscurely to and fro,
the curtain abruptly goes up on a crowded stage, and the
play begins.

II

The account of himself handed down by Alfred,
through the pens of his writers and copyists, is that he
was the grandson of Egbert, the man who finally and for
ever united the inhabitants of England into one nation.
King Egbert had begun his career as king of the West
Saxons, in that part of England which is south of the
Thames and west of Winchester ; and he had extended
a more or less effective rule over the remainder of the

B

country. His predecessors, as described in the English *Chronicle* which Alfred caused to be prepared, are vague, and their deeds are briefly summarized. Even of Egbert, his own grandfather, who was undoubtedly a very real person, Alfred does not tell us much. Of his father, King Aethilwulf, Alfred tells us more. But Alfred himself is the first figure whom we know in detail, " in the round." And when we look attentively at the record, we see the reason. Alfred was the first to leave any statement or personal memoir which has reached us direct. Some gulf cuts his predecessors off from us ; a gulf across which the only hand is Alfred's.

And such a gulf exists. When Alfred, in the year 890, ordered the preparation of the English *Chronicle*, he was at peace after half a lifetime of strenuous warfare. He had several purposes in view. Complete devastation had destroyed some of the most civilized parts of England,[1] and in the holocaust many buildings of importance had perished with their contents. The records and archives which, in Alfred's youth, existed in plenty, had almost wholly disappeared. Unless he and his contemporaries, from what they knew and had preserved, took steps to perpetuate the history of their country, all effective knowledge of the subject might die out with that generation. But Alfred aimed at more than this. He felt the necessity of gathering together the broken threads of national life, and of re-establishing a tradition. Hence, he described the careers of the earlier kings in such a way as to reveal their significance rather than to tell their story. A most important aspect of the *Chronicle* was that it registered the origin of the English and the nature of their claim to England. Baeda had written

---

[1] Mr. Plummer (*Life and Times of Alfred the Great*, p. 13) mentions the Council held at Gloucester in 896 to settle questions of land tenure and the like. The spurious Saxon charters are due to attempts—often very necessary —to replace destroyed title deeds (Birch, *Cart. Sax.* Introd., p. xx).

the history, not of the English state, but of the English Church. His references to secular events are incidental to his main purpose. Alfred, on the other hand, intended his *Chronicle* to be a secular history, and he meant it to continue the story past the point at which Baeda had left it, and to give an outline of the process by which the England of Baeda became the England of Alfred.

III

For a considerable part of the facts, and alleged facts, which Alfred set down in the *Chronicle*, we have to rely upon his good faith, and upon the accuracy of the sources he accepted as authentic. His good faith so far has triumphantly survived all tests ; his sources have not always been quite so triumphant. The original basis round which he gathered the rest of his material was a Wessex Chronicle, or set of annals, preserved most probably at Sherborne. He expanded this from various sources ; of which some, no doubt, were old English songs and ballads ; some may have been oral traditions ; some statements were derived from Baeda, some from authors such as Orosius ; there were also ecclesiastical records, some of which have perished since Alfred's day, while others still survive. Out of such materials Alfred constructed his *Chronicle*, with the object of explaining himself and his methods, and of fixing in a permanent form the claims for which he contended.

IV

According to his information, Britain, once a possession of the Romans, had been definitely evacuated by them. The Britons, unable to hold their own against the Picts and the Irish, had invited the brothers Hengist and Horsa to enter their service. These powerful mercenaries, having settled thus peacefully and legally in Britain, and having conscientiously carried out the service for which they were engaged, were afterwards themselves involved in a war with the Britons. They sent for more help from the Angles, the Saxons, and the Jutes, and established themselves in possession of Kent somewhere about the year A.D. 449. East Anglia, Essex, Sussex, Northumbria, Mercia, and Wessex had afterwards been occupied in like manner and settled.

Each of these districts had been ruled by independent kings, who were subject from time to time to the supremacy of one among their number. This supremacy was a personal and variable authority. It did not belong by any legal right to the king of any particular section of the English. Aelle the South Saxon king had first held it : then Ceawlin the West Saxon, and next, Aethilbert King of Kent. For a short time East Anglia had been dominant. Northumbria had in turn become a very powerful kingdom which at one time dominated England. Last of all came Wessex. The struggle for supremacy among the petty kingdoms had been continuous from the beginning, and after it had favoured one or another in turn, Wessex had proved to be the victor in a contest predestined from the first to end in a united nation.

At the very moment of success, England had been stricken by catastrophe—the Danish invasions. The Danes had appeared in British waters at some time round about the year 800. Since then, another and a different struggle had been waged. It had ended in the Danish conquest of all England north of the Thames. Wessex—that is, England south of the Thames—survived. In this war, Alfred had himself played a leading part. To him, if to any man, was due the survival of Wessex.

Such were the claims which Alfred put forward in

the *Chronicle*. They were addressed to the English, not to the Welsh nor to the Danes. He desired to fix in the minds of the English the principle that the English were a nation, with a long past and possibly a great future ; that England belonged, by some valid and justifiable title, to the English, and that no Danish conquest conveyed any right in English soil. The importance and the sacredness of the English tradition were his theme. His children grew to manhood and womanhood under the impress of the idea that England must be reconquered, and that Wessex alone possessed either the power or the title to undertake the task. All the rights of the English were concentrated in the hands of the kings of Wessex.

When, therefore, the curtain rises on the drama of English kingship, we behold the English driven to their last ditch, and issuing their claim to possess a title to England such as none of their enemies could show. But before we go further, and trace the adventures through which this claim was triumphantly made good, let us inquire how far Alfred's nationalist propaganda corresponded with the real facts of the case.

V

To claim that England belonged to the English may seem like asserting a truism : but the justice of the claim was not, in Alfred's day, indisputable, nor undisputed. The Welsh vigorously disputed it, and put forward a counter-claim to represent the original British inhabitants dispossessed by the Saxon.

There has never been a time (at any rate in Europe) when the questions of legal title and moral right were unimportant in the eyes of men. They have in all ages had their share in moulding public opinion and in guiding the currents of human life. At their worst and weakest they have been powerful weapons in the hands of men who were seeking to escape from the compression of superior physical force. If Alfred took the trouble to derive a valid title from the rather uncertain status of Hengist in Britain, it was because the counter-claim of the Welsh was, if not rebutted, sufficiently strong to convey to others, who could enforce it, a title which the Welsh themselves could not enforce. The reality of this danger is attested by the fact that, some centuries after Alfred's day, the Normans actually did influence public opinion by claiming a title to England through the Welsh.

It will be clear enough, when we come to consider the story in detail, that the English conquest of Britain was not quite so simple as Alfred makes out, and as doubtless he believed it to be. The British were better organized and better led, put up a better fight, and had more influence upon the later course of events, than we might gather from Alfred's narrative. A succession of British over-kings—guletics, as the Welsh afterwards called them—anticipated the unity which Egbert established. If Alfred had lost the campaigns of 876 and 877, he and his predecessors would have disappeared from history very much as the guletics did. The Danes would have wiped out all trace of them, as the English erased the record of the British over-kings. But the guletics left their mark, even if not always their names. In one respect, particularly, they seriously affected the subsequent political development of England down to our own times. They conceived themselves to be, not barbaric usurpers, but the legitimate successors of the Roman emperors who had ruled in Britain.

However difficult it may be to point to any sufficiently formal and legal assertion of the theory that the guletics were successors to an imperial sovereignty, the assumption nevertheless runs through Welsh tradition and through a mass of rich legend which for many centuries the Welsh faithfully preserved—stories of British kings who were Roman emperors, who conquered Rome, and who were sometimes Romans. When, much later in date, we find English kings remaining in significant independence of the neo-Roman empire of Charles the Great and the Othos, and even putting forward a remarkable claim to an imperial independence of their own, it is a natural deduction that they learned the claim from the British guletics. Welshmen seldom make themselves ridiculous through a misplaced humility. They must have ground that imperial claim very resolutely into the consciousness of the earlier English, who, as heathen, may have been acutely aware of their disadvantage.

VI

The serious importance of this theoretical counterclaim—which might at any moment develop indirectly into a threat of a more concrete kind—was not matched by the material power of the Welsh. While the English power remained unbroken, the Welsh claim was little more than political antiquarianism. The English had effectively and permanently dispossessed, not perhaps the British inhabitants, but certainly the British owners. The reality—and to some extent the nature—of the English conquest is shown not only by such historical record as survives, but by the language, the institutions, and the place-names of England. The English conquest was a far more complete one than the Norman. Within five hundred years of the Norman Conquest, the Norman-French language had died out with those who spoke it : but five hundred years after the English Conquest, the English language was still creative, and was afterwards to prove its vitality by overcoming both Danish and Norman-French. Military conquests are often superficial and evanescent. The English conquest of Britain stands out as peculiarly successful in the way in which it assimilated the conquered into the social structure of the conquerors. Here, at least, the conquered were far from leading their conquerors captive. So far as effective occupation is concerned, Alfred can make out his case.

But there are features about the record that Alfred gave us in the *Chronicle* which raise interesting questions to an inquiring mind. The information missing from the *Chronicle* is information we should particularly like to possess. We should much like to know the circumstances in which the Roman city of Londinium passed into the hands of the English : but the *Chronicle* does not mention them. We should very much like to know how, why, and at what time the Roman garden-city of Calleva became a deserted waste for the owls and bats, crumbling slowly beneath the soil which now covers it. We should like to know what became of its citizens. Nearly a thousand years after Alfred, the archaeologists, spade in hand, found the ashes half-raked in the furnaces of the Roman bath at Letocetum, where the furnace-men had fled while drawing the fires : and at Uriconium they found the old man with his money box, who had crept into the hypocaust for refuge, and found it for ever. We should like to know why the first English in Britain had so great a horror of the Roman towns, that for generations they never built on the same sites. Alfred either did not know of these things, or did not think fit to tell us.

VII

The people who preserved for so many centuries the tale of Offa the Gentle, and the heroic tale of Beowulf, are not likely to have been incapable of preserving the thrilling tales of London and Calleva. The Welsh remembered the burning of Uriconium, though they had forgotten exactly when it happened. There are many curious questions connected with the English conquest which may never be clearly answered. Over them rests a silence none the less conspicuous because the written record which has been transmitted to us is in some cases obviously vague, and in others obviously false.

The bitterness of the Welsh is not altogether evidence in favour of the tradition that the English conquest was a cruel one. The earliest documentary evidence is contained in Gildas ; but much of it is rhetoric—with only occasional distinct assertions of fact. The modern historian seems to be coming round to the view that the Roman towns were largely deserted, and their municipal life dead, before the coming of the English. Their plunder can be dug up, if anywhere, nearer Antrim than Thanet. Something else, other than cruelty and devastation, seems to be implicit in the Welsh bitterness. That which the English wiped out with such success and completeness was not the material fabric of a civilization, nor the ordinary population which dwelt in it, but the social and political institutions of the British. Destruction and slaughter are soon forgiven and often forgotten : for after all, the people concerned in it are dead : but the dissolution and absorption of a social system is seldom forgotten and is never forgiven : for the people concerned live and remember and hate.

VIII

We gain support for the belief that the social and political, rather than the moral element was at the root of Welsh hostility, when we consider some of the problems connected with the English conquest. In what force were the English ? The *Chronicle* represents them as few in number, and their invasion as extending over a long series of years. It is certain that the conquest was slow. Even as late as the reign of King Edwin, the bounds of English Northumbria ran little further west than York—and that was two hundred years after the reputed landing of Hengist and Horsa in Britain. Bensington and Aylesbury in the Chilterns are said to have fallen in 571—a hundred and twenty years after the date of Hengist. The British and the English must have been near neighbours for many generations, their frontiers often slight and arbitrary. None the less, they influenced one another little, or not at all. The English advance, though slow, effectively wiped out the language, institutions, laws, customs, and traditions of the British. There was very little give and take. It was supposed, by the historical writers of a century ago, in the light of these facts, that the English actually exterminated the British. Since then, closer investigation has betrayed the fact that the modern population of England is still preponderantly British, and that the old English or " Saxon " type is rare, and only with great difficulty capable of identification.[1] Traces of British customs and social institutions survived in remote corners of the country until recent times. The truth would seem to be that a very rigid, powerful, and exclusive social system destroyed a weaker one. There was no extermination, and no influx of a numerous new stock. All that happened was that the British became thoroughly Anglicized.

Such a conclusion, however, drives us back upon

---

[1] As is well known, it is probably commoner in some parts of the United States than in England itself. The genuine Yank was often a typical Angle : though whether his virtues were always of the class which gave rise to St. Gregory's enthusiastic " non Angli, sed Angeli," must be left to the judgment of Americans themselves.

a fresh set of questions. What was this social system? What was the real significance of the theoretical claim of the Welsh and the effective claim of the English? What was the ultimate purport of the nationalist manifesto which was embodied in the English *Chronicle*? And while we are about it, who were the Danes, and what place did they occupy in the scheme of things? To answer these questions we must recede somewhat from Alfred and observe how he looks when seen in a wider perspective, with the world for his background.

IX

The age in which Alfred lived was governed by a dominating fact which conditioned everything it thought and did. No modern European or American very seriously questions that our age is one of advancing civilization, in which we are moving towards more abundant wealth, more profound knowledge, and more close-knit unity. But in exactly the same way, Europeans in the age of Alfred did not—and, indeed, could not—question that it was an age of decreasing civilization. The fact was far too glaring to be ignored or disbelieved : and it dominated the minds of men. For us to empty our minds of the familiar conditions of the twentieth century, and to see the world as it was in the ninth, needs an extraordinary effort of imagination. We have to realize not only that men looked back to a vast vanished civilization, a golden age of human achievement, but (and this is the difficulty) that they were actually right in doing so.

Alfred was a man who, though a king, dwelt in draughty and inconvenient wooden manor houses which an artist would have loved, but would not have wished to live in. He had no bathrooms, and no very adequate means of obtaining artificial light. His estates were cultivated by poor and imperfect methods ; their productivity was not large in amount nor varied in kind. His clothes were spun and woven by his own household. Though he ardently longed for knowledge, he had very few books, and lived in a world of men who for the most part could scarcely write their names, and who regarded an acquaintance with letters as both unnecessary and undesirable. Alfred needed to employ all his authority and influence as a king in order to find and assemble workmen who were capable of making those luxuries which are so necessary to the nobler kind of ritual in human society. A goldsmith or a book-illuminator was as rare as a king—perhaps rarer. He could not obtain things by ordering them. He spent most of his life in an exhausting struggle to persuade his subjects to live and work in harmony.

Only a robust outdoor man could endure the austerity of life in the ninth century. For such a man it was no doubt a very healthy life ; and it did not lack spiritual grace, sunshine, and beauty. Alfred was not robust. He suffered all his life from a malady to which no man could give a definite name, and which no one could cure. He would have been a happier and a healthier man for a few of those simpler luxuries which are commonplace to us.

Nevertheless Alfred lived, and knew that he lived, in the midst of the wreck of a vast civilization. England was covered with a network of magnificent roads, the like of which—as means of communication—were not known until the railroads of the nineteenth century : it was dotted with the ruins of stone-built and brick-built houses which had been warmed by central heating, and with the badly damaged remains of cities which had once been centres of industry and commerce. His own ancestral kingdom was a small part of one distant province of what had once been a vast empire ruled by great statesmen and protected by disciplined armies. Where he rode on a bob-tailed nag, followed by his scramble of hefty Wessex fighting men, the legions had once swung along with supply-train and siege-train and pioneers and sappers and artificers and auxiliaries—commanded, perhaps, by a man whose quarterly income exceeded the yearly revenues of Alfred, as far as effective purchasing power was concerned : a man who wore silk underclothing, and had a secretary to manage his correspondence. Alfred also had a secretary to manage his correspondence : but it was unfortunately for a different reason. He could not write.

The world had slipped. It had slipped and plunged into an abyss : possibly because it had been a very wicked world. But it certainly had slipped, whatsoever the cause might be : and Alfred was one of the men who were struggling to get back.

X

Alfred had no bad conscience over this matter. Neither he nor his ancestors had destroyed that wonderful world of civilized life. As he had been careful to indicate his forefathers had been invited into Britain after the Romans had left it. He had been careful, moreover, to see that a full genealogy of his father had been inserted into the *Chronicle*. These ancestors had been Angles and Saxons and—on his mother's side—Jutes. They came from Angeln across the sea—fierce, hard-bitten heathens, engaged in an incessant struggle with nature and their fellow-men. They had been glad enough to settle down among the wreckage of Roman Britain, and to reconstruct what imperfect fragments of it they could manage. Ever since, their effort had been to learn the secret of civilization, and to become civilized. Their success so far had not been great.

Alfred, if we may judge by his actions, took a sympathetic—but only an antiquarian—interest in that fierce old heathen atmosphere of war and hardship ; it could still blow a trumpet in his heart, and urge him on to effort ; but he did not want it back. He was divided, as were all Englishmen for a thousand years, between the spirit of adventure and the spirit of discipline and achievement. The ships and the swords haunted a mind which recognized the virtues of peace. It was just because of this duality of mood that the attempt to refound civilization proceeded so slowly. Everything had to be begun from the beginning. Men themselves had to be made, and their minds refashioned. The strength of the tradition which he received was a very significant promise for the future. The Welshmen might put forward what theoretical claim they liked ; the Danes might hold England from the Clyde to the Thames ; Alfred staked his faith on the English power that had no irrefutable theoretical right as against the Welsh, and no perfectly effective occupation as against the Danes. Somewhere, at the root of his motives, was the unreasoned conviction that he represented a cause indefeasible and predestined, that must be upheld to the death, but would probably triumph before that came.

There can be no greatness without that intense conviction. Alfred had no justification to show for it. Without knowledge of the future, he planted his banner of Englishry upon faith alone.

XI

The significance of Alfred's claim on behalf of the English amounted, therefore, to the assertion of their right, in virtue of some quality in themselves, to be the principal agents in the refounding of civilization, in despite of the legitimate claim of the Welsh. If we could put a name upon this quality, we should have described the English social system which absorbed and transformed the British.

The weaknesses which caused the downfall of the Britons are given by Gildas with a force and clarity in remarkable contrast with his usual vague rhetoric. Dissensions, party struggles, and private feuds had been the fatal faults which did all the damage : loyalty and unity had been the qualities which gave victory to the English. This latter was not the spirit of mutual faith which may distinguish a republican aristocracy. It was more primitive than that ; it was loyalty to one among their number. The association of the English was built upon the narrower but very elastic and powerful basis of kingship.

To experience a bond of this kind with one man only is a much easier mental feat than to feel it towards many. Kingship is a more elementary thing than aristocracy : and it has much more likelihood of strength. Loyalty to a king is possible to men who are not yet prepared for the harder accomplishment of equal association. It calls for the adaptation of men's minds to one other mind—not to many other varying minds. It has the strength which belongs to very simple things. Something of friendship enters into it ; something of reverence ; something of hero-worship, that most elementary and widespread of human peculiarities. The English certainly possessed it in great force. From it were derived one after another all their excellencies of social coherence in minor detail.

A force which could lend any people a strength and solidity so great as this was easily capable of wearing down and overcoming the very imperfect forms of association which were all that the British had managed to acquire from the Romans. It was also very easily related to the religious teaching of the Church. That high and spiritual devotion which Christianity taught towards its Lord was easily understood by men accustomed to a similarly exalted devotion in secular life ; and it formed, when adopted, a discipline further strengthening to the secular tie. Tradition is a very important element in all social bonds. The English possessed royal families of very old standing and very high qualities. The mere accumulation, through many generations, of a settled habit of respect and obedience towards them, added infinitely to their strength. By the very circumstances of the case, the British, after four centuries of Roman rule, possessed no royal families so thoroughly tested as the English.

When this tradition of kingship was combined with adherence to the Christian faith, it produced the attitude which Alfred assumed towards the Danes. He considered himself an integral portion of that civilized world the religion of which was Christianity. The Danes were heathen, and could be granted no lot in that heritage. Their aims were not its aims, nor their manners its manners. Neither in object nor in method had the two worlds ground in common. Hence a good many motives combined together to inspire that uncompromising resistance which Alfred showed towards the new invaders. He fought for his kingdom—which was a strong motive ; he fought for civilization, which was a higher motive ; he fought for the cause of God—and when a strong man begins to mix the inspiring vintage of religion with his motive, his courage can become as immovable as the hills.

XII

The English social system was thus constituted in essence by a very few men—the royal families and those kindreds who for generations had followed them. It was a centre without a circumference. That refounding of civilization, upon which Alfred was determined, originated with this narrow group. It could not have originated in any other way. To begin the construction of that infinitely complex web of human relationship and interdependence which we call civilization needs as its foundation an absolutely firm and united group of men, who can transmit across the generations an assured tradition, and can provide the will and the obedience to carry out the most arduous tasks. More especially in the circumstances of the ninth century, the formation of groups of men with interdependent relationships could not be carried out by mere amiable confederation. Any such groups so created would have been broken up by the stress of events as soon as they were formed. The way had to be cleared by a group of devoted and desperate men united in the most sacred bonds and by the most unswerving loyalty—men who walked with death and to whom the command of duty was absolute. At the head of such a group stood King Alfred—a wise, a frail, and a sick man of unbending courage and unwavering patience. We have seen what he knew and what he thought. It is time now to study the story.

CHAPTER II

THE GREAT CHANGE

I

THE reversion of Europe, from the highly organized state which it had attained under the Romans to the state of affairs which we find prevailing in King Alfred's day, is a wonderful and interesting change. We should find it hard to credit did we not know very certainly that it happened. The Fall of the Roman Empire has always been a subject to which the attention of men strays back with a fascinated curiosity. Moralists (always first in the field when disaster comes) preached about it even while it was happening. Political historians traced the events which accompanied it. Edward Gibbon's mighty work is one of the most splendid monuments which ever commemorated what he called the crimes and follies and misfortunes of mankind. Even while civilization fell to pieces around them, contemporaries did not admit that the cord of continuity was cut. The modern scholar sees that in this they were very largely, if not wholly, justified. Something had unmistakably fallen in irretrievable ruin ; something persisted unquenched and unquenchable. What had fallen was the material fabric and external organization ; what survived was the spiritual doctrine and the intellectual principles which mould them.

Every age is liable to economic troubles. The fall of the Roman Empire was an economic collapse so prolonged and so severe, that from it there was no recovery. The industrial and the financial system, the middle classes which embodied its activity, almost the whole urban life of civilization died out ; the military system was involved in the ruin, leaving the agriculturist poorer, more isolated, more defenceless, deprived of some of his markets, but otherwise pretty much as he had been. The government, without revenue, and without the power to make its control effective, gradually disappeared.

II

The difficulty we have in grasping the causes of this process is not due merely to a lack of sympathetic imagination ; for the men who suffered its terrors were even less able than we are to explain why it happened. The conviction of stern moralists that it was God's punishment for wickedness ; the persuasion of cultivated old gentlemen that it was due to neglect of the grand old principles of good taste ; the apprehensions of some that the end of the world was at hand ; the certainty of soldiers that they could soon put matters right if they had sole control ; the prayers, persuasions, exhortations, and infuriated threats of the government to induce men to hold together and carry on—all this still survives in books which few except special students ever read. The real difficulty lies in the complex inter-relation of the political and economic events which ended in the breakdown.

The expansion of one great civilization throughout the known world had been a process only possible through the enterprise of a very vigorous commercial system, and the discipline of a very powerful political control. The political government had for the most part followed on the footsteps of economic enterprise, organizing and making permanent the relations that had begun as commercial relations, stabilizing and protecting, according to the lights of the age, the nexus of mutual advantage that had spontaneously arisen. It is easy to criticize the proceedings of the Roman government, but it is less easy to demonstrate that any other government could have accomplished the work of unification. Its final product was an organized world-state which profoundly impressed the imagination and the moral sense of mankind. Such as it was, it was the highest achievement of the social spirit of humanity. In its search for justice and for peace, and in its pursuit of those spiritual and intellectual activities which are the fruit of ordered life, it immeasurably transcended the untamed, uncivilized world which had preceded it, and by the remains of which it was ringed. A great gulf separated the world of civilization from the wild world of natural man and unbridled competition. Men forgot its faults and remembered only its virtues.

III

This final form of the Roman state was reached after contests which permanently injured the fabric of civilization. Some of the problems of organization proved insuperable. The failure of his predecessors to reach any better solution induced Caesar to turn for his own alternative to a system of monarchy based upon a military guild. Although it secured several centuries of peace and good administration, the imperial monarchy so established was never completely in harmony with the economic power. Through a long series of political struggles from Tiberius to Constantine, self-defence forced it first to limit the freedom of the economic power, and then to organize the state with a rigidity which was a cause of serious weakness. We might count other sources of weakness ; that worship of security and comfort which resulted in the expenditure of wealth more upon those things which gratified the senses than upon those which nourished human power ; the abandonment of agriculture more and more to semi-servile classes which did not share in the healthy tradition of citizenship ; the diminution, therefore, both in the number and the quality of those upon whom the state could rely to carry the burden of trouble when hard times came. All the weaknesses of Roman civilization combined their forces when the disasters of the third and fourth century fell upon it. The margin of safety was insufficient. The plague, brought back from the East by the legions of Marcus Aurelius ; vast ethnic migrations out of Asia, which no man had foreseen, and consequent military pressure upon the frontiers : these were the first shattering blows. The breaking of the frontiers ; general war and disorganization ; incalculable damage to the agriculture and commerce of the provinces followed ; and though the emperors pulled affairs straight and restored order, they could not make good the damage that had been done. Their remedy was the military remedy of sterner discipline and more rigid organization : but these things did not help the agriculturist and the merchant. The economic condition of the empire slipped slowly down. It was this economic slip which was the danger. Everything else could have been saved, if this could have been saved : but the rescuers themselves needed to be helped by the rescued—and locked in this desperate paradox Roman civilization sank slowly into the gulf.

IV

The history of the fall of Roman civilization in Britain cannot be told entirely from British sources. But the general tendencies at work were everywhere the same, and the story of Britain can be filled out from the tale of other countries—and can in turn illustrate them.

Notwithstanding the double sack of Rome by the

Visigoths and the Vandals, Rome did not fall to military conquest. Even if a false economic theory of consumption, rooted in a false moral ideal, undermined the strength of the Roman world, that world did not fall because of luxury or idleness. It is an old and familiar story that the gilded youth of civilization can hold its own with the hairiest cave-man. Roman civilization fell from two principal governing causes, to which the rest were subsidiary. The economic collapse was the first and immediate cause : but its effects were deepened and made irremediable by another, to which we will return in a moment.

The remote origin of the economic collapse was in the strangle-hold which the imperial government was obliged to keep upon its senatorial opponents. In limiting the amount of liquid capital which might be held by one person it just sufficiently tied the hands of the financial men to prevent any exuberant enterprise. Now, we must remember that the system which we know as slavery, while it gave the owner of capital the power to cut wages to their lowest limit, could not give him the power to cut them below a certain level which was indicated by the cost of reproducing the workman. Simultaneously, it saddled him with the responsibility for keeping his work-people whether there was work for them to do, or not. In the settled days of the empire, the supply of labour, servile or free, had become stable. There was no longer any method of deluging the labour market with an indefinite number of hands. Hence the employer tended to become cautious in his operations. Every one of these conditions tended to set up and perpetuate a certain rigidity in the economic structure—a characteristic which distinctly increased with time. The system became one which grew to depend continually more and more upon the sharp division of trades, the closed and privileged guild (often hereditary) which held, developed, and transmitted the entire body of knowledge connected with the craft. There are conveniences in such a system. It is easy to control ; and it is therefore acceptable to comfortable men who are not bitten with any rage for adventure.

But the destruction of such guilds involved the extinction of the knowledge they embodied. It is not necessary that a whole nation should be exterminated in order to bring about its economic collapse when it depends on a system such as this. The first serious breaches would so far involve the general structure that a progressive degeneration, impossible to prevent or stem, would be the natural result. Even the death of certain individuals might mean the extinction of essential functions, the creation of gaps, which nothing could ever make good.

There is no reason to suppose that the Roman system in Britain differed in any marked way from that which was usual elsewhere in the empire ; and there is evidence that it followed the common model. Romano-British civilization needed peace and protection from violence as the first condition of its continuance. From the moment that effective violence reached it, it began to disintegrate. By a natural logic which nothing could prevent, it dissolved away.

V

The men who dealt the deadly blow at Roman Britain were the famous " Picts and Scots." We need to rid our minds of any impression, left upon them by the schoolbooks of an earlier generation, that the Scots came from what we nowadays know as Scotland, or that they were hairy savages bedaubed with blue paint and gnawing bones in caves. The Scots were Irishmen ;

and they were, if not the renowned Fianna of Finn mac Cumhal, then men indistinguishable from them : [1] that is to say, they were splendid fighting men, organized and disciplined, who obeyed great kings and were led by famous fighting chieftains—those great tawny men, with their golden torques and bracelets, their weapons hilted with ivory and silver, their enamelled targets, proud war-horses, and huge deerhounds, who flash, with perhaps a touch of poetic magic, across the oldest Gaelic legends.

The Irish had harried Britain from time to time, with greater or less success. Their most serious invasion took place in the year 367, in the days when the Goths were first proving their importance in the eastern provinces of the empire. This invasion went far beyond anything that they had hitherto achieved. They devastated Britain almost from end to end ; the destruction which they wrought was huge, calamitous, and incalculable. When Theodosius, the father of the emperor of that name, arrived on a special mission to deal with British affairs, the Irish had already retired with their loot ; but he found sporadic raiding parties even in the neighbourhood of London.

Some hint of how Calleva came to be a deserted ruin may be found in the fact that an Irish Ogham inscription has been found scratched on the stonework of the Roman city.

Theodosius saw that order was restored, and that all unauthorized persons were cleared from the country. But the blow had been given. From that day onward,

---

[1] The Irish chroniclers date Finn's life time a century earlier : but the firm and assured tradition that the time of the Fianna extended into the days of St. Patrick is as good evidence of their real date as the calculations of the chroniclers. In this case, the " men of Lochlann " were not Northmen, but English. We hear little more of the Scots after the days of Hengist, and there is no mistaking the fact that the Fianna concluded their career under a cloud.

Britain was staggering beneath the effects of it, unable to recover.

One catastrophe worked hand in hand with another in those days against Roman civilization. The imperial government would not have failed to deal effectively with the situation in Britain, had not its hands been tied by the development of the Gothic wars nearer home. The precise date and circumstances of the Roman evacuation of Britain are very doubtful, and it is now perhaps impossible to determine them with exactitude. But it seems certain that at some date during the struggle with Alaric the government notified Britain that it could expect no help, and must take its own measures. On some definite communication of this kind the Welsh based their claim to be the residuary legatees of Roman authority.

As far as we know, Britain was never reoccupied. What kind of government survived, or arose in Britain, we have no clear information.[1] If the " British Cities," to whom the rescript was addressed, had any importance, it was rapidly lost. The traditions embodied in later chronicles hint at an unsettled state of affairs—local kings in at least southern and western Britain, who were half Roman and half British ; over-kings who claimed rights over the whole land in virtue of Roman precedent ; governments that could not achieve a perfect foothold, nor organize the country. Some necessary connection had been dislocated.

[1] Sir Charles Oman's theory is that by 400 the west of Britain was already, with the approval of the Roman government, providing for its own defence. This would account for the strong stand which this part of Britain later on made against the English (*England before the Norman Conquest*, p. 171 *et seq.*). A definite kingship was being set up by Cunedda and his sons in Wales and the west, which proved to possess far greater strength than the Romanized east of Britain.

VI

Such—varying the names, and allowing for a certain amount of difference in detail—was the story of nearly all the Roman provinces of the west. The express peculiarity of Britain was that the inhabitants claimed the benefit of a formal evacuation, a legal extinction of sovereignty on the part of the Romans.

Men who have lived all their lives amid the impregnable security of settled institutions are liable never to know how hard it is to found them, or to hold them together when all is crumbling into disorder. Habit and tradition play so great a part in their maintenance, that, when these are lost, and we must start anew, we realize with a shock how little the social order is ingrained in mankind—how instinctively men refuse to be organized, and decline either to be led or to be driven.

The case of the British might have been different if knowledge and training had been so diffused that gaps could always be filled by the promotion of intelligent amateurs. There were no amateurs. There were no men who knew enough to carry on. Hard as the existence of the amateur may sometimes be upon the professional, he nevertheless forms a reserve which is of essential importance to civilization at large. Once civilization is so rigidly organized that the destruction of any of its functioning parts is irreparable, it is practically doomed. Before long some eye will penetrate the secret, and, when the chance comes, wreak the mischief that all the king's horses and all the king's men can never again make good.

VII

But behind the economic collapse of civilization under the Roman empire lay a weakness deeper than the economic. Even an economic collapse might have been grappled with and overcome, had any body of men existed who were united with that coherence which had distinguished the ancient aristocracy and the later oligarchy of Rome.

The economic collapse provided a touchstone by which to test some obscure but essential elements in the condition of Europe. When the economic level of Roman civilization was reduced to a point at which the barbaric tribes of the north could meet Roman armies on something like equal terms, the result was an extraordinary mingling of peoples and institutions. Vandals from the shores of the Baltic found themselves in northern Africa ; Visigoths from the Vistula were living side by side with Roman senators in southern Gaul and in Spain ; Ostrogoths from south Russia fought in Italy with Langobardi from the Elbe, led by a Syrian ; Franks from the Rhine and Burgundians of Central Europe were inextricably mixed with Romanized Gauls ; Angles and Frisians and Romanized Britons with Picts of Fortrenn and Irish Gaels. All handicaps were off. Civilized man could no longer depend upon the special advantages that hitherto had given him a long start in the race for success. His victory now must depend exclusively upon his primary virtues—his original qualities as a man.

Let us at this point remind ourselves of the real nature of these primary virtues of the human being. They do not reside in physical strength nor in ruthless will. The race is not to the swift nor the battle to the strong. When the legends and epics of that age came to be written down, their theme proved to be the tragedy of defeated heroes, the sorrowful tale of the strong man who fell to the weak men, and of the swift man who arrived too late. In that age, at least, victory was not to the cunning ; for no legend is more persistent than

the story of the wise man who stumbled and fell. The
primary quality of man as man is his social quality : his
capacity for living and working adequately with other
men, adjusting his mind to theirs, and maintaining
certain faith and unbroken loyalty.

This truth came home tragically to the actors in the
complex drama which was fought out over the ruins
of Roman civilization—and usually it came too late.
When the imperial troops of Belisarius rode into Ravenna,
the enraged Gothic women are said to have spat in the
faces of their husbands at the sight of the men who
had beaten them. Totila understood the truth. If the
virtues of the prize-ring could give men success, King
Teia would have saved the Ostrogothic kingdom in
Italy. If mere Machiavellian craft could have worked
the trick, the eunuch Narses would have risen to be lord
of the world. But none of these things sufficed.

On the secular side of the struggle, civilized man
emerged badly. Long dependence upon his advantages
had destroyed the qualities which had created them.
One truth at least stood out with marked emphasis.
Over the question of reconstructing the secular power,
some of the minor kingships of the north could produce
a social group more solidly united and more powerful
in action than any group created by the Romans. Two
in particular may be noted—the English monarchy and
the Frankish. These two were destined to be the foundation of the new world that was to arise.

VIII

But the Roman world, which could create no secular
group of power equal to these, could produce a religious
group capable of holding its own. The Roman Church
seemed to be the repository of all the moral force which

had once given Rome its universal dominion. If Rome could no longer wield armies or the power of finance, she could wield something even deeper and more effective—ideas. We must forget all thought of religion as a poetic sentiment or a pleasantly insoluble subject for debate, when we think of the Roman Church of this age. The Church was a fighting organization, whose task was, without weapons or physical force, to reimpose upon mankind the scale of values which is the spiritual aspect of civilization. And for its purpose these values had to be unbendable, unalterable, and absolute.

Out of the chaos which followed the fall of the Roman state in western Europe we can therefore perceive two kinds of power emerging. The kingship of the northern peoples was the only secular power capable of recreating the secular state and reorganizing the practical activities of men. But it was indeterminate. It proved capable of going anywhere and doing anything ; but it had nowhere to go and nothing to do. It was willing and even anxious to be given a purpose. It admired the fabric of civilization which lay shattered around it ; it had never had the opportunity to possess such great gifts, which had vanished unexpectedly just at the very moment when it might have seemed possible to seize them. It wished to learn the secret of Roman greatness. The Church was all purpose and no power. It could confide the secret of Roman greatness. It could—and it intended to—give determinate point and purpose to the powerful secular kingship.

The Church was, of course, scarcely dealing with woolly lambs in the persons of these English and Frankish kings. The Roman military man, and the cultivated Roman civilian with his tradition of delicate literary paganism, had often been difficult to deal with ; but the northern kings, the victors of a struggle for survival which still bore traces of the natural world of the wolf and the wildwood, were much more formidable material. Their wonderful advantage was their malleability. Caught in that critical moment of transition, when they had drifted out of their heathen world into one that was still in principle, at least, civilized, they could be moulded as the tough old hard-set material of the Roman world never could be. For centuries they were to remain a difficult problem : fierce, manslaying, polygynous men with a genial and generous side to them, a mixture of good and evil, baffling to the moralist. It was of little use presenting such men with poetic ideals or hazy sentiments. They had only too much of these already. Doctrine, hard, definite and unbending was what they needed. They got it. The Roman Church, with the tradition of Roman law behind her, presented them with a faith once delivered to the saints and not now to be tampered with. That faith might sometimes be forgotten, but it was never changed.

IX

The disappearance of the commercial and industrial classes of Roman civilization left the world to the agriculturist. There are, probably, no circumstances (short of the absolute savagery of the " Food Gathering " stage) in which the craftsman and the merchant are not to be found in the human community ; and every agricultural village needs its smith, its carpenter, and its pedlar, whether as permanent members or as journeymen who visit it on periodical occasions. But there is fundamental distinction between such commerce and industry as this and the system of special production for a competitive market which prevails in civilized lands. The ancient world shared with the modern all those features which we familiarly know as " capitalism " : the com-

petitive market, the division of labour, the mass-produc-
tion of commodities, the buying and selling of money
and credit. The fall of this system left Europe a land of
self-sufficing agricultural estates. Much as these might
vary in detail, they followed one another in their self-
sufficingness.

Not very much evidence has survived concerning
these estates in Britain ; but on the Continent they were
usually large. The largeness of the estates which covered
Roman Europe was due not only to economic but to
political causes. For a century before the final catastrophe, the government was compelled to impose higher
and higher taxation, and to exact its payment with ever
increased rigour. The result was the destruction of many
of the old proprietors of standing, and a general movement to sell out to men who were prepared to take the
responsibility of dealing with the revenue authorities.
This did not mean the creation of great uniform estates
(" ten thousand acres in a ring fence ") farmed on one
system by their owner, but rather the accumulation of
remarkable congeries of mixed properties, the old and
real owners of which hid behind the protection of a
nominal and legal owner. Such a system often has great
advantages for everyone concerned. The legal owner
was rich enough and powerful enough to stand up to
the government. With the change of times and days,
he took over the task of standing up to the new kings,
and, at least in southern Gaul, he served as a useful
intermediary between the king and the agricultural
producer. In Aquitaine, the old Roman proprietor of
this type survived to become the haughtiest of feudal
seigneurs, woven into the social fabric with a multitude
of various rights, customs, and relations to those below
him and those above him. Often however—and in
Britain, almost universally—the Roman proprietors had

to give way to new men, who were installed in their places by the kings.

Whether the old proprietor survived, or whether an Englishman or a Frank stepped into his place, alike in either case these great holders became ever less of economic and ever more and more of political importance. They interfered hardly at all with production ; they did little to make the tenures uniform or systematic. Beneath the cover of their existence, the agriculturist pursued his own way, and was guided by the terms of his own occupation.

X

The political evolution of Europe was profoundly influenced by this characteristic. In spite of the largeness of the estates that might be held by one man, no strong general influence was at work. A purely agricultural society is subject to a number of social troubles peculiar to itself. It almost inevitably tends to break up into smaller and smaller units, as if it were crumbling into sand. It grows progressively more and more a collection of small isolated bodies, simply aggregated together without any real interdependence. It develops ever more local separatism. Its component units tend to develop customs of their own, varying widely, and whatsoever was originally common becomes individualized and differentiated. We can see this tendency clearly enough in later centuries, under feudalism : but in the days when feudalism was systematically described by jurists, the tendency was already towards great national unities. In these earlier days of which we are now thinking, the tendency was all to differentiation. Latin itself was not only breaking up into the Romance languages, but even into dialects of them. English itself broke into dialects.

Commerce and industry are binding forces which bring men upon common ground, give them mutual interests, and unify their customs and habits. A society which has no commercial system, but creates all its products locally, has no binding force which can hold it together. It cannot act collectively. It ends by forgetting how to think and feel collectively. It can be, sometimes, a warm, cosy, contented life, in which men thoroughly enjoy their freedom to drift passively upon the current of their own irresponsible idiosyncrasies. But if human society and its common life have any spiritual gifts to give men, such conditions as these are not the conditions under which they can be received.

XI

This crumbling of society into small local units was an additional reason why it was upon the northern kingship that political revival almost exclusively depended. No circumstances similar to those of the ancient city-states brought a sufficient number of men into the close daily contact which will in time unify them into an aristocracy [1] : and in those cases in which the circumstances rendered this otherwise possible, the time was too short. The royal groups of the north had meanwhile, being ready-made unities, obtained a start which put them ahead of their competitors. Least of all was any such thing as democracy possible save for the most limited and local purposes. All the conditions of the old Roman agricultural system conspired to prevent it from developing political powers out of its own resources. The very methods by which the former government had kept control of its subjects rendered them, when the control was removed, liable to break up into small units.

[1] The exceptions are the Italian cities, e.g. Venice.

The stress of life in the catastrophic days which followed still further broke them up, interrupted communication and prevented common action. We need not feel surprise, therefore, if after the economic collapse which wrought so vast a change in the aspect of civilized Europe, its people were unable to create among themselves any effective secular government, and that power drifted rapidly into the hands of the only social groups which were ready and able to wield it—the kingships of the north.

CHAPTER III

THE DIVINE KINGS OF THE NORTH

I

THE social ancestry of the English was a very respectable one. In common with all the peoples of northern Europe, they had been organized on the tribal system : an old and honourable model which, in its day, had known many varieties, and many degrees of efficiency. By the beginning of the Christian era the old system had somewhat declined from its ancient wealth and splendour. Ever since contact had first been established with Roman political civilization, in the days of Caesar's wars in Gaul, the tribal system had been steadily decaying. The Roman invasions of Germany and the failure of the tribal leaders to deal with them, had shaken its prestige. The example of Roman institutions—and especially of that particular institution with which the northern peoples came into closest and most decisive contact—the military guild with its semi-divine head— had provided a new and profitable model for imitation. Migration, trade, military service—the overflow of an expanding population—shook the domestic power of a social system which depends, for its effectiveness, much upon peace and tradition. All the events which, for four hundred years, had shaken central and western Europe, had tended partly to discredit and partly to supersede the tribe : and at the time when the English entered Britain it is probable that their own tribal institutions were in an advanced stage of disintegration. As was no doubt the case in all the great migrations of that age, the change had been amply sufficient to strain the tribal organization past its power to recover, and to throw control into the hands of those men—the kings— who represented the new political form of social structure.

The native British system was in no better case. There had been a time when the British also had been organized on a tribal system : and fierce Welsh mountaineers for centuries after the English conquest kept their ancient institutions more or less intact. But wheresoever the British system had been in contact with Roman civilization, the tribe had tended to dissolve before the influence of political institutions. Hence society at large was no longer a powerful and stable structure in the old tribal sense ; and it had not yet become one in the later political sense. Standing in transition from one form to the other, it was weak, delicate, in danger of destruction by the first foe, unable to act strongly or decisively—a loose, ramshackle, disintegrating, purposeless thing, whose advantages had vanished, but whose faults remained. Amid this process of dissolution one thing stood out as a clear, simple, and definite force— indeed the only real force to be found in the community —the kingship.

II

Perhaps the accidental contact of social customs drawn from an old system and a new was responsible for the change undergone by the idea of monarchy when it was taken up by the North Europeans. The royal group, which for centuries past had been establishing itself in imitation of the imperial Roman monarchy,[1] was a strictly political construction. That is to say, it did not

---

[1] The real effect of the Roman influence can be seen from the case of Ireland, where it was absent. The Irish kingship remained tribal, and no strong political organism was ever created in Celtic Ireland. The whole subsequent history of Ireland was influenced by this fact.

depend upon blood-relationship for any considerable part of its power. Nevertheless it was affected by tribal custom. Whether the practical disadvantages that attended the principles of co-optation and election in the model influenced the views of the copyists, we cannot tell ; but it is certain that the operation of the principles was modified by a custom drawn direct from the older system. The right to the kingship became an exclusive privilege of certain families.

The evolution of Roman monarchy into the northern kingship was determined largely by the influence of tribal customs. The kings of the English—like those of the Goths, Swedes, Danes, and Norwegians—made what seemed to later ages the extraordinary claim that they were descended from gods. This divine descent, however, was neither imaginary nor unmeaning. It was real, in that they do seem to have been directly descended from priest-kings who were regarded as incarnations of the gods whom they served and represented. Such priesthoods were usually the privileges of tribal castes. There may have been a good deal of variety in the exact processes by which the members of these sacred castes became the heads of military guilds [1] ; the fact remains that the old religious chiefs were transformed into kings whose work was political.

Such sacred descent could not give them a power they were not able independently to make good by their own force of character ; but it fulfilled, whether by accident or design, a most urgent need and a most

[1] See Chadwick, *Origin of the English Nation*, pp. 174–5. The Goths, according to Jordanes, said that they (i.e. their eponymous tribal caste) came from Sweden. The Langobardi show many signs of a Scandinavian ancestry. The genealogy of the kings of Deira consists of almost pure Scandinavian names. The early history of north-western Europe seems, indeed, to consist chiefly of the formation of political organizations around nuclei which, when examined, prove to be Scandinavian sacred tribal castes.

indispensable function in the scheme of politics. When
Gaius Julius Caesar the dictator was contemplating the
foundation of the imperial Roman monarchy, he sought
to isolate the monarchy and to exclude it from competition. He himself could claim descent from Julius and
from Aeneas, and therefore, remotely, from gods ; but
the remoteness of the claim, and the cheery scepticism
of an educated and civilized world, were drawbacks to
its effectiveness. Caesar's successors attempted to reach
the same end by the method of posthumous deification ;
but the western emperors never succeeded in putting the
monarchy beyond the reach of damage by competition,
and the worst political disasters of later Rome were due
to the feasibility of asserting pretensions which had no
ground but the power to enforce them.

The northern kings started with advantages denied
to Caesar. Their divine descent was not remote ; and
it was accepted as a matter of course by their subjects.
Alfred himself—a devout Christian—did not hesitate
to insert his father's divine pedigree into the *Chronicle*.
According to the genealogy he gave, King Aethilwulf—
and therefore Alfred also—was descended not from one
god only, but from three : Woden, Sceaf, and Geat.[1]
The existence of these old heathen divinities, and of
their cults, is known independently of Alfred ; and
there is reason for accepting his pedigree without serious
question. The effect, which was far more profound in
heathen and tribal days, was to achieve precisely those

---

[1] Woden was apparently a Celtic god, connected with the number 9 and
with ruling Celtic tribes which settled in the north : he became the typical
god of Scandinavian political kingship. Sceaf was an agricultural god of
the Danish islands. Geat is probably Saxon, and may be ultimately Swedish.
The three names together indicate that King Alfred's forefathers united the
claims of Scandinavian, Danish, and Saxon royal houses. By these gods
the reader is to understand the priests who represented them, and who bore
their names. Beowulf himself (*cf.* Clarke, *Sidelights on Teutonic History*, ch. i)
shows signs of having been the incarnation of a bear-god.

objects at which Caesar had aimed. It circumscribed
competition and it secured a legal title to the succession.
To buy or to snatch a crown became almost impossible.
In virtue of these limitations the northern kingship
became infinitely more stable than its model.

III

But although it owed so much to the tribal system,
the kingship derived all its practical power from its
political, not from its gentile construction. It grew in
strength through its remorseless policy of seeking out the
best men it could find, and of organizing them into what
the Romans called a " comitatus " or companionship.
The comitatus was the secret of kingship.[1] Its members
were chosen from any source, and their personal attain-
ments were the sole qualifications taken into account.
They had no mutual relations : they had relation only
to their chief, the king, on whom they absolutely depended.
Their protection was that he, in turn, depended for his
power solely upon them. Political society evolves direct
from this comitatus, or companion-group. The modern
European state is an expansion, complication, and
specialization of this primitive group.

Out of the companion-group the kings drew their
ministers, their delegates, their military organizers, and
" special service " men. The devotion of the companion
to his lord became something famous and immortal,
hymned in somewhat of the same strain that the psalmist

[1] Professor Chadwick has described at length the construction and
importance of these chosen Companion-groups (*Origin of the English
Nation*, pp. 166–74). He did not exhaust the evidence. The comitatus is
somewhat misunderstood if we look upon it as a " body-guard." It really
included all the men who were necessary to the work of the king and who
stood to him in a certain sworn relation. The " Prince " in the old fairy
stories, with his varied circle of helpers—including magicians and Wise
Beasts—is the type !

addressed to his God, or the mediaeval troubadour to
his lady's eyebrow. It was by no means an irrational
sentiment. Kingship was the medium through which a
new conception was revealed to northern Europe—the
" career," the individual reward for individual merit.
Tribalism had been, with all its virtues, an old man's
affair, conducted by seniority and by tradition. Kingship
found a place for the young man, and pay for him.
The idea of the career open to talent was fundamental
to kingship, as it had been to the Roman monarchy. It
formed the magnet which drew to the kings all the brains,
energy, and ability which were to be found in northern
Europe.

The position of the king as paymaster of vigorous
and ambitious men made his financial aspect a very
important one. He was, moreover, the heir to the
Roman custom of pensioning off veterans with gratuities
or with grants of land—a custom as old at least as the
days of Marius. The fund out of which these responsibilities were discharged was the king's own property. It
was constituted by a number of payments which at this
early stage were still private contracts rather than legal
liabilities—charges for the protection of land or goods,
for the enforcement of justice and the like. Spoil of war
similarly passed into the king's possession ; and most
of it remained there. Naturally enough, he would
almost certainly be a landowner in his own right ; and
as his own land would be particularly well protected,
we might expect it to be especially prosperous. Out of
this revenue—all of it private property—he equipped his
followers. In so far as this equipment represented
capital expenditure, he regarded it as still his own.
The unconsumed remnant of his equipment returned to
him on the death of his servant. This was the " heriot,"
as it came to be called.

To leave the deep permanent mark it left upon later

theories of politics and laws of property, this principle
must originally have been held in the most rigid and
uncompromising form, over a long period of time. The
king was an owner of capital ; his property was the source
of all the wealth held by the Companions. They very
often had nothing else.

IV

Neither record nor tradition has preserved any
account of the steps by which the new kingship spread
into the far north of Europe.[1] Among the monarchies
which grew up was the English,[2] on the eastern coast of
the Danish peninsula, just where, opposite the islands,
the broken coast turns round towards Mecklenburg—
between Flensborg and Slesvik, north of Kiel Bay, which
is still marked " Angeln " on the map. They were close
neighbours of two other peoples—the Swaefe[3] to the
south-east, and the Langobardi to the south. The
Swaefe gave their name to the Swabian Germany of the
Middle Ages. The Langobardi drifted to Italy and set
up there as the dreaded " Lombards." The English
were to go another way.

On the west coast, fronting on the North Sea, were
Saxons, known to the Romans in earlier times as

[1] Apparently, however, it spread by a north-easterly route, across the
upper Danube, through the old dominion of Marbod, to that vast continental Gothland which is now Poland. There Irminric founded his
kingdom : and kings from that region seem about A.D. 300 to have established kingdoms in and about Slesvik, from which arose the English, Saxon,
and Danish monarchies. The Frankish was almost the last to arise. The
Swedish had an independent growth ; and the evolution of the Norwegian
kingship can be read in detail in the first two books of Snorri's *Heimskringla*.

[2] The inhabitants of England have never, in historic times, called
themselves Angles with an A. They call themselves English. The word
must originally have been indistinguishable from the Scandinavian Yngl
(in " Yngling "), and was a tribe or caste name, not a territorial.

[3] I.e. the Suevi, of whom the chief were the Semnones. Tacitus
regarded the Angili as belonging to the Semnones, and Ptolemy calls them
the " Suevi Angili " : from which we may conclude that the Angles were
at one time under Suevic domination.

"Chauci." The Chauci had come into profitable contact with Rome, had served in her armies, and had seen Tiberius himself among them. They had been in close association with their Frisian neighbours, who had watched and absorbed the lessons furnished by the Roman fleets of Drusus, Tiberius, and Germanicus, and who had begun the first experiments in ship-building and sea-raiding which were destined to change the military situation in Europe. From the year 286 onwards the Saxons bulked larger and larger on the horizon of the peoples to the south and west. Their raids extended to the Orkneys on the north, and on the south to the Garonne. The threat of their landfall gave rise to the famous Roman defences of Britain known as the Saxon Shore. A " seat on the Board " that governed the Saxon adventurers was worth possessing, though difficult to gain ; and accordingly their direction was contested by more than one of the tribal castes which gave monarchies to Europe.

At some time between the years 300 and 350 a man fiercer than themselves intervened against them—King Helgi " Hunding's-Bane." He slew their King Siric and ruled their land as a conquered country. Helgi had a repute that lasted long in Scandinavian tradition. He belonged to one of those monarchies which failed in the struggle for survival. He was the son of Sigemund Waelsing, whose legend survives in the Icelandic Volsung Saga (though the Danes thought Helgi a son of Hroth-wulf Kraki), and a king whose harshness was a by-word. He died at the hands of an avenger of blood, leaving the Saxons to fall under the domination of the English kings who stepped into his place.[1]

---

[1] Chadwick, *Origin*, pp. 298–301. Saxo, p. 51. In his *Studies*, p. 410 ff., Professor Chadwick suggests that Offa, not Helgi, was the king who suppressed the Saxons of the North Sea coast : but Saxo's testimony is clear on the point that it was Helgi, and the character ascribed to the latter does not

V

The history of the kings of the English, as we have it from the earliest Danish historian, is evidently derived from a lost epic which once was well known both in Denmark and in England. Centuries after the days of King Alfred, the fragments of it were still remembered among the English. In it speak and act, in full and natural humanity, some of those men whose quaint names Alfred briefly recounted in his father's genealogy.

It centres round King Wermund and King Offa ; and though the story comes to us in an imperfect form, filtered through the Latin of a thirteenth-century monk, it bears every sign of having passed through the hands of a master of the art of story-telling. Its dramatic grip and emotional appeal are tremendous. The men for whom it was made would have needed no help to understand the particular force of the parable of the Prodigal Son. To-day, in an age in which fatherhood means less than once it did, the appeal may not be quite so tremendous ; but to the man who composed the poem, and to the audience for whom he made it, the relationship of father and son was clearly a great emotional fact which could be played upon to the point of tears. And this is historical evidence of some value respecting the temper of mind and moral nature which are hidden behind the short official entries in the *Chronicle*.[1] Since

---

agree with that of Offa. By the count of generations, both Wermund and his contemporary Wig fall into the first half of the fourth century—330 to 340. There is independent evidence for dating Helgi a generation or two before 375. Finally, Saxo shows us the ancestors of the West Saxons as under-kings to the ancestors of the Mercians. The cumulation of this evidence indicates that the Saxons came under English rule early in the fourth century, and *before* the date of Offa.

[1] See what Mr. R. W. Chambers has to say on the place of heroic poetry in the Dark Ages (*Widsith*, pp. 183–4).

those days we have come to think of maternal feeling
as the only feeling of its kind. Fatherhood has become
a trifle ; at the worst a jest : and an age which feels in
this way has lost touch with one of the great spiritual
forces which have moved men in the past, and have
helped them to explain their relation with the divine
creative power of the universe.

VI

King Wihtlaeg, son of Woden, who stands at the
head of the genealogy of the Mercian kings, reigned in
Angeln somewhere about the year A.D. 330, in the days
when Constantine the Great was at the height of his
power, and when Eburacum in Britain had given an
emperor to Rome. The Saxons were already a power
upon the North Sea. Their first great ventures had
begun sixty years earlier ; and by now the huge fortifica-
tions of the Saxon Shore were being built along the
British coast from the Wash to Southampton. The
coming and going of fleets from Slesvik, the knowledge
of new worlds and new peoples that they brought back,
and the profit of their plunder, stirred the whole of the
north.

Wihtlaeg was the first of a line of kings who succeeded
direct to the ancient priest-kings. His advent to power
implied that the old laws and sanctions were dwindling
before the new ideas let loose by the Saxon seafaring,
and that the sword had to be called in to protect that
which once had been protected by its own sanctity.
To be a near neighbour of the Saxons in those days no
doubt called for a hardy heart and a strong hand.
Wihtlaeg seems to have possessed both. He intervened
in Jutland to reassert the rights of the kings of Leire ;
he allied himself with the rulers of Skane and Seelund ;

he defeated the Jutish king,[1] whose widow, according to the ancient customs, he married. Wihtlaeg reigned long and peacefully, and died in his bed.

Wermund, his son, who succeeded him, was as prosperous and successful a ruler as his father, and reigned long. Until he was an old man he was childless. Then he begot a son, Offa, who grew up to be a huge and solemn youth, so slow, so serious, and so silent that there seemed very little prospect that he would ever prove useful in business either public or private. Wermund accordingly married him off to the daughter of Freawin, a king in Slesvik—an alliance which he hoped would support Offa better than his own brains were ever likely to do.

Freawin, however, had his own misfortunes to contend with. The Swaefe, under their King Eadgils, a famous fighting man, entered Slesvik. A great battle was fought ; and Freawin fell.

Eadgils followed up his advantage and advanced into Slesvik. The sons of Freawin now sent to their over-lord, who was at Jellinge ; and Wermund raised the host of the Angles, and came to meet Eadgils. A second great battle was fought. Eadgils was wounded, and the Swaefe retired.

But the death of Freawin seems to have been the personal act of Eadgils himself ; a blood-feud was on foot, and according to the ancient custom Freawin's sons Ket and Wig took it up. The story is that they made a journey into the land of the Swaefe, and caught Eadgils alone. He offered to fight them both at once. They declined this offer. Ket undertook the combat ; but when he was beaten down, Wig intervened in his defence and slew Eadgils.

---

[1] This king, by allegation of Saxo, p. 106, was no less a person than Amleth, or Hamlet, who was to be heard of again by the English, later on, under different circumstances !

The English and the Danish Kings

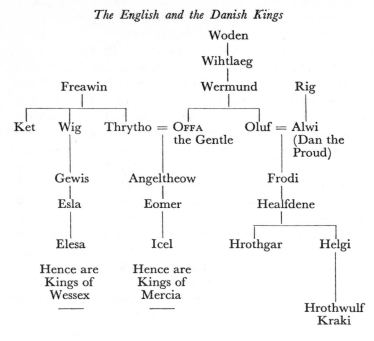

Wermund, one of the new political kings, a modernist
and a realist, who saw the affair from its practical side,
received Ket and Wig with honour, granted them the
rank of their father, and was glad to be quit of a dangerous
foe. The North, however, in the fourth century of the
Christian era, was not yet prepared to endorse political
proceedings so modernist and realistic as this. Public
opinion was against Ket and Wig, on the ground that
they had broken the immemorial laws of honour in
personal combat. The blindness which fell upon Wermund in his old age was no doubt, in the opinion of the
world, a judgment upon him for entertaining cynical
and Machiavellian principles. So, apparently, thought
the Saxons. Whether or not their moral indignation

was particularly deep, the occasion was certainly convenient for repudiating the suzerainty of the Angles.

The Saxons, therefore, sent envoys to Wermund to
bid him give up the kingdom which he had held too
long : for he could not be accounted a king whose spirit
and whose eyesight alike were darkened. Or if he had
a son who would meet a Saxon champion, let him agree
to stake the issue on a single combat. If he would do
neither, then the sword should decide.

King Wermund was by now a broken man. He could
not defend his revolutionary moral ideas. He could only
answer that it was an ill thing to taunt him, whose life
had been brave and honourable, now that he was old
and blind ; his position seemed to him to deserve sympathy rather than taunts. Why could not the Saxons
wait until he died ? But rather than give away his
heritage, he would accept the challenge, blind or not.

The envoys informed him that a Saxon king would
shrink from fighting a blind man : but they delicately
suggested that his son, perhaps, would take up the
challenge on his behalf.

VII

The embittered silence which followed was broken
by a voice which Wermund did not recognize. He
inquired who was speaking.

They said : " It is your son Offa."

He answered : " It is enough that foreigners should
jeer at me. Do you too insult me ? "

They assured him that it was Offa who had risen to
ask permission to speak.

Wermund said : " Whosoever he is, he is free to
say what he thinks."

Offa accordingly spoke to the Saxons, and said : " It
is an idle thing for you to claim a kingdom when not

only its king, but all its brave men are at its service. The king has a son, and the kingdom an heir. I will fight, not only your king, but also the next bravest of the Saxons."

The envoys laughed, for they knew the reputation of Offa. But the challenge had been accepted, and the combat was therefore ratified and arranged. The feeling among the Angles was one of simple astonishment.

When the envoys had gone, Wermund praised the man who had spoken for the courage and the confidence he had shown, and said : " I would sooner give up my kingdom to him, whosoever he may be, than to an insolent foe."

They insisted : " It is your son Offa." So Wermund called him near, and touched him, to make sure of this ; and certainly the limbs were the limbs of Offa.

He said : " Then why have you not spoken before ? "

Offa answered (and, we may imagine, gruffly) : " I had nothing to talk of." [1]

Wermund asked : " And why did you challenge two men instead of one ? "

Offa answered : " To put right the death of Eadgils."

Wermund said : " You have judged all things rightly."

VIII

Then, as a variant on the story of David, began the arming of Offa. He was too big for any coat of mail, and he burst all those that they managed to get upon him. He was too large for any other man's arms. At

---

[1] This is the story related by Saxo : but Offa means that since his father had endorsed the proceedings connected with the death of Eadgils, he, Offa, had had nothing he cared to say. This may cover a historical fact that Offa led a party of opposition to his father ; and his silence may not have been quite so lengthy as the historian makes out (Chambers, *Widsith*, p. 87).

last one of Wermund's own coats was cut away up the left side—the shield side—and patched with a strap and buckle, by the old king's order. Wermund directed him to be careful in choosing a sword upon which he could rely. Several were put forward ; but Offa shook them and broke them. He broke every sword they brought. Finally Wermund remembered his own sword Skrep, which he had buried in the earth when he could no longer use it. He bade them lead him out into the fields.

They led him over the ground while he questioned them as to his bearings : and at last he found the spot and drew the sword Skrep out of its hiding place. Offa saw that it was old and worn.

" Shall I try this too ? " he asked.

Wermund answered : " If you shake this and break it there is nothing left for such strength as yours ; so leave it alone."

IX

The ground was marked out on an island of the river Eider, where Rendsburg now stands. The banks were crowded with people. Offa took his ground alone. The Saxon king was assisted by a champion famous for his strength. King Wermund took his stand upon the end of the bridge, intending to throw himself into the water if Offa fell.

There was a long silence, for they were manœuvring for ground,[1] and Offa, doubtful of the old sword Skrep, parried all blows and waited for his opening. Wermund, thinking that this must be Offa's lack of skill, moved

[1] This kind of fighting is perfectly historical. It was highly stylised and subject to rigid rules. The strokes were given alternately. No rough and tumble was allowed. Hence the manœuvring for stance was nine-tenths of the art. This manœuvring, which was invisible to Wermund, is used in the story to intensify the dramatic suspense. If the old man could have seen the intermediate stages by which Offa obtained the stance he wanted, he would have known what was coming.

quietly towards the western end of the bridge, ready for his son's fall.

Then he heard Skrep speak.

He said : " I hear my son's sword. Where did it strike ? "

They answered : " Right through the man."

He moved back to the middle of the bridge.

Then Offa, luring the second Saxon into position, turned the blade of the sword Skrep round, fearing for the strength of the edge he had already used, and smote his second stroke.

Said Wermund : " Again I hear my son's sword."

And when the judges declared the result, the blind old man wept. It was remembered in England, nine hundred years later, that King Wermund gave his realm into the hands of his son Offa, standing upon the bridge : though where the bridge was, no man knew.

Offa, the chronicler tells us, won the name of " the Gentle " because of his forbearing spirit, but we may suppose that it was not the Saxons from whom he obtained this admirable name.

Fifteen hundred years or so after Offa fought his duel on the Eider, a Cambridge scholar pieced together the remaining fragments of the tale.[1] In Jutland, where Wihtlaeg had put down Amleth, a new king came to the front—Alwih, the son of Rig. Alwih and Offa had wars together, and in the end Alwih married Offa's sister Oluf. The son of Offa was Angeltheow, who was the father of Eomer, and Eomer was the father of Icel, who was the first of the Mercian kings in England. But Alwih rose to be " Dan the Proud," the first of the great Danish kings, who gave his name to Denmark ; and the grandson of Alwih and Oluf was Healfdene, whose grandson was the famous King Hrothwulf Kraki ;

[1] Professor Chadwick in *The Origin of the English Nation.*

and that is why the tale of Beowulf lasted long in England, and the tale of Offa long in Denmark. Each nation told the other's story.

Offa's wife, Thrytho, the daughter of Freawin, was famous for her temper and for the way in which she had treated her suitors. But she made a good wife to Offa, once she was safely married to that large and forbearing man. And Freawin's son Wig, who slew Eadgils, was the father of Gewis, who was the father of Esla, who was the father of Elesa ; and Elesa (so the genealogists said) was the father of the man from whom came the West Saxon kings, including King Alfred. And Alfred duly recorded the genealogy in the English *Chronicle*.

As for the manner of life these men lived—the modern archaeologists report it to have been what they themselves, in their extant poems, declared it to be—the active outdoor life of a fighting aristocracy, whose kings had in their service goldsmiths and ironsmiths not to be despised for their craftmanship : a life grown strange and romantic to us, because of its remote archaism, but neither strange nor archaic to them. They were such men as the Goths whom Sidonius knew a century or so later, when he described young Sigismer, " in red flame mantle, with much glint of ruddy gold and gleam of snowy silken tunic. But the chiefs and allies who bore him company were dread of aspect. They wore high tight tunics of varied colour hardly descending to their bare knees, the sleeves covering only the upper arm. Green mantles they had with crimson borders, baldrics supported swords hung from their shoulders, and pressed on sides covered with cloaks of skin secured by brooches.[1]

---

[1] Gibbon observes, with his habitual felicity : " In the most inclement winter, the hardy German was satisfied with a scanty garment made of the skin of some animal." That is to say, our reputedly poor ancestors dressed in that style for which a modern woman has to pay from four to five hundred pounds.

No small part of their adornment consisted of their arms ; in their hands they grasped barbed spears and missile axes ; their left sides were guarded by shields which flashed with tawny golden bosses and snowy silver borders." [1] So Sidonius tells us. In those days the Goths were still rich with the unimaginable plunder of Rome. No king of the Angles would have claimed that abundance of wealth ; but he could still have drawn from his treasury the inlaid swords and the splendid helms which long afterwards were found at Thorsbjerg and Nydam, the cups and the horns that were filled for the regaling of Beowulf.[2]

X

It was round about the time when Offa was reigning in Angeln that the force which set the balls rolling appeared in Europe. The Huns, like the Scythians before them and the Mongols after them, emerged from the eastern steppes and began by shattering the great Gothic realm which Irminric, the patriarch of all European kings, had built up along the Vistula. Fleeing before their foes, the Goths crossed the Danube and took refuge in the Roman empire.

The fame of the deeds that followed was known in Angeln. When Roman governors attempted to hoodwink and break up the Goths, the latter revolted, defeated a Roman army at the battle of Hadrianople, and burnt the emperor Valens in the house where he had taken refuge. By the year 400 the Goths, under their famous King Alaric, were shouldering their tilted wagons over the Alpine passes and pouring into Italy to begin those campaigns which ended with the sack of Rome and the

---

[1] *Letters of Sidonius* : Mr. O. M. Dalton's translation, vol. ii, p. 35.
[2] Chadwick, *Origin*, pp. 185 ff. Sidonius saw the Saxon ships at Bordeaux, with fierce, turbulent oarsmen, blue-eyed, with shaven foreheads. *Letters of Sidonius* (Dalton), vol. ii, p. 155-6.

burial of Alaric, with all his treasure, in the bed of the river Busentinus, where no enterprising treasure-seeker has ever found him again. They then settled in Gaul, around Arles.

That this blow fell upon the empire just when it was suffering under economic difficulties was no doubt an accident ; but the coincidence of the two was more than it could bear. Up to this point, the British garrison had intervened often enough to restore the balance of affairs on the Continent : but after the defeat of the expedition in the year 407, Britain was never regarrisoned. The cities of Britain were notified that they must look after themselves.

The sack of Rome was serious ; but the abandonment of Britain was more serious still, for it unpinned the northern defences of the empire. The drive of the Huns was pushing all the fighting tribes of Central Europe in a struggling mass upon the Rhine. They burst through in 405 under the leadership of Radagaisus, only to leave their bones in Italy. The Vandals and the Burgundians were next forced through the gap, and the civilized land of Gaul was overrun. The thunder-clouds thickened and darkened with the accession of Attila to the rule of the Huns. He seemed likely to swallow up Europe. It was in 451 that he crossed the Rhine. The storm burst at Châlons, where on the Catalaunian Plains he was met and beaten by the combined Roman and Gothic armies : one of the great and lurid crises in the history of mankind. The Huns rolled away again, to dissolve and disappear : but they left their consequences behind them. One of the most fruitful consequences might have been found down by the lower Rhine, which is nowadays the southern part of Holland. There, on the river Yssel, then known as the Sala, dwelt Merovech, king of the Salian Franks.

It would be difficult to exaggerate either the obscurity

of that monarch and his realm or the profound intelligence which (since he handed it on to his descendants)
he must have possessed. Three years after the battle of
Châlons the world was still seething. Aetius, the last
Roman of genius, and the victor of Châlons, had been
assassinated. Next year, still greater sensations could be
gossiped over on the Sala. The emperor Valentinian
was murdered ; while King Gaiseric, after leading his
Vandals into Africa, slipped across and sacked Rome—
which was more than Hannibal had ever been able to do.
When, two years later, Merovech died, he probably
pointed out to his son Chilperic that they lived in an age
suited to private enterprise ; and he no doubt exhorted
him to grasp what he could.

We know nothing at all of Merovech, save that he
existed and that he claimed the descent of a sacred tribal
caste. But he stood in suspicious proximity to a vortex
of events which it will be interesting to examine.

XI

Throughout the period of confusion the Franks had
been extending their rule over the neighbouring country.
Their task was to hold the dominion so acquired. Whether
or not they were aware that possession of the Rhine
depended upon the attitude of Britain, they made
their first step, just after the battle of Châlons,[1] to
isolate Britain and get it into the safe keeping of their
friends.

The tale that has come down to us is a fragmentary
one. King Hnaef—who was apparently a Jute—came

---

[1] We are not necessarily held to Baeda's calculated date of 447. By his
own evidence any date between 449 and 455 may be right ; and various
considerations make it highly probable that Hengist went to Britain in 452,
after the battle of Châlons. See R. W. Chambers, *England before the Norman
Conquest*, pp. 134, 101, 81 *et seq.*

to Frisia and was there slain in the hall of Finn Folc-
walding, the Frisian king. It was a noteworthy occasion
for more reasons than one : for the comitatus of Hnaef,
instead of falling with their lord, as in honour bound,
treated with the foe and retired.[1] One of them bore a
famous name. He was Hengist.

Now, Hengist was not a Jute. He was a Frisian,
and a man who had served in the Roman army under
Valentinian III. He is likely enough to have fought at
Châlons. Our natural surprise at seeing such a man in
the comitatus of a Jutish king is softened when we
observe his subsequent actions. Far from taking the
comitatus back to Denmark, he went instead to Britain,
and there took service with Vortigern, one of the British
kings, against the Picts and the Irish. The equipment of
this expedition was prepared upon the Rhine, in the realm
of Merovech.[2]

It is difficult to resist the conclusion that Hengist
had brought Hnaef to Frisia, and, after his doubtless
regretted death, had carried out the plans Hnaef had
not lived to fulfil. His action certainly came at a moment
markedly convenient to the Franks.

We know of the subsequent proceedings of Hengist
chiefly from English sources ; so we may presume that
his conduct is shown in the most favourable light possible.[3]
He was one of those adventurers who, as in the cases of
Cortez and Pizarro, are liable to be regarded with very
mixed feelings by a grateful posterity. He was appointed
a camp in the Isle of Thanet, which dominated the
Roman port of Rutupiae and the short continental route

---

[1] See the whole story in Clarke, *Sidelights on Teutonic History*, ch. v.

[2] Thurlow Leeds, *Archaeology of the Anglo-Saxon Settlements*, p. 99.

[3] As Mr. Chadwick shows (*Origin*, p. 33 *et seq.*), the account in the
Historia Brittonum is mainly from an English source. For the traditions
respecting Hengist, see Elton, *Origins of English History*, p. 363. He seems to
have been a person of importance in Frisia.

into Britain. He was provided with supplies, and undertook the defence of Britain against the Picts and the Irish ; and also, apparently, the defence of King Vortigern against Ambrosius Aurelianus, a person whose identity will become clearer in a moment. If any men in contemporary Europe were capable of dealing with the Irish, it was men of the type of Hnaef's comitatus—six-foot, fifteen-stone killers who foamed at the mouth and threw fits of homicidal mania on the battlefield. They did their task well.

All the traditions point to Hengist as a cunning and crooked diplomatist rather than a blue-eyed hero. He seems to have taken observant note of the general possibilities of the country, and its political condition. To deal with Ambrosius Aurelianus might be (as it proved afterwards) a proposition of a nature far more serious than the rounding up of Irish raiders. Hengist suggested that he should be allowed to enlarge his forces.

Vortigern assented. Sixteen ship-crews accordingly arrived to join the three which Hengist already had [1] : and with them came Hengist's daughter Hrothwina. Their arrival was marked by a great welcoming feast, at which the wine flowed freely. Vortigern succumbed. His marriage with Hrothwina put him securely into Hengist's pocket. Kent was her marriage settlement. These things hardly added to Vortigern's popularity with his subjects. He had drifted into the position of ruling by aid of a comitatus of foreigners ; and effective though such a rule might be, it was bound to be the prelude to serious domestic trouble. There was already a sub-king of Kent who was stricken with alarm and grief at this transfer of his kingdom into the power of Hengist.

---

[1] If Hengist's ships were of the " Tune " model, he may have had 135 men in his first three ships. Sixteen more ships brought his forces up to 720 men.

Hengist enlarged his forces still further. Octa and Ebissa brought forty more ships. These were sent north to deal with the Picts and Scots near the wall of Hadrian, not against Ambrosius Aurelianus. That Hengist was playing a double game is obvious from the course of the story. We may legitimately doubt the " Picts and Scots near the wall of Hadrian." The objective of Octa and Ebissa may have been a little nearer at hand. Whatsoever the truth in this respect may have been, Hengist's forces were diverted away from the purpose for which he had been allowed to raise them. Vortigern, consequently, was soon in difficulties, and had to make serious concessions to Ambrosius Aurelianus. His own people took steps to depose him. His son Vortimer stepped into his shoes, and Hengist was requested to leave Britain. The burden of providing for his army—it was by this time more than a comitatus—had never been contemplated, and was now intolerable.

But it was too late.

XII

We shall probably never know how far the diplomacy of Hengist extended ; most of the details are lost, and they were no doubt felt from the first to be of the kind that it is prudent to cover up with a decent veil of silence. By reading between the lines, however, it is possible to discern a good deal. Hengist did not leave Britain. He established himself firmly in Kent, and it was there that the first struggle took place. Four great battles were fought during a period of eighteen years. According to the *Historia Brittonum* they were defeats for Hengist ; according to the *Chronicle*, they were victories—a divergence of report not unknown in later times when publicity has been more carefully secured. We are only told of

Vortimer that he died, begging his men to bury him by
the colossal statue of Rome that stood near the channel
of the Wantsum, looking across to Thanet—where, though
dead, he might still face the foe.[1] They could not do so.
They buried him in London ; from which we may
deduce that his victories were not of the kind that win
wars.

Vortimer's death threw power back into the hands
of Vortigern, who was still very much under the influence
of Hrothwina. It was accordingly possible for Hengist
to enter into negotiations. He seems to have been the
initiating party of the Peace Conference which sat to
arrange the terms of compromise. The conference
broke up in disorder, in which the Franks had so much
the best of the exchanges that three hundred of the
British leaders are said to have fallen, and the charge is
definitely made that Hengist planned a massacre, and
not only made the British drunk as a precaution, but
actually gave a pre-arranged signal. Geoffrey of Mon-
mouth goes into details, and tells us of Eldol, the *dux* of
Gloucester, who, armed with a stake, fought his way
successfully out of the Peace Conference. The *Chronicle*
preserves a dignified silence respecting the episode.[2]

Vortigern was spared. He purchased his freedom by
ceding the three provinces which are now known as
Essex, Middlesex, and Sussex.

---

[1] *Hist. Britt.*, c. 44. Geoffrey, vi, 14. That Geoffrey was following a
source by no means imaginary or worthless is proved by the fact that the
monument he refers to has recently been excavated. The proof of its
character gives Vortimer's alleged request far more point than Geoffrey
himself realized. His latest editor, Mr. Griscom (1929) believes in the
reality of Geoffrey's sources.

[2] The *Historia Brittonum* hints that neither party was as sober as it might
have been. They may have been under misapprehensions concerning one
another's intentions, and their subsequent recollections may have been
imperfect. But both Saxons and Franks were skilled in the use of the knife
—the seaxe in one case, the scramasax in the other—which suggests that
Colonel Bowie's exploits several centuries later were a case of heredity.
See Baeda, ii, 9, where the man Eomer is evidently an expert.

The fate of Vortigern is tragic enough. His prestige never recovered from the blow. Abandoned by his friends, hated by his people, he wandered about seeking a refuge until, brokenhearted, he met an ignominious end. Had he been a luckier king scandal might have been less busy with his name.

The way was now clear for the entry of more important actors upon the scene.

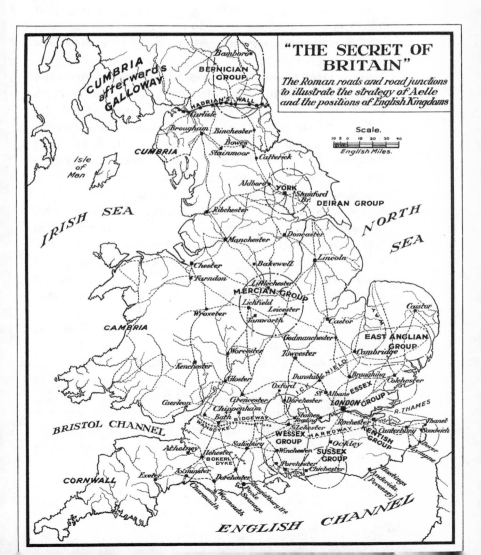

CHAPTER IV

THE ANCESTORS OF THE ENGLISH KINGS

I

THE fall and death of Vortigern opened a fresh and dramatic chapter in the struggle for Britain. Ambrosius Aurelianus entered the war, and Aelle was fetched to meet him.

It is clear enough that Vortimer had not driven the invaders into their ships. Hengist had carried fire and sword from one end of Britain to the other : a process which was not stayed until, after devastating town and country, it reached the other side of the island and " dipped its red and savage tongue into the western sea." But it is equally certain that Hengist had not established himself firmly in any part of Britain save Kent. That keen and successful business-man acted with an astuteness which has received less commendation from posterity than might have been expected. Kent, from its position with relation to the Continent, had always been the richest part of Britain and the customs barrier of its foreign trade. Hengist proceeded to make himself safe by transferring the task of conquering Britain to broader shoulders than his own. Since he could not carry out the task himself, he had nothing to lose by doing so, and he had much to gain.

The grant of something resembling a legal title to Essex, Middlesex, and Sussex furnished him with valuable assets. He was in a position to supply any new partners, not only with such a legal title to portions of Britain, but with information which would enable them to make good by military means any claim they chose to advance to the rest. The secret of Britain was the secret of the Roman roads.[1] Hengist had been many years in Britain. He had—if we are to believe Gildas—been over most of the country, either as a friend or as a foe. He was therefore aware—he could hardly be unaware—of those facts respecting the course of the Roman roads, and the position of the road-junctions, ignorance of which for fifty years prevented the Danes in a later century from successfully invading Britain.

No trace survives of the negotiations, nor of the terms upon which the transfer was effected. But that the English kings arrived in Britain at some time is, of course, without question ; and that, with the arrival of Aelle, the conquest passed out of the stage of private enterprise into royal hands, is equally assured. If the transfer were based upon the representation that the rest of Britain was as wealthy and civilized as Kent, this is only what might be expected of Hengist.

II

Before this threat, Britain closed into unity. Ambrosius Aurelianus was the refuge to which all the British turned, as chickens to a hen—and his wings were wide. It was the year in which Count Ricimer was assassinated at Rome ; and perhaps the rise of Ambrosius—himself a Roman by descent—was one of the results of that wave of anti-Germanism. But five years were to pass. Then the return blow came : in 476 Odovacar the Rugian

---

[1] We must carefully distinguish between the idea of the English settling along the rivers (which is true) and the idea of their conquering England by sailing up the rivers (which is a flat impossibility). Britain could only have been conquered by properly organized military action along the roads. Anyone who has walked up the Thames beyond Kingston, or the Stour or Avon above Christchurch, will know how impossible it would be to force such avenues against any serious defence.

overthrew the last Roman emperor of the west, Romulus Augustulus, and became King of Italy : and in the year following, Aelle arrived. It may be true, as the *Chronicle* informs us, that he and his sons came in three ships, though that statement sounds like a line from a song : but we may take it that far more than three followed and preceded him.

The conquest of Britain was now begun in earnest.

The distribution of the English kingdoms in later times furnishes us with a strong hint as to the strategy adopted by Aelle. For the English to advance westward from Kent presented insuperable difficulties. The great forest of Anderida, running right up north-west, created a bottle-neck between wood and river Thames in the wild heaths and marshes of Surrey beyond Kingston. The routes westward (there were not many) were easily defensible. The only great Roman road ran to London. There may be some connection between these facts and the difficulty which Hengist found in making himself master of Britain. The Danes later on experienced a similar difficulty in advancing westwards from a base in Kent. They resorted, accordingly, to another plan ; and Aelle seems to have adopted a variant of the same strategy which they afterwards employed.

Essex was an early, and certainly an important English kingdom. It was large—including probably most of Middlesex and Hertfordshire, with London, and extending south over the river into Surrey. How far it reached to the north is unknown. A glance at the map will show the importance of Essex. From Colchester the Roman roads (then in comparatively good condition) radiate west, north, and south. Colchester was a strategic centre. It could not, in those days, be acquired save by the previous acquisition of Kent. A map of the Roman roads is the best illustration of the significance of

Colchester. By the routes it commanded, armies could be thrown into East Anglia and the Midlands, and could capture London, cross the river southward, and link up with the English on the Sussex coast. When we find that the Mercian kings represented the direct and the senior royal line of the English, there is little difficulty in guessing the truth. Aelle's chief attack went through Colchester, and penetrated towards the Trent valley ; and it was commanded by the king of Angeln, the Icel who appears in the genealogies. Icel was then to turn south, and press towards Gloucester and Cirencester and the Thames valley. The occupation of East Anglia would be an incident in this great scheme, while the establishment of the kingdom of Essex would have included the capture of London, the acquisition of Surrey from the north, and access to the Roman road (the Stane Street) which led down to Chichester.

We know from the *Chronicle* that Aelle himself undertook the task of reducing the southern portion of the Saxon Shore, that stretched along the coast of Sussex. His capture of Anderida is reported : [1] and his own kingdom was Sussex.[2] His turning movement round the great forest would give him the narrow coastal strip that reaches to Chichester and Portchester : the forest still lay impenetrable. It was this part of the plan, which he conducted in person, that went awry. No record has come down to us of the campaigns of the king of Angeln. We only know that he successfully carried out his own part of the work ; for we find the Mercians safely in

[1] His object was the iron mines. See the Ordnance Map of Roman Britain. This district (the Cleveland of ancient Britain) had a certain independence of its own (*Chron.* s.a. 1011). Its seaport was for many centuries one of the chief ports of England.

[2] Had Aelle succeeded, his " Sussex " would have comprised the whole of England south of the Thames save Kent : i.e. the Wessex of Ina, but not the Wessex of Egbert. It was not altogether to Hengist's interest that Aelle should succeed too well.

Mercia. But about Aelle's part, which met with disaster, we have a small amount of worrying and difficult information. He certainly reached Chichester. If Portchester was not seized, its capture was assuredly intended. The Jutes seized the Isle of Wight, and reached the Hampshire coast as far as the Avon and Hengistbury Head. Then something went very seriously wrong. They never got any farther.

They had, in the Isle of Wight, the point of access to south-western Britain—the great rich land that was in after years Wessex. If they could have won it, Ambrosius would have been nipped between the armies of Aelle and the armies of Icel coming from the north. But no such event came to pass. The forest still cut them off, and they could not win through to the inland districts. They must have been repulsed along the line of Portchester and Winchester : and they never reached the great road-junctions of Axminster and Dorchester.[1] It is the British sources that tell us of the twelve great battles of Ambrosius, and they seem to have been no myth. The *Chronicle* claims two victories for Aelle, and it mentions a third battle which it does not venture to assert that he won. One of his victories was the sack of Anderida—and even to-day, at Pevensey, the huge walls of the Roman citadel stand stark and bare as Aelle left them. The war culminated in a crushing defeat of the English at Mount Badon, the site of which is unknown.[2]

---

[1] It seems just possible that Aelle had erroneous information, and was looking for Axminster in the neighbourhood of Hengistbury Head. The correct position of Axminster is exactly the kind of point of which Hengist himself might have been ignorant ; for pursuit of Picts and Irishmen would never have taken him there.

[2] Mr. Thurlow Leeds suggests that the defence of Ambrosius consisted of the Wansdyke—a huge earthwork eighty miles or so in length, stretching from the Bristol Channel at Portishead to the foot of Inkpen Hill in Hants, with a second line of defence at Bokerly Dyke, eleven miles south-west of

Hengist died in 488, for in that year his son Aesc silently succeeds to the kingdom of Kent. Aelle, after 491, silently vanishes out of history. He had failed, and his countrymen covered up his failure with a profound silence which fifteen centuries have not broken. We do not know when he died, nor where ; nor his kinship. His name is not included in the royal genealogies of the English. His repute survived in a curious, haunting way. We can guess that he was a great man, for he ruled all the English ; and the silence that covers him is as great as he was. But deeds speak louder than words. A map of England, as it was a century later, tells us more eloquently than any chronicle the greatness and the deeds of Aelle.

III

The deeds that so speak were not wrought only in Britain. The English expedition to Britain was organized and equipped during the reign of the Frankish King Chilperic, the son of Merovech. Chilperic did not live to see its fruit. His son Chlodovech ("Clovis" as the French call him) was satisfied that his own hands were now free ; and, accordingly, four years after Aelle's

Salisbury. If this be so the Battle of Mount Badon was probably an attempt of the Mercians to pierce this defence. It would lie right across the Fosse Way, while Bokerly Dyke would intercept any turning movement from the east, via Silchester (E. Thurlow Leeds, *History*, vol. x, p. 97 *et seq.*). This view is accepted by Messrs. Crawford and Keiller, *Wessex from the Air* (1928), p. 230. Sir Charles Oman, on the other hand, thinks the Dyke a boundary (*Quarterly Review*, Oct. 1929). The deeds of Ambrosius are obviously those traditionally attributed to " King Arthur," and there can be little mistake in identifying him as the original " Defender of Britain." The problem is : was there also, in addition, an actual King Arthur, guletic of Britain, later than Ambrosius, to whom the deeds of Ambrosius were attributed ? Or is Arthur one of the old British pantheon ? A good deal that is mysterious would be cleared up if by happy chance both explanations were true ! Sir Charles Oman is disposed to accept the historicity of Arthur as a successor of Ambrosius, *England before the Norman Conquest*, pp. 200–1, n.

F

landing in Britain, Chlodovech let loose his Franks. He had Soissons, his crucial conquest, the heart of later France, in his hands before the death of Hengist. In the year in which Anderida fell, he put down the Ripuarian Franks and joined them to his own kingdom. The men who fought the battle of Mount Badon knew that Chlodovech had defeated the Alamanni, conquered Burgundy, beaten the Goths and taken their treasure-hoard, had extended his rule to the Pyrenees, and had died, five years before, a baptized and catholic king. That European force which we know of as France had come into being : and Ambrosius Aurelianus must have been aware that a great bar of conquest cut him off from Rome. These were indirectly part of the deeds of Aelle.

When Aelle died, the English remained as they were, holding the south-eastern coast and waiting for better times : while the defeat at Mount Badon left the kings of Angeln in occupation of the northern midlands, bestriding the Trent, with a certain indefinite power stretching south towards the Thames, perhaps as far as Oxford, but pushed forward into a position which was dangerously exposed on the north, and none too safe on the south.

Still, no power could now come across Gaul to dislodge them.

IV

Forty years of peace followed the battle of Mount Badon. But it was a peace during which the English incessantly prepared for a further advance. Gildas tells us that as soon as the generation which knew Ambrosius Aurelianus had passed away, Britain was once more torn by intestine feud and party strife. A general and united resistance was never again organized against the English.

The next stage of the conquest of Britain is marked by the rise of a group of three royal families, which include the two families of Bernicia and Deira, and the family of Wessex. This group of three royal families had a common origin. While the Mercian kings claimed descent from Wihtlaeg, these others claimed descent from Beldaeg. The first two families went north of the Humber, where they began the conquest of that long narrow strip of coast which runs from York up to Bamborough. The third went south, to the other flank of the Mercian position.

When the war re-opened, a startling change had come about in the arrangement of the parties. The man who succeeded to the position of Aelle as general commander of the English was Ceawlin of the West Saxons. But the identity of Ceawlin is a problem which may well baffle the closest inquiry. King Alfred had a perfectly straight story to tell upon the subject. According to his account, Ceawlin was the son of the West Saxon King Cynric, who was settled on the Hampshire coast ; and Cynric was the son of Cerdic, who had led the West Saxons thither ; and Cerdic was a direct descendant of King Freawin, who was a descendant of Beldaeg. Such is the official record endorsed by King Alfred. Nevertheless it is almost impossible to believe it. Although Alfred and his West Saxon predecessors alleged that Wessex was conquered from the south, all the archaeological evidence is in favour of the belief that it was conquered from the north. The third stage in the conquest of Britain begins in the year 556, when the battle of Banbury in Oxfordshire was fought : and that was just forty years after the battle of Mount Badon. Ceawlin, therefore, enters upon the scene in Oxfordshire, as we might have expected from the evidence of archaeology. The strong presumption is

that he was either a Mercian or a Middle Angle, who
came down the Icknield Way [1] (along which any man
may yet walk with pleasure, if he cares to do so), and
that he started out from somewhere near Cambridge—
that grand " centre of dispersion " from which the kings
of Bernicia, Deira, East Anglia, and Wessex all alike set
out on their various journeys.

A few years later, Ceawlin succeeded Cynric as king
of the West Saxons. With his accession we are conscious
that a new power has arrived upon the scene. The little
Wessex which for forty years had clung precariously to
the coasts of southern England is suddenly transformed
into a powerful kingdom advancing with giant strides
into the impregnable strongholds of Britain. The
Northumbrians were finding the greatest difficulty in
making their way north : but Ceawlin found none in
making his way west. After a side-blow at Aethilbert
of Kent, to repress his perhaps too officious interest in
the new enterprise, Ceawlin cleared the Chilterns of
the last of the independent British, and turned west.
Gloucester, Cirencester, and Bath fell into his hands as
the result of the battle of Derham.[2] Seven years later
he entered the Severn Valley and established the province afterwards known as the kingdom of the Hwiccas.[3]
These campaigns cut in two the position of the southern
British, parted the north Welsh of Wales from the west

[1] This route would enable Ceawlin to turn the eastern flank of the
Wansdyke. Under 552, the *Chronicle* tells us that Cynric had taken Sarum
—i.e. turned the Bokerly Dyke from the south or the east. See Mr. Thurlow
Leeds, *History*, x, p. 97, and *Archaeologia*, lxiii, p. 159.

[2] The British kingdom represented by these cities was, Sir Charles
Oman thinks, the ancestral realm of Ambrosius Aurelianus (*Quarterly
Review*, Oct. 1929). If so, the idea that the battle of Mount Badon was
fought on the Wansdyke must be abandoned. Tradition is not unanimous ;
but the preponderating voice places the kingdom of Arthur south of the
Wansdyke.

[3] This may have been Cunedda's kingdom (*ibid.*) Ceawlin was seizing
and occupying definite and organized regions—not unorganized wilderness.

Welsh of Devon and Cornwall, and rounded off the
Mercian conquests. They were hammer-strokes of a true
war-smith, and they were never obliterated.

V

Aethilbert—a worthy descendant of Hengist—was
prepared to profit by the proceedings of others. He
bided his time until Ceawlin had wrought his work and
had no more to do but to reap the results. Then
Aethilbert entered Wessex in force. On his return from
a campaign Ceawlin was met by the fresh and undamaged army of Kent. He died two years later,
probably in exile, while his brother Ceol reigned in
Wessex as an under-king of Aethilbert, who stepped
into the shoes of Ceawlin as over-king of the English.[1]
Hengist, if he knew, must have smiled.

It was only four years after this that the mission of
St. Augustine landed—perhaps not wholly unexpectedly
—on the coast of Kent, and received a friendly welcome
from Aethilbert. Times were changed. Aethilbert in
Kent was in closer touch with the ideas and tendencies
at work upon the Continent than were most of his
contemporaries in England. He showed the typical
shrewdness of his family in his attitude to the missionaries. He knew what Chlodovech had done by making
terms with the Church. He proceeded—with caution—
to follow in the footsteps of that intelligent statesman.

The next step in the conquest was taken by the
Northumbrians, who had been struggling, with varying
success, against the British in the north. In 607
Aethilfrith, the grandson of Ida the Flame-bearer, led

[1] Archaeological evidence confirms the statements concerning the widespread influence of Aethilbert. Thurlow Leeds, *Archaeologia*, lxiii, p. 196.

the host of the Northumbrians to Chester, and there inflicted upon the British a great defeat which cut Cumbria away from Wales, just as the victories of Ceawlin had cut Wales away from Cornwall and the south. From this time forward the English possession of Britain was no longer in question. The Mercian salient had been levelled up, and it was only a matter of time before the last remaining provinces of Britain passed into the hands of the English.

VI

The period which immediately succeeded the age of the conquest was one of mutual distrust and dissension among the English royal houses. Aethilfrith of Bernicia had acquired his power by absorbing the kingdom and driving out the sons of Aelle of Deira. Edwin took refuge with King Redwald of East Anglia. The attempts of Aethilfrith to obtain the extradition or murder of Edwin were unsuccessful.[1] He had good reason for anxiety, for Edwin ultimately persuaded Redwald to intervene on his behalf. The defeat and death of Aethilfrith at a battle on the Idle were followed by the restoration of Edwin to Northumbria, and the succession of Redwald to the over-kingship. Redwald did not enjoy his dignity long. His death paved the way for Edwin to grasp at the supremacy.

Edwin was the first of the great kings who made Northumbria the most powerful and the most progressive province of England, and perhaps of Europe. Northumbria might very easily have united the whole of England under her own sway, and anticipated by two hundred years the later success of Egbert of Wessex,

---

[1] There is some ground for believing that Edwin and Redwald were cousins. If so, Redwald's support of Edwin is explicable.

had it not been that Northumbria was itself constructed
out of two separate kingdoms. Neither the Bernician
nor the Deiran house could permanently gain the upper
hand. Their contests so fatally weakened their common
cause that Northumbria failed to realize the full results
that might justly have been expected from the brilliance
of her start. Baeda recorded for subsequent ages the
history of the men who lifted Northumbria to the front
rank ; and we can hardly reckon it an accident that
their deeds were immortalized by infinitely the best,
wisest, and greatest of early English historians.

Edwin had been married to Quenberga, the daughter
of the Mercian King Cearl : and it was no doubt with
the approval and support of the Mercians that Redwald
had acted. Edwin's second marriage was more ambitious.
He sought an alliance with Kent through Aethilberga,
the daughter of Aethilbert and sister of Eadbald, the
reigning king. The marriage was agreed upon with
certain stipulations concerning her religion, which
Edwin accepted. He even made tentative feelers in the
direction of joining the new faith himself.

The policy of Edwin attracted the marked attention
of his royal rivals. The death of Aethilbert and the
accession of Eadbald in Kent had been accompanied by
a reaction against the religion introduced by the
missionaries. Edwin's marriage was the first sign that
Christianity might have a career before it in England.
No one seems to have supposed that Edwin's policy was
dictated entirely by a disinterested admiration for the
moral beauty of the new religion. To judge by their
conduct, his contemporaries attributed to him intentions
of a more prosaic and more political nature. An alliance
between Northumbria and Kent might, owing to the
topography of Britain, profoundly affect the military and
therefore the political situation. The West Saxons were

the first to take alarm. An unsuccessful attempt on their part to assassinate Edwin was followed by the realization of their worst fears. He promptly appeared in Wessex in arms. The defeat of the West Saxons was accompanied by the death or execution of all the men who had shared in the conspiracy. A year later he was baptized.

This was a very practical assertion of his supremacy. With Kent neutralized and Wessex suppressed, Mercia's independence was not likely to last very long. The year which saw the defeat of the West Saxons therefore saw also a new and formidable event—the awakening of Mercia. For a full century and more the Mercians, as if they had borne the chief burden of the invasions, had lain passive, taking very little part in English affairs. With Penda, they awoke, and began to justify the old repute of the kings of Angeln. Penda was placed upon the throne by a *coup d'état* of the heathen party at the expense of the pro-Christian reigning branch of the royal family.

VII

Penda—" old King Penda "—was a famous man in his day, and a man of character. Probably few modern Englishmen will need to look far to find examples of his type. He was a confirmed old-fashioned heathen, unalterably opposed to the new foreign religion introduced by Aethilbert, played with by Redwald and adopted by Edwin. As the *Historia Brittonum* tells us, " he was never baptized, and never believed in God." Baeda has somewhat more to tell us. For all his heathenism, Penda did not interfere with freedom of thought, nor obstruct the preaching of Christianity among the Mercians if anyone wanted to hear it : on the contrary, he hated and despised half-and-half men, and openly expressed his contempt for those who did not act up to the principles they professed. Round Penda concentrated the resistance to the new faith. He is said to have been fifty years old when he came to the throne.

Penda turned first to Wessex. He defeated King Cynegils at Cirencester and compelled him to enter into an agreement with him. It was impossible for the Northumbrians to assist Wessex, and Kent gave no help. Penda perfectly realized, and consistently exploited, the advantage of his geographical position. Edwin was not strong enough to cope with him. The great Northumbrian king fell in battle at Hatfield Moor on October 14, 653, in his forty-eighth year. Cadwalla, the king of Gwynedd, was the stalking-horse which Penda employed. Times were indeed changing when an Englishman would call in a Welshman against another Englishman.

But Penda partly over-reached himself. Cadwalla set up in York and began a reign of terror. A year later, one of the exiled sons of Aethilfrith of Bernicia saw his chance, and made a bid for fortune with a small but devoted host. He was a Christian of the Irish Church, and had the churchmen upon his side. The religious zeal of this little band of desperate crusaders proved a stronger thing than all the policy of Edwin. They defeated and killed Cadwalla at Denise's Burn, and began a second period of Northumbrian greatness.

The tide was against the ideas of Penda. The accession of Oswald was followed almost immediately by a fresh change on the part of Wessex, and the baptism of King Cynegils. Oswald was present at Dorchester to act as sponsor for this important convert. Cwichelm, the son, and Cuthred, the grandson of Cynegils, soon followed his example. The sons of Redwald had already made the change. Oswald's overthrow by Penda at Maserfield, five years later, changed nothing. Oswi his brother stepped into his shoes, and Oswald was soon

working miracles. Fate itself seemed to fight against
Penda. King Cenwalh of Wessex, Cynegil's son, having
married Penda's sister, was indisposed to break with
the powerful Mercian by accepting the new religion, but
he evidently found his wife as difficult as her brother, for
he ended by repudiating her and taking prompt refuge
in East Anglia, where he spent a year in meditating over
the faults of the Mercians and the advantages of the new
faith. His baptism was rewarded by his immediate
restoration to Wessex—a fact which he could hardly fail
to notice. The next to go over was Penda's own son,
Peada, who held the under-kingship of the Middle Angles.
Penda raised no objection.

But Penda himself was irreconcilable. He declined
all overtures from Oswi, and the two kings at last met
for the same kind of test that Penda and Edwin and
Penda and Oswald had tried. Penda's host was a vast
one. Thirty commanders, some of them kings, served
under him, including many Welsh. Oswi relied upon his
own comitatus of picked fighting men. His trust in this
supreme weapon of northern kingship was justified. In
the famous battle of the Winwaed, which the Welsh called
" Gai's Field," Penda fell with most of the " thirty kings " ;
and heathenism in England—as a principle, if not as a
practice—fell with him.[1]

The victory at the Winwaed made Northumbria the
supreme power in England. For fifteen years after it,
Oswi was the over-king of England. He died in his
bed on February 15, 670, in the fifty-eighth year of
his age.

[1] Baeda, *Hist. Eccl.*, iii, 24. *Chron.*, s.a. 655. Professor Lethaby considers
that the Ruthwell Cross was erected, and inscribed with Caedmon's poem,
in memory of this victory. *Archaeological Journal*, lxx, p. 151 (1913).

VIII

It is noteworthy that the death of Penda had no effect whatsoever in stopping the revival of Mercia. Penda had been the strenuous champion of lost causes ; when they were abandoned, Mercia was none the worse. His son Wulfhere began, long before the death of Oswi, to build up a power firmer and better based, taking full advantage of the new currents that were beginning to flow through the nation's life. Penda's policy of Welsh alliances was dropped. The Mercian kings became Christian, and accepted the new ideas. Even during the lifetime of Oswi, Wulfhere crossed the Thames, extended a very effective power into Wessex, and reached the Isle of Wight. This was far more than his famous father had ever succeeded in doing. It was moreover Wulfhere, the son of Penda, who put the last touch to the conversion of England by becoming godfather to Aethilwald, the quiet and remote King of Sussex, who dwelt dreaming by the southern sea.[1]

The rise of Mercia was still further advanced by the decline of Northumbria. For fifty-one years the Northumbrians had exercised the supreme power in England. Ecgfrith, Oswi's son and successor, met with unexpected disaster in the fifteenth year of his reign. He fell in battle against Bruidhi mac Bili and the Picts of Fortrenn, on Saturday, May 20, 685. The battle of Dunnichen Moss undid all the work of the great Northumbrian kings. The Picts and Cumbrians who had been subject to Ecgfrith established their freedom ; and his successor ruled over a kingdom much fallen from its old magnitude.

The kingdom of Kent was also declining in power.

[1] Baeda, *Hist. Eccl.*, iv, 13. *Chron.*, s.a. 661. Biship Wilfrid baptized Sussex in the year 681, and taught the inhabitants (so Baeda tells us) sea-fishing. Apparently a small community of Irish monks already dwelt at Bosham, but were not much heeded.

In 676 Aethilred of Mercia ravaged it ; and in the year of Ecgfrith's fall it, like Northumbria, was in confusion and unsettlement. The competition began to narrow. Mercia and Wessex seemed to be the only runners left in the race.

While the Mercians were consolidating their power north of the Thames, the West Saxons were extending theirs south of it, a task which they pushed forward despite many difficulties and interruptions. Cenwalh had carried the boundaries of Wessex to the borders of Devon. His death in 670 marked the end of a royal succession from Cutha, the brother of Ceawlin, which had lasted unbroken for seventy-three years. After passing into the hands of Aescwin, a descendant of Ceawlin's brother Ceolwulf, the kingship went back to Centwin, Cenwalh's brother ; and finally, since the logic of the situation could not be denied, it settled in the hands of direct descendants of Ceawlin, in the persons of Caedwalh and Mull, of whom we first hear in this year of events, 685. This return to the direct line of Ceawlin seemed to mark an era. Caedwalh and Mull began their careers by the seizure of the Isle of Wight, Sussex, and Kent, thus breaking the bounds which Wulfhere had set to the extension of West Saxon power eastward.

The king who followed Caedwalh, the famous Ina, belonged to another branch of Ceawlin's family. He kept Sussex, and seems to have exercised a beneficial over-lordship in Kent. A change was coming, not only over the kingdoms, but over the kings. Caedwalh had gone to Rome and had died there. Aethilred of Mercia, the son of Penda, after a successful reign of twenty-nine years, entered a monastery. Coenred his successor, together with Offa of Essex, went to Rome in 709. Ina of Wessex followed in 728, and died in Rome after a long and busy reign in which he had fought, and legislated,

refounded Glastonbury and made Wessex supreme in
southern England. None of these kings sought any
refuge from failure. They were able and successful men.
But the feeling of the age was changing. The sisters of
Ina shared his religious tastes. Aethilbald, the Mercian
king who followed Coenred, reigned forty-one years—a
certain sign that nothing was wrong with Mercia.
Aethilbald's long reign was largely occupied in struggles
with Wessex, in which he mostly had the advantage.
He was followed by a successor in whom the power of
Mercia reached its culmination—the great Offa. Not
only was Offa practically king of all England—though
he is not named in the list of the eight—but he reigned
thirty-nine years. He and Aethilbald between them
governed Mercia for a continuous period of eighty years :
and this was an advantage of no mean order when
Wessex was unsettled and distracted.

Offa drove the West Saxons from their hold north of
the Thames. The move had been long impending.
It had been foreshadowed in 702, when the bishopric
of the West Saxons was divided into two. From the time
of the loss of Dorchester the centre of the West Saxons
was shifted to Winchester. Feud and civil war distracted
Wessex. Part of this was perhaps due to the deliberate
policy of Offa, whose methods never erred on the side
of undue scruple. The kingdom gained a temporary
respite by the accession of Berhtric, who compromised
with the over-shadowing Offa, married his daughter,
and carried out his policy. Ealhmund, a descendant of
Ina, became sub-king of Kent as part of the same arrangement. It seemed as if the long struggle were over, and
that the Mercians had won in the race. The man who
had given them victory bore the famous name of that
son of Wermund whose story long lived both in Denmark
and in Britain.

IX

At the last moment came a sudden and dramatic change.

The kingdom of Kent was an indispensable factor in the reckoning of all statesmen who aimed at supremacy in England. It was the direct door to the continental trade ; it was the means by which England had first been conquered and had then been held. Aethilbert's power had been Kentish. He had struck down the West Saxon supremacy of Ceawlin. Even Edwin had allied himself with Kent. Caedwalh had attempted to seize Kent as the preface to a new chapter in West Saxon power. He had not permanently succeeded. The triumphant Mercia of Offa was founded upon his control of Kent.

Ealhmund probably owed his kingship in Kent to rights conveyed through his wife or his mother.[1] Marriage did what the sword of Caedwalh could not do. All the efforts of the Mercians to suppress the independence of Kent only thrust the claims of the Kentish crown more effectively into the hands of Ealhmund's son Egbert. There were men, even then, who thought Offa's methods self-defeating ; who thought that the power of Mercia waned because it was built upon blood, and who desired a political power more human and more generous, with greater respect for the liberty and personality of its subjects. And it is certain that Offa himself created the circumstances which ultimately destroyed his policy.

Now, some years previously Charles the Great, the Frankish king, had requested from Offa the hand of a Mercian princess for his son Charles. Offa, foreseeing the object of this benevolent proposal, stipulated for strict reciprocity and the hand of a Frankish princess for his own son. It is instructive to note that very strained

---

[1] Oman, *England before the Norman Conquest*, p. 388.

relations followed. This Mercian princess, there is reason to think, was no less a person than Eadburga, who had been married to Berhtric the West Saxon king. With the political chess-board so arranged, Providence prepared to transform the game completely into the favour of Wessex.

Even when the first Northmen were raiding Lindisfarne, and men at large were wondering what this new portent might mean, Ealhmund in Kent died, leaving his son Egbert to succeed him. Offa himself died in 796. His son Ecgfrith held on to the government for a few months, and died also. The new Mercian king, Cenwulf, had not the prestige of Offa. The heir of the ancient kings of Kent, Eadbert Pryn, therefore determined to make an effort for his own rights. It is highly probable that his kinsman by marriage, Egbert, was in sympathy: for both as a West Saxon and as a Kentishman Egbert might be only too glad to see Mercia weakened. And Charles, we may be sure, looked on with warm approval. It is unlikely that he would grudge support to so worthy an object as the weakening of Mercian power.

Eadbert might have succeeded, had not the Mercians managed to divide the Kentish interests. Offa had planned to set the seal upon Mercian supremacy by making Lichfield an archbishopric. Old Archbishop Eanbert of Canterbury had been charged with the crime of resisting this proposal, in collusion with Charles. By surrendering this scheme, the Mercian king brought over Aethilweard, the new archbishop of Canterbury, to his side. With the ground so prepared, King Cenwulf entered Kent in 798. Eadbert Pryn fell into his hands and was put out of the way by the method of blinding and mutilation. The more prudent Egbert took refuge in Gaul. But the death of Eadbert simply meant that the hereditary claims of Kent had now passed in the female line to Egbert, who united the rival houses of Ceawlin and Aethilbert.

The death of Berhtric in 802 was followed by the prompt return of Egbert from Gaul. His claim to Kent might need to wait ; but in his claim to Wessex he had no competitors. On the very day of his elevation the Mercians crossed the Thames in force. They were met by Alderman Weohstan and the Wiltshire men, and a fierce contest took place. Both commanders were slain, but the Wiltshire men held their ground. Offa was dead ; Charles had over-reached himself ; and in Wessex stood Egbert—and the fleets of the Northmen were already upon the sea.

A long story had turned a definite chapter, and the next chapter is new.

CHAPTER V

THE RELATION OF BRITAIN
TO EUROPE

I

THE return of Egbert meant much more than might appear upon the surface. Egbert had fled to the Franks, and the man who in these days ruled the Franks was a greater man than Offa ; a greater man than any who was to rule in Europe for many a long year to come—Charles the Great. And nothing political took place in Frankland without Charles having a finger in the pie. An English royal exile did not arrive without the knowledge of Charles—nor leave again. Aachen was a mighty school of politics and warfare ; and Charles was wise and foreseeing.

But who and what was Charles ?

To illustrate his significance, let us glance over the relationship in which England stood to the Frankish realm.

There are a number of formulas by which we can briefly and graphically describe the main features of European history ; and one of them embodies some very curious facts connected with the position of the British Isles relatively to the Continent. The history of Europe has consisted largely of the results produced by the interaction of the southern civilization centred round the Mediterranean with the northern civilization centred round the Baltic. The two areas are strongly contrasted in climate and in the type of human mentality which they produce. We frequently express their difference by some of their specific characteristics. One is a beer-drinking, and the other a wine-drinking world ; one built the high-pitched roof and gable, the other, the low-pitched roof and pediment ; one is, on the whole, a world of fair-haired men, the other mainly a world of dark-haired men ; and deeper than any of these external features go profound differences of mental character too subtle to be caught in any single phrase, but illustrated by the greatness of the north in mathematics and psychology, and the greatness of the south in art and jurisprudence.

The line of contact and distinction between them is indefinite, and moves northward or southward from time to time ; but, broadly speaking, it is represented by a geographical feature—the Rhine. European history might easily be written in terms of a struggle for possession of the Rhine frontier. When we leave the ground of recorded history, and enter that world of dumb facts which is the province of the archaeologist, those facts are still best explained on the same terms. According to whether the Rhine is under the control of northern or southern powers, Europe is swayed by one influence or the other.

The geographical relation which gives especial importance to Britain is that the British Isles are an outflanking wing of the Rhine frontier. The struggle for the Rhine has a way of becoming a struggle for either the possession or the alliance of Britain. As far back as we care to search, the attitude of Britain has been a decisive influence upon the course of events in Continental Europe. When we find the Celts, in the dawn of history, practically masters of Europe, we find Britain Celtic. When Roman civilization pushed north, and for its own protection seized the Rhine, it confirmed its grip by seizing Britain also. As long as it held Britain, no breach of the Rhine frontier by the Northerners was ever permanent. Serious as some of these breaches were, in each case the damage was repaired and the frontier once more made good. The occupation of Britain by the English was the decisive fact which transformed Europe again from a southern to a northern polity : and northern kings were soon reigning where Roman emperors and Roman governors had once ruled.

II

We have already seen what ground there is for suspecting that the Frankish kings were the men who arranged and financed the English conquest of Britain ; and we have noticed the speed and permanence of the conquest of Gaul by the Franks, once Britain was in English hands. The cynical and remorseless intelligence of the Franks pointed out to them the direction in which their interests lay. They proceeded to confirm their hold upon Gaul by adopting the Catholic faith. They had a great deal too much at stake to permit them to be philosophically indifferent to the views of the English. If the Frankish power, now in unity with its Gallo-Roman elements, were to hold its own against the heathen nations north and east of the Rhine, it must not only beat them in war, but absorb them into the same cultural scheme—that is, into the same religious faith. The conversion of England enabled the Franks to build up their empire beyond the Rhine, and to spread Christianity in northern Europe. By the time of Egbert the Franks, under the leadership of their great Arnulfing kings, had extended their rule over Alamannia, Bavaria, Frisia, and Saxony. Italy itself, and its Langobard owners, fell to them. They turned back the Moorish attempts to conquer Gaul and Italy, successfully defended Europe against the invasions of the Avars, and made an effective frontier against the Slavs. They did what

Drusus and Germanicus could not do : they created an
Elbe frontier. They seemed to be rebuilding the mighty
dominion which had been overthrown. They were
striding towards empire : and to those who preserved
the memory of former days it might well seem that as
the Illyrian emperors from the Danube had restored the
Roman dominion after the age of the Thirty Tyrants, so
Frankish emperors from the Rhine might restore it after
the age of the Goths and the Vandals.

The Frankish Court thus became the centre of
western Europe, the focus through which all the surviving
traditions of Europe—political, religious, military or
artistic—were transmitted. Charles himself—Charles the
Great—the man who entered romantic mythology as
" Charlemagne," just as Ambrosius Aurelianus entered
it as " King Arthur "—Charles was very nearly the ideal
of an old northern king. He was strong, skilful, and able ;
a sportsman, a soldier, but not a saint ; a keen judge of
character, a hearty trencher-man, a lover of enlighten-
ment. His intellectual ability was as notable as his
physical strength. He did on a large scale, with permanent effect, those things at which men like Offa of
Mercia or Edwin of Northumbria laboured on a small
scale. He was the pattern on which ambitious kings
modelled themselves.

Now, this was the man to whom Egbert of Wessex
had fled : this was the man at whose court he spent
some of the most impressionable years of his life.

III

An intelligent observer—and Egbert, to judge from
his subsequent career, was intelligent—could not have
lived three years in that clearing-house of knowledge and
ambition without becoming a much wiser man. That

Charles was tending straight towards the revival of
Roman dominion is obvious enough. Through all that
he did ran a consistent purpose of political consolidation.
He illustrated by example the advantages of a large
political unit, governed with strictness and discerning
tact, over a congeries of small independent governments
plunged into incessant strife : advantages in wealth, in
dignity, in human happiness—all the things which arrest
the eye and strike the imagination—as well as in those
less obvious things of the mind, intelligence, learning,
and the social stability they help to create. He showed,
moreover, the way to these advantages ; his methods
were based upon tested experience, and could be learnt.

To a man who had grown up in the narrow, blinkered
world of southern England, absorbed in its local quarrels
and isolated by its local interests, it must have been a
singularly enlightening experience to dwell for a time in
a place to which came regularly all the news of Italy,
Spain, Gaul, central Europe, and the North ; in which
there prevailed a sense of the largeness and the unity
of the world : a place with which the emperor at
Constantinople, the patriarch at Jerusalem, and the
caliph at Bagdad were in communication. The Roman
empire was far more than a legend at the court of
Charles : it was a reality. And Charles acted as if it
were a reality. He did what no man had done for
centuries : he intervened in British affairs. He was in
more or less regular communication with Offa of Mercia.
He could exert diplomatic pressure on the rulers of
England. He was in touch with Ireland. Whether or
not he conceived the idea in theory, he certainly recognized in practice that the power which controlled the
Rhine must have Britain upon its side.

This was not all. Egbert had every opportunity for
realizing vividly another set of facts, no less striking.

Charles had beaten down the resistance of the old Saxons, suppressed their independence, and secured it by transporting several thousand families into Neustria, on the coasts of the Channel, where he settled them. Egbert is hardly likely to have regarded this without interest of a somewhat personal sort. He himself was a West Saxon; and there is no particular reason for assuming that he was ignorant of traditions which Baeda and the churchmen knew—that the Saxons of England were descended from the old Saxons, and had originally come from Old Saxony. The conquest of his kinsmen was recent, and it was famous; it suggested more than one train of thought.

The influence of the Frankish court upon the later kings of Egbert's house is clear enough. Egbert's son married a Frankish princess: his grandson, Alfred, showed in many of his methods and tastes the effect of Frankish example. We shall see, as we proceed, the many ways in which this influence manifested itself. It was with Egbert that it began.

IV

All these things gave particular point to the claim of the English kings to be independent of Rome, sovereign rulers in their own right. Very few royal documents of Egbert's reign have survived. In those which we possess, he states his royal title with considerable reserve. He is "Egbert Rex," and nothing more: all else is left open.[1] He does not claim, as Cenwalh had claimed, the haughty title of "Basileus Westsaxonum." He owed Charles too much to challenge his claims; and he owed himself too much to admit them.

[1] He was originally "Rex Occidentalium Saxonum": but even later on, in 833, he was not, like Aethilbald of Mercia, "Rex Britanniae," but only "Rex."

Egbert's accession to the crown of Wessex took place in February 802. He was still at the Frankish court— he may even very probably have been with it in Rome— when the work, the ambition, the intrigue, the warfare of four generations were rewarded. On Christmas Day, in Saint Peter's, in the year 800, Charles was crowned emperor of the West.

Cordial as were the relations of Charles with the Church, there were certain undercurrents which profoundly affected the destinies of Europe. The Pope took the Frankish king unawares, and scored one of those diplomatic points which create inexpugnable precedents for the future. The crown was placed unexpectedly upon Charles's head as he knelt at the altar. He swore afterwards that had he known beforehand of the Pope's intention, he would never have entered Saint Peter's that day ; and we may well believe him. The right which the Pope then asserted in practice—somewhat sharp practice—remained ever afterwards a prerogative of the see of Rome. But Charles, though he was unable to deny the accomplished fact, and saw no way of repudiating the papal claim, had never intended to receive the imperial crown in that particular way, nor with that particular implication that the Pope had the right or the power to bestow it.

It marked for ever the fact that the empire which Charles thus acquired was not that of Augustus, Vespasian, and Diocletian, but belonged to a new political world, based on utterly different conceptions. And along this path the English did not follow. Neither then nor at any other time did any English king—save John and Henry III—admit that his sovereign title derived from the Church. The Church ranked, indeed, among the great forces which he consulted, and which accepted him and ratified his title ; but it was never allowed to be more. The secular political state in England remained, as it had always been, an absolutely self-sufficing power. Egbert continued with stolid patience to be " Egbert Rex."

V

Charles had some fourteen years more of life to live as emperor. During those years he so established the prestige of the revived Roman empire that he made it an integral part of the political conceptions of Europe. The essential unity of Europe as one great polity was reasserted, and it remained sometimes a fact, but always an inspiring and engrossing theory. To the great Frankish kings of the house of Saint Arnulf we owe the preservation, the confirmation, and the transmission to modern days of this conception of Europe as a single and united polity. It was all the more important to fix and assure this conception, because the way to its perfect achievement (which we have not reached yet) was through a period of disunion and differentiation in which, but for their work, all remembrance of unity might have been utterly and for ever lost.

The restraint—we might almost say the indecision— which England has always shown towards the great political movements of the Continent (and has shown especially when they have taken dramatic or idealistic forms) she showed towards the Frankish empire. She never allowed herself to be drawn into its circle. That she was profoundly and permanently influenced by it we shall presently see. But that course which she has taken so constantly in later times, she was taking then—she learnt from the new imperial movement, she sympathized with it, she even sided with it ; but she preserved her distinctness and her separate individuality. It is probable enough that Egbert, king of the West Saxons, would have hesitated to say, in so many words, that beside the vast empire which stretched from the Elbe to the Straits of Messina he set up another empire, as eternal, as absolute, and as individual : the empire of Wessex. But what his tongue would not utter, and what even his thoughts might not let him think, his actions betrayed. " Ego . . . basileus Westsaxonum " was certainly running at the back of his mind.

More than that was running in his mind. He had the gift which belongs to so many of those men who found dynasties and start great states upon a career of power— the gift of patience and industry. After the first fierce battle which had secured his safety and supremacy in Wessex, his reign passed many uneventful years. The Mercians let him alone. Not until the year after the death of Charles do we hear anything exciting of Egbert. In the thirteenth year of his reign he invaded Cornwall.

Egbert's invasion of Cornwall carries us straight back, by another road, to the subject of Charles and the Frankish empire.

VI

It was under the Arnulfing Franks that that welding together of the Roman civilization with the northern was first begun, which we think of as " mediaeval." The Middle Ages may in one sense be a period of time ; but what we most of us really mean by the word " mediaeval " is the mental atmosphere of Frankish Gaul. While this atmosphere may be repellent to some types of modern mind, it was (and in part for exactly the same reasons) still more repellent to the fierce race of seamen, peasants, and hunters who dwelt round the Baltic, and from whom a good many types of modern mind are descended. They clung uncompromisingly to their faith in the dark

godheads of the north. Something else may have entered
into their feelings concerning the Frankish empire—their
contempt for men whom they regarded as of inferior
race and status. The Goths were still remembered with
admiration, and the English, possibly, with respect ; but
the Franks were not recognized in the heroic legends of
the north.

The completion of the work of Charles the Great was
therefore marked by a reaction against it which we must
now begin to follow in detail.

The ruthless ferocity with which Charles had crushed
the Saxons was an irritant rather than a warning to men
who regarded even the formidable Saxons with a touch of
haughty patronage. Many causes doubtless conspired to
one result : jealousy of Frankish power, apprehension of
its further advance, abhorrence of its theology, increasing
knowledge, dynastic changes, commercial enterprise—
all the causes, in fact, which in later centuries sent
Elizabethan seamen illegally trespassing in the Spanish
seas. But the result was a series of great wars which
extended over almost the whole European continent ;
they were of vast magnitude and crucial importance ;
and their aim was a heathen reconquest of Europe.

Charles had had warnings and premonitions. His
Elbe frontier had lifted a curtain upon a strange and
almost unknown world, which began to awaken and to
move before the face of southern civilization. Strange
kings emerged into view, with their " grey-browed
counsellors, thunderous warriors, curl'd veterans "—
and, above all, their fleets. When the mists blew a little
from the seas of the north, they revealed something of
which the world had not dreamed before—the true, sea-
going fleet.

It was these fleets that caught the south by surprise.
The true terror of them was revealed only by slow,

successive steps. They harked back to a remote ancestry ;
but they reached their full perfection only just about
the time when their use was provoked. The ancient ship
of the Baltic peoples, as old at least as the Bronze Age,
was a many-oared galley or war-canoe, capable only of
coastal work. The Mediterranean galleys of the Greeks
and Carthaginians did not directly influence the far
north. The sea-going ship was evolved first, apparently,
in the English Channel, by men who had seen the
Mediterranean galley, and who improved it into a vessel
more suitable to the northern seas. The ships which
Caesar saw among the Veneti of the Channel coast
traded to Frisia. It must have been such vessels as these
and not Mediterranean galleys, which were employed
by Drusus, Tiberius, and Germanicus, in their naval
operations along the Frisian coast, and which certainly
reached the Elbe, and possibly the Jutish peninsula.
The men of the north were quick to learn. The advent
of these ships along their coasts gave rise to a series of
ingenious improvements in ship-building which often
far outstripped their models. Cheapness of construction,
low working cost, and mechanical efficiency went hand
in hand. By the third century the clinker-built whale-
boat was already constructed, a true keeled rowing boat
of the modern type ; and its invention was signalized
towards the end of the century by the appearance of the
Saxons in the North Sea.

But the rowing boat, even if it were capable of such
extended operations, had its limitations, both of size and
of seaworthiness. The fifth century saw the construction
of a ship which was no longer a galley with auxiliary
sails, but a true sailing ship with auxiliary oars. The
change was crucial ; and this was the age of the English
conquest of Britain and the moving of great fleets and
large bodies of men across the sea. But although the

sea-going ship had been created, the deep-sea sailor had not yet been trained. Three centuries passed before the northern seamen were ready : when the improvement in the details of the sailing ship, and the rapidly growing experience of navigators, saw the advent of real fighting fleets which could range across the open sea, circumnavigate the British Isles, reach the Mediterranean, Iceland, and Greenland, and carry men with certainty to any indicated place. The " wicking " age is the age of the deep-sea ship.

VII

The nearest and most graphic parallel to the invention of the northern ship is the invention of the aeroplane. Both similarly cut right across all the accepted rules and the accustomed methods of war. When the first wicking raid fell upon Lindisfarne, men were stunned as they were by the first air raids eleven hundred years later. The invaders came like a bolt from the blue ; and back into the blue they went. But there were very serious differences. To improvise an answer was far harder. Ships could be built ; but neither the seamen nor the sea-going experience could be created to order.

The north had, in fact, done that thing which from time to time it is in the habit of doing : it had sprung a surprise upon civilization. It did so when it invented the horsed car which broke so many Asiatic and Egyptian armies two thousand years before Christ ; it did it now with the ship ; it was to do it again with the firearm and with the aeroplane. The sea-going ship was the military answer of the north to the empire of Charles ; and it was destined to be a very terrible answer indeed.

But it was a military answer to a political fact. The

issue which was joined between the two antagonists was
therefore whether the military ingenuity of the north
could break the political organization of the south, or
whether the south could hold itself intact. In the latter
event it would be only a question of time before the
political ideas of the south so permeated and converted
the north as to change the relationship between them,
abolish the profound differences which were the basis of
their antagonism, and give them a common ground of
mutual interest and mutual sympathy. We shall see
how the problem worked itself out to solution.

All great wars have a natural tendency to become
wars of exhaustion. A good deal would depend upon
the extent to which the political civilization of southern
Europe could, by its superior productivity, outlast the
resources of the still semi-tribal north. The contest
opened at a time when the south had, for the moment,
shot its bolt. Charles died in the year 814, when the
Frankish empire was at the height of its power. It was
never again to be so powerful or so united. The north
came fresh to the struggle, and its power was rising in a
curve which had not yet reached its maximum.

VIII

Those first quiet years of Egbert's reign were lived
while the threat from the north grew gradually more
ominous. After the sack of Lindisfarne the presence of
raiders off the western coasts of Britain became constant.
First Jarrow and then Lambey in Glamorganshire was
attacked. The Isle of Man suffered ; Skye and Iona ;
the Irish coast was involved. There were raids against
Frisia and Gaul ; but it was nevertheless the raiders in
western waters who were the most serious feature of
the situation. The damage they did was at this stage

perhaps not very great; it was their presence itself that was alarming, and the opportunities they found for exploration and the gathering of definite geographical knowledge.

All this was by-play—reconnaissance work which was made to pay its own expenses. The centre of interest was still upon the Elbe. That great Danish king, Sigfrith (known in legend to later ages as " Sigurd Hring," the victor of Bravalla), had regarded the Saxon wars of Charles with interest. He had not intervened, but he had extended protection to the Saxon chief, Widukind, when the latter sought a refuge with him, and he had been in diplomatic communication with Charles. His successor, Guthfrith the Proud, took a stronger line. He attacked Frisia, and gave the Franks to understand clearly that he was not to be trifled with. They were a little astonished at Guthfrith.

That the raids in the Irish seas were no casual adventuring is clear from their sudden cessation while Guthfrith was carrying out these naval operations in the North Sea. Guthfrith's career came to an abrupt end in 810, when he was assassinated. Some political meaning lay behind the episode of his murder, for the succession was disputed and at least one of the rival candidates proved to be under Frankish patronage.

The death of Guthfrith relieved the Franks of anxiety on the Elbe, but greatly increased the anxiety of Egbert of Wessex. The western seas filled again with raiders. The Irish coast was harried. Northmen of Norway, as well as Danes of Denmark, were on the water. Along the Elbe frontier, Franks and Danes watched one another : but the trouble was little likely to come to a crisis there. The real attack was developing slowly in the western British seas.

IX

Egbert's invasion of Cornwall is doubtless closely connected with these raids, and was perhaps a part of the resistance which for a few years discouraged them. Cornwall—the " Bretland " of the Northmen—was always an important strategical point for their fleets. The time had not yet come for them to seize that shore in force. They had not turned Land's End and gained the Wessex coast. But Egbert's interest in Cornwall marked the beginning of a new chapter in his reign.

The Wessex to which he had succeeded had been a kingdom without unity or vigour, depressed beneath the dominance of Mercia. After thirteen years of Egbert, it began to be capable of great deeds. Throughout those thirteen years Mercia, once so powerful, had been slipping gradually into that state of disunity and indecision in which formerly Wessex had dwelt. The influence of Charles did not diminish, but increased as Egbert's reign grew longer. Egbert understood, it is clear, those bracing and subtle arts by which men are disciplined, enriched, and taught to act together. This much we need not set down wholly to the account of his Frankish education in politics. But when the period of waiting and recovery was over, he knew how to utilize the moral results, and to what ends. These things we may attribute with much more probability to his Frankish training.

Charles had died the year before the Cornish expedition. A little time passed : and then King Cenwulf of Mercia died, and Mercia slid a little further into chaos. A very little time passed : and then the new King of Mercia, Ceolwulf, was thrust out by his people, and Bernwulf reigned in his stead.

The cup was now full. The events which began rapidly to follow show clearly that Egbert had foreseen them and prepared for them—had even, perhaps, shared in their creation, and smoothed the path of their advent. Great and sudden movements are not made upon sudden decisions. Twenty-three years of preparation had made Wessex ready.

Early in the year 825 Egbert seized Cornwall. From Devon he advanced westward. A great battle was fought near Camelford—Slaughter Bridge still bears the tradition of ancient fight. The place of the battle betrays its cause and its object. Camelford is close to the " Bretland " coast, and it was fought in order to seize and hold Cornwall against invasion by sea. King Bernwulf of Mercia, who doubtless possessed private information concerning the other items that were due to appear on the programme, was at Swindon with a Mercian host before Egbert could return to meet him. The crash at Ellandune was a great and fiercely fought battle, with a heavy fall of men : but it was decisive. As a result, Bernwulf fled back into Mercia ; and the whole of the ancient dominion of Ina, the whole of England south of the Thames, fell into the hands of Egbert.

He sent his son Aethilwulf into Kent to drive out Baldred, the Mercian regulus. Not only Kent, Sussex, and Surrey gave in their submission to Aethilwulf, but Essex also. At one stride, Wessex was over the Thames.

Events proceeded rapidly. The king of the East Angles now called upon Egbert for protection against Mercia. Bernwulf staked his chance upon the reduction of East Anglia before Egbert could arrive. He failed ; he fell in the battle that was fought ; and he left Egbert master of a third of England.

A pause befell after these victories. Four years passed before Egbert was ready for his next great step. Then he entered Mercia and completed the conquest of England up to the Humber. Later in the year he pushed

northwards and invaded Northumbria. At Dore he was
met in conference. The Northumbrians offered terms
which were satisfactory to him, and he withdrew his
army and returned home.

In three campaigns, therefore, with a vigour worthy
of Charles himself—and with a rapidity and completeness which Charles might have envied—he had made
himself master of England.[1]

X

He aimed at more than England. He entered Wales
in the following year, and established some kind of
supremacy or suzerainty. Wiglaf of Mercia seized the
opportunity to return, and to take possession of his
throne. Egbert allowed him to stay there—on what terms
we are not told : but since peace prevailed in England
the terms were probably satisfactory to both parties.

The rule which Egbert in this manner extended over
the whole of England was the final and conclusive
assertion of her unity. Its terms, and the details of its
arrangements, would not have satisfied a mediaeval
lawyer : it was a hegemony, rather than a solid and
unified kingdom : it was a small replica of the Frankish
empire of Charles, with the same diversity of local law :
but the principle of unity which Egbert's over-lordship
represented held good for ever. The sovereign independence of the smaller kingdoms was never again
permanently made good. Much had to happen before
the full fruits of Egbert's actions were garnered : but
from this time forward England became one nation and
one state—and so men felt it to be.

[1] *Chron.*, s.a. 825–9. He was not, as the *Chronicle* alleges, the eighth,
but the tenth Bretwalda, or over-king of the English : Aethilbald and
Offa of Mercia being the eighth and ninth. See Professor F. M. Stenton
in *Eng. Hist. Rev.*, xxxiii, p. 433 *et seq.*

XI

He was none too soon. The raiders were working their way round from Ireland into the Channel. Their topographical knowledge was expanding. The next campaign of Egbert was fought much nearer home, and at a point which bore a sinister significance. He fought a fleet of thirty-five Danish ships at Charmouth ; and the Danes left the field with the honours of the battle. Now Charmouth is in the Channel itself, and it stands close to one of the heads of the great Roman road—the Fosse Way—which, beginning at Exeter, runs north-eastward across England. They had found, or they were trying to find, one of those strategic points which were to mean so much in later years. The secret of the Roman roads was not far off discovery when the Danes could take the trouble to fight a serious battle at Charmouth. But perhaps it was not discovered yet.

Two years later still, Egbert fought his last campaign. The Cornishmen were apparently no lovers of English rule. Danes were always quick to detect and exploit the political weakness of their enemies. A fleet arrived in Cornwall, and the united army of Cornishmen and Northmen pressed eastward. Egbert met it at Hingston Down. The *Chronicle* assures us that he won a great victory ; and it is certain that the Northmen never reached Wessex, nor any of the points of strategic importance. But Bretland continued for many a long day after Egbert to be a settlement of Northmen and Danes, and an advanced base for their fleets : and even to-day the northern coast of Cornwall shows vivid signs of their presence. Though they never reached Wessex, it would seem to be equally true that Egbert never again saw the Cornish sea.

XII

He died a year after the battle of Hingston Down, in the thirty-seventh year of his reign. Of his character as a man we know nothing by direct record. No poet sang him ; no annalist praised him. No breath of excited admiration has magnified his fame or distorted the picture of his personality. We know him only by his actions. This fact alone would give us a very strong hint of the truth. As far as we can judge he was a wise, prudent, and sober man who never committed a single good nor a single bad action through motives of passion, nor inspired a single romantic thought in his people. He attended, throughout a long reign, strictly to business.

But his life's work had vast and far-reaching effects. At the very last moment before the storm broke—while the Danes were slowly feeling their way to grips with the Frankish empire—Egbert had transformed the situation. What now confronted the Danes was no longer a feeble and disunited England, a ready base for their descent upon the south, but a united kingdom attached by sympathy to the empire of Charles and the world to which it belonged. Whatsoever the Danes now did would need to be done in the teeth of an English power which barred the way. With Egbert, England definitely parted from the world of the north, and ranged herself with the civilization of the south of Europe.

XIII

She so ranged herself upon terms characteristically her own. Not a single word has survived to tell us of the private thoughts and intentions of Egbert : and this too is typical. We only know that he acted in a way implying solid sympathy with the Roman civilization which the Frankish empire represented : and implying equally the purpose of maintaining the absolutely independent sovereignty of the realm he governed. No doubt he himself left it at that, and never sought to probe deeper into the political mysteries of the future.

CHAPTER VI

RAGNAR LOTHBROK, AND THE DISCOVERY OF THE OPEN SEA

I

THE representative who embodied the awakening of the northern nations, as Hildebrand embodied Papalism or Calvin the Reformation, was a man as remarkable as Alfred, but one who has grown to gigantic and mythological proportions when seen through the distorting glass of legend : Ragnar Lothbrok. So little reliable evidence has survived concerning his personality and his deeds that his mere existence has been doubted : yet when the evidence (however fragmentary in its present form) is carefully examined, it is coherent enough ; and it seems difficult to account for some of the events of ninth-century history save on the hypothesis that Ragnar was a reality.

To understand the personality and activities of Ragnar, we need to know a little of his antecedents. In the early years of Charles the Great that process of political unification which had brought the Frankish empire up to the Elbe, and had united England under the rule of the Mercian kings, Aethilbald and Offa, had similarly concentrated the old local kingdoms of the western Baltic under one supreme government. The Danish king, Harald Hilditann, controlled a sea-empire circling round the Danish islands, and including Jutland, Slesvik, Skane, and Vermland, and probably at least the southern part of Norway : besides (if one were to believe the saga-men) the coast of Wendland along to the Oder.

At some time before the year 777 Harald's power was challenged by one of his northern feudatories, who held Vermland. It pleased the Danes in after ages to tell and to believe a picturesque story that Harald grew very aged—though the dates do not quite bear out his extreme age—and was called upon by Sigfrith Hring to retire upon this ground.

The real reasons for the civil war which broke out were most likely connected with the more usual motives of men—the command of trade-routes, the incidence of taxation, differences over high policy, and the desire of men who were consciously strong to hold the reins of power. The great battle which decided the contest between Harald Hilditann and Sigfrith Hring was fought at Bravik on the Swedish coast, and for centuries afterwards was vividly remembered on account of the number and the fame of the fighting men who took part in it. The host of Harald was levied from Denmark, Wendland, and Gothland ; that of Sigfrith, from all the lands of Norway and the Wick and from Vermland. The assault of the great champion, Hubba the Frisian, upon Sigfrith's wedge-array all but shattered it : but after Hubba had fallen, riddled with Norse arrows, the onslaught of Starkad Storwerksson upon Harald's host turned the fortunes of the day. Harald was slain—by, it is said, his own host-leader, Bruni. Hring stopped the fight after the fall of Harald, and offered terms which the Danes accepted.

In this way, according to their own account, the supremacy of the Dano-Norwegian sea-empire passed from the Danes to the Norwegians.

Sigfrith Hring ruled for some twenty years or so. His contact with Charles the Great and the Frankish empire has already been noticed. The accounts of his reign given in northern sources are too contradictory to be accepted in detail ; but they agree in depicting him as a great ruler who sacrificed his power at home to the exigencies of his imperial policy. Revolt broke out in Denmark during his unusually prolonged absence from that portion of his dominion. His young son Ragnar was at first put forward as a rallying point for his friends : but when the revolt grew too serious, Ragnar was sent for safety to Norway. The return of Sigfrith once more changed the position of affairs. A battle was fought, in which he was victorious ; but he died of wounds received in its course.

II

That Sigfrith's victory was real, and that he did die soon after it, would seem to be confirmed by the subsequent events. Ragnar was too young to undertake the rule of a great kingdom. The man who stepped forward to take the place of Sigfrith was Guthfrith " the Proud," the " Hunter-King," the hereditary king of Westfold in Norway. Guthfrith married Alfhild, Sigfrith's widow and Ragnar's mother, and to this legal title to the succession he added the material power of an able soldier and of a king securely based on an old and stable kingdom.

Guthfrith reigned twenty years, and he became an even more famous man than Sigfrith. So seriously did Charles take him that in 799 only the urgent call of the Pope drew the emperor reluctantly away from the project of a Danish war. The next year, however, on his return from Rome, he built ships and began fortifying the Frisian shores against the raids of Guthfrith's fleets. Four years later, in 808, war began in earnest. Guthfrith boldly laid claim to Frisia and to Saxony. He proposed nothing less than the conquest of Germany and the repression of Frankish power.

Moreover, the operations of Guthfrith were no mere border forays. They were serious campaigns. His forces were strung out on a line some two hundred miles long. In the east his land army crossed the Elbe, and proceeded to put out of action the Slavonic Abodriti who were in alliance with Charles, and who were in a position to attack his communications if he advanced south : while westward, his fleets hovered on the North Frisian coast, doing much damage. Charles tried to grapple with the real difficulty—the naval. He built ships as swiftly as possible ; he erected moles and fortified bridges to bar the mouths of the rivers. His whole position was unmistakably on the defensive. Guthfrith also was busy. He built the first Danewerk, for the better definition and protection of his dominions in the Jutish peninsula.

Guthfrith was not ready to move again until two years after this : but then his action was swift. It fell this time upon Frisia. Charles, at Aachen, was dumbfounded to hear that the Frisian defences had been forced : a fleet of two hundred ships had landed an army in Frisia : three battles had been fought, and Guthfrith had withdrawn only after receiving a formal capitulation. Nor was his withdrawal a retreat. He had returned north to bring down fresh reinforcements, and to carry out his usual administrative business at home. Charles was roused to more serious action than he had taken since the prime of his days, when he was without dispute the greatest European soldier of his time. The Frankish levy was raised in full force. He took up a position near Verden, where the Aller flows into the Weser above Bremen. There Charles the Great awaited in person the advance of Guthfrith the Proud.

III

The news which actually arrived was unexpected. Guthfrith was dead. The Danish fleet had returned north. Hamburg—not the great Hamburg of to-day, but the little Hamburg from which it sprang—had indeed been captured by the Wiltzes : but the whole advance of the Danes had been broken up.

The story of Guthfrith's death was known to the Frankish chronicler, though he did not deign to record what seemed, no doubt, to a churchman, the sordid details of a sensational scandal. It is to the journalistic instinct of the Northmen, which we inherit from them, that we must turn for the facts.

Guthfrith's marriage with Alfhild, the widow of Sigfrith, had resulted in the birth of a son, a half-brother of Ragnar, known in northern history as Olaf " Geir-stead-Elf." Alfhild probably died some time before 810 ; in any case, Guthfrith applied for the hand of Asa, daughter of Harald, King of Agdir in Norway. Harald refused. If he scented some project of employing his daughter's marriage to get Agdir out of the hands of his sons, into the hands of Guthfrith, his suspicions were to some extent justified by the results of his refusal. Guthfrith employed force. He entered Agdir, slew Harald, and married Asa. This may have occupied him during the blank year 809. The possession of Agdir was a small profit to set beside the consequences which followed. Asa waited until her son was born—the child who afterwards was to be the famous Halfdan the Black, named after Guthfrith's father and brother. Then, when Guthfrith came to visit her, she had him assassinated.

The feud was a purely personal and domestic one ; but it shook to pieces the Scandinavian sea-empire which Sigfrith Hring had taken from Harald Hilditann. It had political results of the most far-reaching kind, which we must trace in outline, for they came home with no trifling force to the successors of Egbert of Wessex. Guthfrith left no undisputable successor. There were a number of heirs who laid claim to his hegemony, and a prolonged struggle took place between them.

First, however, Guthfrith's nephew, Hemming, made peace with Charles. The contest for the heritage of Guthfrith then developed. It was fought, not between individuals, but between boards of kings. One group, the " Sons of Guthfrith," which must have included Ragnar, Olaf, and Halfdan as well as Harek and Sigfrith, represented the Norwegian power of Sigfrith Hring ; the other, including Ragnfrith and Harald, represented the old Danish power of Harald Hilditann's family. The sons of Guthfrith ultimately drove Harald to take refuge in Germany. Harek was the man who, as president of the board of kings, assumed the nominal rule of Denmark ; but whether his power was quite what it purported to be is a question. Harald appealed to the emperor for help.

Lewis the Pious, who now occupied the throne of Charles, could not grant help to a heathen. Harald therefore made the critical decision and was baptized at Mainz. With Norwegian support the sons of Guthfrith fought a battle at Ullakr, which was not decisive. They succeeded, however, in forcing Harald to take refuge again in Germany. Two years later, the Franks endeavoured to secure the interests of Harald by negotiation, backed by a demonstration in force along the Eider. They were not definitely intending war, but rather the exercise of pressure, a great part of which was to be moral. This plan was frustrated by Harald himself, who made a raid into Denmark and harried there. The sons of Guthfrith instantly crossed the Eider and by a surprise attack inflicted a crushing defeat on the would-be demonstrators.

The sons of Guthfrith were now strong enough to contemplate an actual invasion of the Frankish empire. It was probably at this point that a certain divergence of opinion and policy began. The ministers of Lewis the Pious had scarcely shown adroitness. They had by this time convinced at least one singularly able man that he could not live in the same world with them ; and they had evidently persuaded him that if not by one means then by another he must break the Frankish threat. The Franks regarded the menace as sufficiently serious to justify the emperor in taking the field in person. Other interests, however, intervened. Olaf Geirstead-Elf died about this time ; and Westfold, as well as his mother's father's kingdom of Agdir, came into the hands of Halfdan the Black.

The accession of Halfdan made a considerable change in the situation of affairs. He had ideas and intentions quite other than those of Ragnar. He had no sympathy with imperial schemes. The old kingdom of Guthfrith had been slipping into chaos while Olaf was devoting his attention to the southern wars. Halfdan carried his Norwegian people with him ; and from the date of his accession a decisive rift began in the sea-empire of Harald and Sigfrith Hring. Halfdan settled down to the steady business of building up a compact national kingdom.

IV

Ragnar does not seem to have interfered in any way with Halfdan. After the death of Olaf Geirstead-Elf he began to devote himself to other schemes of a much wider and more complex character. In 831 he was in Ireland ; and it is shortly after this time that we begin to notice a new policy and new methods among the raiders. Ragnar turned his energies from the Frankish borders to the western seas. His reasons were sound. On land the Danes had no advantage over the Franks, but on the water they were completely masters of the situation ; and Ragnar proceeded to exploit to their full extent the possibilities placed in his hands by control of the sea.

The whole history of Ragnar and of Ragnar's sons is a singular one. It struck even his contemporaries as singular. It bears no likeness whatsoever to the history of men like Charles or Alfred the Great. He was a very famous man, whose memory fascinated the interest of succeeding generations just as that of Napoleon fascinates ours. His power was not the formal, official power, which accompanies the rulers and commanders of mature political states. It was a personal power, much more like that of an influential banker or company director. He had no more authority than he could at any given time get men to give him. It was a strangely anonymous power. Secrecy and silence wrapped Ragnar about, until we begin to suspect that they were intentional. No pomp or Oriental magnificence surrounded him. No mediaeval kings-of-arms stalked before him. Reading the Christian chroniclers, we see vast armies and fleets, great expeditions ; we see cunning policies adopted, profound plans made ; but we see no author. For all that we could tell, these armies and fleets and policies and plans might be the result of mere accident and drift and confusion, if it were not that such things do not come by chance ; and if it were not that every now and then the name of Ragnar slips out unexpectedly, in connections which confirm the general accounts of northern historians. He sat in the background spinning his web of war and statecraft, while other men took the nominal leadership. His own countrymen, when they came to record his deeds, did so with strange mistakes which almost suggest that they had been mystified of set purpose. There was a twist or kink in Ragnar that was not uncommon among the men of the heathen north. He could not do anything quite straight ; he could not be ever quite candid. His mind was tied into a knot like one of those involved decorative dragons which northern men graved on their doorways and on their tombs.

V

The increased activity which followed Ragnar's presence in Ireland is visible between 830 and 840. A chain of settlements was built up along the Irish coast. The plunder of the great shrines and monasteries of Ireland was a profitable speculation. Ireland was not then the poor country it afterwards became ; it was almost untouched by serious war, and bullion had been accumulating for over a thousand years—ever since, in the Bronze Age, Ireland became a gold-producing country.[1] But no less important, to a man with long views, was the strategical advantage of an Irish base. The Irish question began with Ragnar.

It was certainly from Ireland that the threat slowly developed. Wicklow was established in 835 : Dublin in 836. Southern and central Scotland were reconnoitred. The attack upon Charmouth happened in the last-named year. The occupation of Cornwall came two years later. Meanwhile, the first of the grand fleets had tested the Frisia-Flanders route. It spent three years in attacking

[1] We have no guide to the amount of bullion taken out of Ireland by the Danes; but, even judged by modern standards, it must have been large —and gold was far more valuable then than it is now. Its effect upon Denmark was exactly that of Mexican and Peruvian gold upon Spain. When the boom was over, Denmark returned to the normal, where it has remained ever since.

the continental coast as far south as the Loire, but it hardly touched England. The Danish leaders were still exploring, gathering information, and acquiring experience. They had not yet penetrated the secret of England. When, in 839, Egbert died, they were still endeavouring to reach the Franks without possessing an English base : and it was becoming ever clearer that they would not succeed.

But soon after Egbert's death the threat grew more ominous. In 839 the " great royal fleet " of Thorgest arrived in Ireland. The policy of Thorgest was exceedingly definite. He set with system about the task of reducing the country. He built a fortified camp on Lough Rea, captured Armagh, the chief seat of Irish religion, and made himself abbot of the monastery. He is said to have set his wife, Otta, over the Abbey of Clonmacnois, where she sat on the altar and gave answers like the Pythian priestess of the Delphic oracle. No royal person of the name of Thorgest, nor of any name like it, is known ; and it is noteworthy that his capture and death at the hands of King Maelseachlann in 843 made little difference.

VI

While Thorgest was maintaining and extending the Danish hold on Ireland, the main fleets were engaged in much more serious work. Coming down by the Frisia-Flanders route, the main fleet attacked the English ports from Lindsey down to Kent, tested London and Rochester, and spread as far as Southampton and Portland. It had no notable success ; but England was not its immediate objective. It crossed to Etaples, worked along to the Seine mouth, and sacked Rouen. It took its time. It pushed up the Seine and in 845 arrived at Paris.

This was the greatest expedition so far undertaken by the Danes, and its leader was Ragnar. The city was hastily evacuated. Ragnar was exploring and testing rather than contemplating serious conquest ; he allowed himself to be bought off by seven thousand pounds of silver bullion, and in addition took, as souvenirs, a few decorative objects from the churches of Paris. The public opinion of the age triumphantly pointed to the result. Bad weather fought against the Danes ; a plague-mist followed them ; dysentery broke out, and the retreat, though safely effected, was almost a rout.

In the meantime, another fleet had carried out an exploit no less remarkable. Starting from an Irish base, the sons of Ragnar had worked their way south to Spain. It was purely a voyage of exploration. The Moors were astonished and interested at the northern shipmen. The contact so established was followed by a certain amount of communication between the Irish ports and the ports of Spain. At least one Moorish embassy reached Ireland, and left on record an interesting description of what it saw there.

The Danes were reaching farther and farther south, in ever increasing force. The Spanish Moors were the first people they had encountered who also belonged to a non-Roman world outside the Frankish empire.

VII

The prolonged absence of Ragnar, and the disasters of the French campaign, had shaken his position at home. In 850 there was serious revolt in Denmark itself. A battle at Gronsund was followed by the reduction of Seelund and the restoration of Ragnar's authority. Considerable changes were made in the local government of Denmark, and the under-kingships were redistributed.

His return home evidently, had a reason. It was becoming ever more obvious that, in order to reach Gaul effectively, an English base was indispensable. The attack upon England was bound to come sooner or later, but the methods by which it could be conducted were not yet clear. Great strides had been taken towards the discovery of the true strategical routes, and the correct bases for fleet operations in the western seas ; but the Danes seem so far to have had no great acquaintance with the topography of England, nor any definite knowledge of the military methods which would be required.

A year after the suppression of the revolt in Denmark, the first tentative attack on England was made. Three hundred and fifty ships took the Frisia-Flanders route. An advance party of Danes had already occupied Thanet, whence they were expelled by Aethilwulf's eldest son Aethilstan, the under-king of Kent, before they had gathered the information necessary to guide the plans of the expedition. Aethilstan died of his wounds. The incertitude of the Danish leaders with respect to England, and the imperfect intelligence they had gathered, are illustrated by the curious nature of the plan of invasion. It was never repeated.

The fleet sailed into the Thames. Canterbury was taken by storm : Rochester next. The fleet then proceeded to London. Here it defeated the Mercian army of King Beortwulf. Turning south, the Danish army followed Stane Street—which was strategically a blind alley. Aethilwulf advanced with the main forces of Wessex. With the Roman roads at his disposal, he would have no difficulty in concentrating the levy either at Chichester or at Winchester. He was swift : for he met the Danes at Ockley, just south of Dorking : and at that place was fought a battle which ended in the destruction of the Danish host—" the greatest slaughter of the heathen army " says the *Chronicle*, " that we have heard of up to this day."

VIII

These two defeats—the failure of the expedition to Paris, and the disaster at Ockley—drove the Danes still farther afield in their search for the secret they needed. Ragnar, still feeling his way, returned to Ireland. He spent some time in securing the country pending a long departure, and a whole year afterwards at Dublin, in the actual preparations for it. Taking into account the novelty of the experiment, and the resources at his command, the voyage he then made was probably as great an adventure as the later voyages of Magellan and Drake. His fleet crossed the Bay of Biscay, sailed down the coast of Spain, went through the Straits of Gibraltar, and doubled the Spanish peninsula, reaching the mouths of the Rhone. He went some way up the Rhone ; but the prospect of fighting his way back overland was too dangerous to be faced. He preferred to attempt Italy.

He got as far as Luna, which he took by a stratagem, and he is said to have had designs upon Rome itself. After ages asserted that when he came to Luna, he mistook it for Rome, and went no farther—an explanation ingenious enough to have had its origin in Ragnar's own mind. But the voyage was too long, and they had come too far, and Rome was too formidable a city—how formidable, he may only have realized when he saw Italian civilization for himself. He sailed back the way he had come, and arrived home after a voyage of three years.

At some time between the years 862 and 866, Ragnar died. He was alleged by the later saga-men to have

I

been captured and slain by King Aelle of Northumbria ; but the death of Ragnar is of a piece with his life— elusive, mystifying, and doubtful. The outline of his career can be roughly tested by the agreement of the independent narratives of the northern and the Frankish chroniclers ; but the minor details given by the former can never now be verified, nor even made to agree with any other known facts.

IX

The Mediterranean voyage was the greatest of Ragnar's achievements, as it was the last. He had been a discoverer and a marker-out of paths, rather than a successful soldier or statesman. He was the man who first realized the potentialities and the principles of naval war. He demonstrated the possibility of moving great fleets over immense stretches of sea ; he conceived the first idea of those chains of naval bases which have since become the foundation of British naval power. We can hardly point to a single great success he won. Most of his enterprises were, in the military sense, failures ; and sometimes disastrous failures. His real success was in the originality and usefulness of the ideas which he passed on for other men to develop. And at any rate, his failures were triumphantly far from the seas and coasts of Denmark.

There can have been few men who exploited to better profit a somewhat slender stock of advantages. In addition to those which he received from his birth and early training there were others which we cannot doubt he deliberately acquired. He was evidently well acquainted with the classical methods of besieging fortified places—at least, his sons employed them, and tradition attributed them to Ragnar. The military tactics employed by his sons had affinities with Roman methods. They employed the Roman roads, mounted infantry, and the system of earthwork fortification. They also knew the ancient sea-routes southward from Britain to the Mediterranean. These coincidences seem too numerous to be wholly accidental.

Irish monasteries contained more things than plate and vestments. They contained libraries, and men who were capable of reading them. But Ragnar must have been a remarkable man to have grasped the possible amount of useful information that could be acquired by such means ; and he remained for many a day the only Northman who ever troubled himself to acquire it.

X

It it be possible to estimate the personality of Ragnar from the hints and suggestions buried amid the legends of later times, we might infer him to have been not the noble blonde beast of the legendary sagas, but a subtle, twisted, and accumulative man, somewhat of the type of Louis XI of France or Henry VII of England. But there must have been a streak of inspiring romantic imagination in him—a sense of the sea and of the adventure that lies in seafaring—which, in spite of the fact that it continually led him to over-shoot his mark, would explain the hold he had upon the Danes, and the tremendous tradition he left behind him. He became the typical representative of the wicking age, who embodied that new world of the open sea which was the gift of his country and generation to mankind.

Whatsoever his personal failures, he had been a bold experimentalist. He gathered, and bequeathed to his sons, a body of knowledge, an established fame and a full treasury—gifts which they proceeded to use.

CHAPTER VII

KING AETHILWULF AND THE CAMPAIGN AGAINST ENGLAND

I

THE reign of King Egbert marked a definite period in the growth of the English kingship. When Egbert died and Aethilwulf stepped into his shoes, we are conscious that a great change had come to pass. It was a change in the moral atmosphere, rather than in anything else. About Aethilwulf there clings an air of security, and even of antiquity. Although he was the son of a man who had fled overseas for his life, and had spent some years in exile, yet Aethilwulf lived in an atmosphere of firmly established and immemorial right. The old sense of peril, of instability, of impending change, of hourly doubt, had disappeared. He creates in us the impression that he was an old man—though, in actual fact, he died younger than many of the contemporaneous kings of Europe. And this feeling reflects the truth that Aethilwulf did occupy, almost first among English kings, a perfectly assured position, based on the unanimous consent of his subjects. What had once been hazardous and questionable had slipped quietly into being a matter of course.

The supremacy over all England had passed into the hands of men who embodied a new spirit. The royal house of Wessex was torn by none of those dramatic feuds which had rent the lines of Northumbria ; it breathed none of that fierce and impatient temper which had marked the Mercian royal family. Even when they played their part in terrible events, the West Saxon kings

did so with a curiously gentle and amiable air. Most of
them were good men, even when judged by the standard
of far later and more exacting ages. One of them—
Alfred—was almost a saint, and perhaps missed canoni-
zation only because of a touch of sober realism which
forbade him the eccentricity of working miracles. They
dispensed altogether with that apparatus of intrigue,
murder, imprisonment, and repression which some
dynasties have felt indispensable, if not to their happiness,
at least to their security. They were destined to reign
for over two hundred years, and to demonstrate that
amiable virtues can be a good investment for kings.

II

The battle of Ockley, fought twelve years after the
accession of Aethilwulf, was a decisive one. The rest of
his reign was not disturbed by any serious war. Even
with the Danes ravaging the coast of the Continent, and
the Northmen building their naval bases in the Irish
Sea, England still seemed able to hold herself secure.
Wales was the only point of danger. The year after the
battle of Ockley, the Danes made an attempt to reach
England through Wales, and actually penetrated as far
as Shropshire. Aethilwulf and Buhred of Mercia seem
to have agreed that the Welsh were perfectly able to
bar this road if they had a sufficiently strong motive
for wishing to do so. Buhred accordingly married
Aethilwulf's daughter as a mark of good faith, and the
two kings, in 853, entered Wales together. The demonstration was successful. Rhodri ap Merfyn, realizing the
situation, undertook to prevent the passage or settlement
of enemies.

Aethilwulf felt safe enough to undertake a journey to
Rome in 855. The effectiveness of his Welsh policy was

demonstrated during his absence. In 855 the Danes made a second attempt on Wales. They were defeated by Rhodri, and their leader, Orm, slain. Wales was therefore never to any serious extent settled by Danes or Northmen, and remained permanently a buffer state securely protecting central England on the west.

III

The proceedings in Wales, however important in their way, were less important than certain obscure skirmishings to which Aethilwulf paid, apparently, no very great attention. Small parties of Danes landed in Thanet and Sheppey, near the short sea-route from the Continent, and defied all local efforts to eject them. These reconnoitring parties were in all probability a far more serious danger than the English realized. Some-one seems to have been trying to gather more definite information than the Danes had hitherto possessed on the subject of the topography of England. According to the Danish chroniclers, Hingwar, Ragnar's son, was in England round about this time ; and it is all the more possible that he was present in Thanet or Sheppey, in that the visitors showed a fighting power which hints that they were no casual raiders, but a picked comitatus. Alderman Ealhere of Kent was slain in an attempt to expel them.

We shall see, later on, that the conduct of the next invasion of England showed complete and intimate acquaintance with the geography of the country : and we shall note the identity of its leader.

IV

The visit of Aethilwulf to Rome was important. It was the first such visit ever paid by a king of all England. Coming so soon after the battle of Ockley, it had something of the nature of a diplomatic mission to mark and confirm the adherence of England to the cause of Christendom. Aethilwulf did something more : he took with him his youngest and favourite son, Alfred, then six years of age.

King Aethilwulf had been married to Osburga, daughter of Oslac, a Jute of the Isle of Wight, descended from the family of the Jutish conquerors Stuf and Wihtgar. Alfred was his fifth son. This Jutish strain in Alfred is worth noting. How little the strict rule of primogeniture had as yet affected kingship is illustrated in his father's attitude towards him. At four years old Alfred was sent to Rome. In sending so young a child upon a journey which, in those days, was so long and so dangerous, and accompanied by such serious risks to health, Aethilwulf's motive must have been personal and dynastic. Pope Leo IV received the child, graciously adopted him as his spiritual son, and invested him with the consular insignia, which Alfred apparently thought was the holy anointing of a Christian king.[1] It is more difficult to surmise Aethilwulf's purpose in taking him on the same journey again, two years later. Asser, who probably received his information in after years from Alfred himself, says that it was because Aethilwulf loved him more than his other sons. Osburga, apparently, was dead, and the king preferred to keep Alfred under his own eye.

There can hardly have been another English king who, before he was ten years old, had twice visited Rome. Quite as important as the moral impression produced upon Alfred by the vast and venerable city,

---

[1] This incident is discussed in Mr. Stevenson's *Asser's Life of Alfred*, note to ch. 8. The investiture was in keeping with the traditional train of thought Alfred had received from his predecessors. The rite of anointing became the peculiar privilege of the English, the French and (later on) the Scottish kings. See J. Wickham Legg, *The Sacring of the English Kings*, p. 5.

and by the great ecclesiastical monarch who now represented its power, must have been the experience of
the journey thither and back ; the sea-crossing, the rivers
and hills of Gaul, the huge mountain chains that barred
the entrance to Italy, the olive and the vine of that land
where the old civilization was scarcely dead, if ever it
did die. The civilization of Italy changed, rather than
perished.

Before he was out of childhood, therefore, Alfred had
seen Frank and Burgundian and Gaul, Lombard, Tuscan,
and Roman, and had heard them speak in their own
tongues. He had seen two popes,[1] and sat at the feet of
an emperor : he had learned something of the size of
Europe, something of the meaning of its racial differences,
something of its topography. No learning out of books,
however good, could have given him the education he
thus received from his own childish experiences. The
observation of a young child is keen, wide, and un-
prejudiced. What he sees is never forgotten. These
journeys are part of the secret of Alfred's later character
as a king.

V

Aethilwulf remained a year in Rome. The visit was
thus no hasty trip, but a stay sufficiently long to have
allowed Alfred time to see much, and to become acquainted with the unbroken tradition of Roman civilization. He heard Latin spoken as a living language by
men to whom it was their mother-tongue. Rome itself,
the city, was in those days comparatively intact ; not,
indeed, undamaged by war and decay, but still so near
to its virgin state that to a child—and perhaps to any
Englishman of the day—it must have seemed a wonder
of glory and magnificence.

---

[1] Benedict III became Pope in 855.

No modern eye has looked upon the Rome which King Alfred saw and lived in. In later centuries the old city was gradually pulled to pieces to build mediaeval Rome. He must have seen libraries, and have become accustomed to the idea that men could and did read the books in them. Long before he could understand the full import of what he had seen, he must have acquired a store of memories which later on enabled him to see the state of England in its true light. That Aethilwulf should have had the wisdom to give Alfred a year in Rome is sufficient of itself to prove him a man of understanding. It was enough for a life's work. It went far towards forming the man we now remember as Alfred the Great.

VI

On his way home, Aethilwulf married Judith, daughter of Charles the Bald, king of the West Franks, the future emperor. Aethilwulf could hardly be in Gaul, and marry Charles's daughter, without meeting Charles himself : and if he met him, then Alfred also met him. Two great neighbouring rulers, such as were the king of the Franks and the king of the English, had much to say to one another.

Charles had his own difficulties to contend with, and his own ideas concerning the right method of dealing with them. He had been deeply involved in all the dramatic events attending the breaking up and division of the empire of Charles the Great ; and although his life has all the air of being a losing fight, and his policies seemed to be failures, yet that lost battle ended in the creation of modern France, which is no failure. Like most French rulers, he lived and governed upon a somewhat larger scale than his English contemporaries. He wielded larger armies, and struggled with more formidable social forces. The marriage of Aethilwulf and Judith was a pledge of mutual understanding between the two kingdoms. How far, in the circumstances of the day, they could actually help one another was perhaps doubtful ; but the expression of sympathy and alliance against a common foe was no idle gesture.

Charles the Bald had, moreover, a point of contact with the English king which was of a peculiar nature.

The English had learnt from the Welsh those doctrines of the imperial sovereignty of Britain which, in spite of their sympathy with the moral and religious unity of Roman civilization, made them indisposed to admit its political unity. Egbert had been prudent in his dealings with the subject : but Charles himself was being driven by circumstances into a position resembling the English. As king of the Franks he was not inclined to admit more imperial control than he could help. His own claims to the imperial crown were rather more a claim to an imperial sovereignty in Gaul than a claim to the supreme rule *urbis et orbis*. The alliance of Charles and Aethilwulf thus took place at the time when ideas of national sovereignty were first stirring. The nations themselves were hardly as yet in existence. But a common interest that can scarcely be defined can often be felt. Charles had an interest in associating himself with the one people in Christian Europe which privately maintained in theory, and managed publicly to maintain in practice, its political independence.

Besides this, the idea of local independence was " in the air." Charles's great vassals were already contemplating those claims which, a little later, gave rise to the great fiefs. Nothing could be more natural than that, when everyone was preparing to assert a sovereign independence, the king also should assert it. Europe was drifting slowly towards the creation of a landed aristocracy ; not merely a landed upper class, but an aristocracy in the true sense, an organized caste of land-holding soldiers who formed an order based upon personal service and personal relationship, not upon official position and administrative law. This, which contained the seeds of immense changes for Europe, was arising spontaneously as a result of the difficulties created by the Danish wars.

Charles and Aethilwulf were thus not likely to lack subjects for intimate conversation. No matter how delicately they might feel it expedient to tread, there were burning themes for discussion which only reigning kings could discuss. Alfred betrayed, in later life, some knowledge of the military methods which Charles employed against the Danes. It is needless to doubt that he saw some of them with his own eyes : that he saw the new stone-built castles and fortified bridges : that he saw Charles himself, and could form an estimate of how much strength there was in Gaul, and what manner of men the Franks were. The acquaintance with the Continent which Egbert gained was repeated in Alfred. The Christian kings were assuredly linking themselves together in at least sympathetic unity, if no more, against the threat from the north.

VII

The incidents of Aethilwulf's return to England proved that some idea of all these things was stirring at home. His eldest son, Aethilstan, had died some years before, after the sea-fight at Sandwich in 850. Aethilbald, who now ranked as the eldest, put forward claims which were distinctly hostile to Alfred. Aethilbald's demands for a " division of the kingdom," backed by Ealhstan, bishop of Sherborne, and Eanwulf, alderman

of Somerset,[1] were really a claim for the execution of a
definite act of settlement and succession. The suggestion
was not unreasonable. Aethilwulf had given Alfred
certain moral claims which, unless a definite settlement
were made, would put him, a child, into a position of
advantage over his elder brothers. None of them had
been anointed by the Pope. The king's marriage with
Judith had not been in all ways popular. Aethilwulf
regarded her in the Frankish fashion, as his queen, and,
to some extent, as an actual sharer of his throne. This
was not in accord with the old tradition of Wessex
kingship.

Aethilwulf's policy was indeed open to a good deal
of suspicion from the more conservative members of his
court, who may have seen in it distinct signs of a tendency
—even if not an intention—to define a new international
royal caste marrying among itself, and to draw the line
in such a way as to exclude the junior branches of the
old tribal caste. The whole situation had a precedent
still fresh in the minds of elderly men. It was the same
situation which had existed when Lewis the Pious
attempted to push forward the claims of his youngest
son—who, it is highly interesting to note, was no less a
person than Charles the Bald himself. In that case the
elders had intervened, and after a disastrous civil war
had divided the empire. It looked very much as if
Aethilwulf were a new Lewis, and young Alfred a new
Charles.

There the likeness stopped. Either the sons of Aethilwulf were much more good-natured men than those
of Lewis the Pious, or Aethilwulf was a much more
dexterous diplomatist than Lewis—and possibly these

---

[1] Professor Chadwick has indicated the probability that these aldermen
were the old " sub-reguli," and members of the junior branches of the
royal house (*Studies*, ch. viii).

alternatives are both of them true. The settlement which was finally executed made provision for the claims of the elder sons, and also achieved the main point which Aethilwulf wished to secure, and Lewis the Pious had signally failed to achieve—the preservation of the unity of the crown in the hands of his chosen successor.

Aethilwulf himself elected to retain the kingdom of Kent [1]—not for its unimportance, but for its importance. It was an investiture which like the modern principality of Wales, was frequently given to the king's eldest son or prospective successor. Aethilbald was given Wessex. The arrangement (which has come down to us as the " Will of Aethilwulf ") was peaceably effected and systematically carried out ; and the good faith shown by all the parties to the compact was the direct cause of the survival of Wessex and the restoration of the English crown by West Saxon kings. It prescribed that on the death of Aethilwulf the over-kingship should pass to Aethilbald, while Aethilbert succeeded to the sub-kingdom of Kent : and that the remaining brothers should succeed one another in the same way, in order of age. The result was that the rights of any sons were passed over in favour of the rights of the brothers. If Alfred lived, he was thus certain to come to the throne in due course, and he would then be in a position to make a fresh act of settlement according to his own views.

This arrangement did not owe its existence to the greed and ambition of the sons of Aethilwulf. Its terms show plainly that a good deal was surrendered by the elder brothers, who cannot have been unaware that they were sacrificing the interests of their possible children. Alfred, in later years, rehearsed its terms without the

---

[1] Stevenson, *Asser's Life of Alfred*, note to ch. 12. It should be emphasized that in this arrangement Aethilwulf was not being pushed into a subordinate position. Kent was the cornerstone of his kingdom.

least suggestion that it was unfairly partial to himself. The object was to preserve the unity of England—in which it succeeded [1]—and in the hands of the man best suited to rule. But this last is an insoluble problem the difficulties of which at last drove statesmen to accept the workable though arbitrary rule of primogeniture. It was such experiences as those of Lewis and Aethilwulf that at last forced primogeniture on a perhaps not too enthusiastic world.

Men parted with reluctance from the idea that some form of deliberate choice was morally necessary in settling the succession. In their efforts to avoid the results which sometimes followed from strict primogeniture they resorted again and again to the peculiar collegiate type of monarchy which we see illustrated in such forms as the sons of Guthfrith, the sons of Ragnar, the sons of Aethilwulf, and the sons of Gunnhild, in which we almost find monarchy taking the shape of a board of kings. Aethilwulf's act of settlement was perhaps the soundest in theory and the best carried out of all these royal boards. He actually secured the important point that supreme control should rest in the hands of one brother at a time. The amiability and loyalty of the house of Wessex thus counted as a valuable political asset, making for the stability of the crown and of the very young and unformed nation to which it was slowly giving substance and shape.

King Aethilwulf died some two years after his return from Rome. Something of his prestige and augustness peeps from the mighty genealogy which the annalist

---

[1] Aelfric, writing a century and a half later, will not even copy from his Latin original references to two Caesars or emperors reigning at the same time : " but I everywhere speak of *one* emperor as being concerned in the persecution of the martyrs ; just as our own nation is subject to one king, and is accustomed to speak of one king and not of two " (Aelfric, *Lives of Saints*, ed. W. W. Skeat, E.E.T.S., p. 5).

sets down for him. He traced Aethilwulf back to the ancient gods. We know very little in detail of the old king : but the hints we have—the battle of Ockley, the Welsh campaign, the education he provided for Alfred, and the act of settlement contained in his will—imply a man powerful, prudent, and wise. He was one of those men whose greatness consists not so much in any great deeds they themselves do, as in the skill and forethought with which they provide for the successors who are to follow them.

VIII

Aethilbald reigned two years and a half—an uneventful reign—and the reign of Aethilbert who duly succeeded to the crown, was equally uneventful until the last of its six years. England pursued the even tenour of its way untouched by serious trouble. It was in 861, the first year of Aethilbert, when Alfred was twelve years old, that the famous incident occurred which has crept into every history of England. He received no early book-learning ; there was very little to be acquired, and it is probable that Alfred had already learnt in Italy as much as the educational resources of England could have taught him. He lived an outdoor life, and was an ardent huntsman. But he listened with attention to the English poems which were recited at meal-times. What they were, no man can now tell : but they may have been any or all of the tales whose sole remaining trace is the catalogue of heroic names in *Widsith* : and there may have been others, one or two of which (such as the tale of Cynewulf and Cyneheard) were embodied into the English *Chronicle* : and some may have survived as late as the days of William of Malmesbury and Henry of Huntingdon : robust and dramatic tales, whose main motives consisted of doing what no one else dared to do, and of dying in the last ditch. Judith noticed his interest ; and one day she showed him and his brother Aethilred a book of English poems, promising it to the one who should first learn it. Alfred was the first, and won the book.

Now Judith was the great-grand-daughter of Charles the Great : and Charles had once collected a book of ancient Frankish poems. This book (for which a modern scholar would gladly give the shirt off his back) Lewis the Pious with impious piety destroyed, on the ground of its heathen tendencies—a loss for which there is no compensation. That Judith should possess a similar book of English poems shows that Charles's example was not without its imitators. But who gathered the poems, and what they were, are problems over which imagination may linger fruitlessly, though fondly.

The real point of the story lies in the evidence it affords us of the interest which Alfred took in the traditions and spirit of his own people : and the fact, which is of no small importance, that others before him had troubled to collect them. We may gather that all the sympathy with Roman civilization which was shown by the ruling house of Wessex did not divert them from their own tradition.

IX

It must have been during the reign of Aethilbert that Ragnar Lothbrok died. It is improbable that they heard of it at Winchester : improbable that they knew more of him than the vaguest rumour. Ragnar had masked himself close during his lifetime. His death threw open the flood-gates and let loose the inundation upon England.

All very great events have a quality of surprise about them. Ragnar's death was, we may infer, rather nearer to 862 than to 866 : for the events which began in the latter year needed preparation. They were not casual events. They fell upon England not only with the unexpectedness but with the force with which a similar storm fell upon Belgium in 1914. A new mind, a new man had stepped upon the stage, who, in the practical conduct of war was a much greater man than Ragnar.

The events began ominously. In 865 a party of Danes wintered in Thanet.

No stout King Aethilstan was present to eject these strangers at the cost of his own life. They bargained with the Kentish men, who promised them money, presumably in order to avoid the taking of supplies by force. But before the money was paid, the Danes began to forage in eastern Kent. The problem was never cleared up ; but apparently the Danes found the money delayed, and suspected that the English were employing the interval to gather men. They may have been right in their suspicion : but they had guilty consciences, for in the spring of 866 the fleet of Hingwar, Ragnar's son, arrived from Denmark.[1] The storm had burst.

The English did not realize at first the full import of the proceedings which began to follow one another with increasing rapidity. Hingwar, from Thanet, shifted north into East Anglia. The move was destined to be terribly familiar to Englishmen in later years. It was the regular opening gambit of a Danish invasion : not now experimental, but made in full knowledge and foresight of the completed game.

Hingwar negotiated with the East Anglians. They supplied him with horses—for which that part of England has been famous since the days of the Iceni—and he undertook to preserve the peace with them. This was the old policy in Cornwall and in Wales : but no Egbert

---

[1] For Hingwar, the "lost Napoleon" of the Danish wars, see Mr. Collingwood in *Scandinavian Britain*, pp. 84–8.

or Aethilwulf arrived upon the scene. The death of Aethilbert and the succession of Aethilred may have paralysed the action of Wessex. Hingwar spent a year in East Anglia : and by the end of that time there can have been very little concerning the topography of England which he did not know.

From Cambridge the roads northwards were easily accessible. Hingwar, with his mobile mounted columns crossed the Humber early in 867, and occupied Northumbria. By the autumn, York had fallen easily into his hands. With York as his base he was in touch with Ireland, and commanded all the network of Roman roads which had long ago been designed, by men who knew their business as soldiers, to converge on the strategic centre of northern England. York was never again to pass into English possession on the old terms.

He laid his plans with evident knowledge of the political conditions of the country. He could never have walked into York as he did, had not Northumbria been torn by party divisions which, while hitherto convenient enough to Wessex, were now to be utilized against her. The Northumbrians consulted together during the winter, and sank their differences. Before spring was well advanced in 868, a united host appeared before York. The assault on the city was allowed to make some headway ; the Northumbrians were already through the gate, when Hingwar sprang his ambuscade. The fall of men was great and disastrous. So fatal was the slaughter, that the battle of York Gate, on March 1, 868, was practically the end of English Northumbria, the great realm of Edwin and Oswi, Baeda and Caedmon.

From his proceedings, it is clear enough that Hingwar had come to make a permanent conquest. Northumbria was not ravaged. Any plundering that occurred was on a trifling scale, and affected only the more wealthy centres where portable wealth could be seized. The land itself remained undamaged. Hingwar set up a new king who, whether from motives of self-interest or for the benefit of his country, was willing to conduct the government of Northumbria as a deputy of the Danes.

X

Wessex had not yet moved. Any attempt to strike at Hingwar without the assured support of the local English would have been a step too dangerous to risk. If the extraordinary mobility of the Danes—which was to be amply demonstrated a year or two later—were already impressed upon the minds of the West Saxon leaders, it would be easy to understand their caution. Long before an army could arrive from Wessex, the Danes would have stamped down any merely local effort. The unity of England was moreover so imperfect that the old kingdoms had a natural tendency to act as independent units without reference to the whole. East Anglia had, without second thoughts, made a separate peace. These two factors combined to restrain Wessex from hasty action.

But a certain reaction of feeling took place after the capture of York. That Wessex was in active communication with the local powers we can see from several facts. Alfred's marriage took place this year, and his bride was Edburga, a daughter of Aethilred, the alderman of the Gaini, of the royal house of the Mercians. During the marriage feast he experienced the first attack of some sickness which he and his age could neither cure nor explain. It was destined to haunt him all his life, though it does not seem to have impaired his practical activity. We may infer, too, that both Mercia and East Anglia were listening to diplomatic representations which were not without effect upon their attitude.

Hingwar in 868 recrossed the Humber and seized Nottingham. King Buhred at once called up the Mercian levy and sent to his over-lord for help. But before the Wessex army could arrive, Buhred had changed his mind, and had entered into a separate treaty with Hingwar, who then, in execution of its terms withdrew to York, while the disappointed Wessex army returned home frustrated.

We are not told the nature of, nor the consideration for, the treaty. Very possibly Hingwar secured it by telling one half of the exact truth : viz. that he did not intend to remain permanently in England, nor to march against either Mercia or Wessex. On such an understanding it might well seem the wisest plan for Mercia to bargain with him. He could have struck his blow long before King Aethilred could have arrived.

But Hingwar—a true heathen—had far other plans. In the ensuing year he marched, not against Mercia or Wessex but against East Anglia, where Edmund, the under-king, was beginning to realize the full meaning of the Danish invasion. Whatsoever illusions King Buhred of Mercia might be under, Edmund evidently grasped at last the truth that the Danes had come to stay, and that he had made terms with foes with whom compromise was radically impossible for a Christian. Hingwar, carrying out with elaborate scruple the exact letter of his compact with Buhred, avoided Mercia, marched through Lincolnshire, crossed the fens, and entrenched himself at Thetford.

XI

It was now that the presence of the over-king of England was needed ; but he was not there. Whether Edmund ever called upon him to come is unknown. No tradition to that effect ever survived. The East Anglian king measured the force of his own unassisted kingdom against men and tactics novel to him, and far more formidable than he can have realized. He assaulted the Danish camp. Some accounts say that he fell in the defeat which ensued. The later accounts—which the northern traditions endorse—say that he was captured, and upon refusing either to rule under the heathen, or to abjure his faith, was tied to a tree, shot full of arrows, and finally beheaded. The impression made upon men by this event shows some of the reasons why it happened. Edmund was regarded as a man who had staked his life for Christendom.

Hingwar and Hubba are named as the men personally responsible for the martyrdom of Edmund. The great abbey of Medehampstead—which Kings Peada, Wulfhere, and Aethilred had built to commemorate the victory of the faith over their father, old King Penda—was plundered and burned by heathen far more cruel than Penda had ever been. The whole of East Anglia fell into the power of the Danes.

The grim lesson was effective. When the Danes advanced upon Wessex, no man stirred to her help.

XII

The final reduction of England was now close at hand. Hingwar seems to have been so confident of the result that he left affairs in the hands of King Halfdan (commonly believed to be one of his brothers, and a son of Ragnar) and went north, where he effected a junction with Olaf the White, the Norse king of Dublin, besieged and took Dumbarton, subdued Strathclyde, and in the following year returned home to Dublin, leaving the whole of Britain from the Thames to the Clyde in Danish hands. In Dublin he died twelve months later ; so that he, who had all but conquered England, never lived to see how unexpectedly much more there was destined to be to that story.

King Edmund had perished on November 20. By Christmas, moving along the Icknield Way, the Danish host was at Wallingford. On December 28, it occupied Reading, and began to throw up a great earthwork between Thames and Kennet. The aim was Winchester, the capital of England.

We may believe that King Aethilred and young Alfred had made ample preparation, for the defence of Wessex was conducted with skill and effect. The host of Wessex was massed south of the Thames between Reading and Winchester. On December 31, the last day of the year, the Danish advanced posts came into contact with its van. Alderman Aethilwulf, who commanded it, drove back the Danes from Englesfield, and the whole army pressed on to Reading. There, four days afterwards (January 4, 871) the Danish camp was assaulted. The fall of men was heavy : Alderman Aethilwulf was among the slain. Finding it impossible to force the Danish entrenchments, King Aethilred retreated along the Ridgeway. Halfdan now followed ; and on January 8 the two hosts came into contact again at Ashdown. Even at the time, the importance of the battle there fought was recognized. Its results decided the fate of England—and very possibly the whole future of Europe, and with it the fate of the world.

XIII

Old Bishop Asser, who knew no more of war than a mothers' meeting, has transmitted to us an account of the battle which in all probability he derived from Alfred himself. It is a very vague and muddled account, as we might expect ; but as the information which was given him must have been perfectly clear, it is worth while to see if his story can be unravelled.

He tells us that the Danes divided themselves into two bodies, and began to prepare defences. They had two kings among them, and several earls ; so they gave the middle part of the army to the two kings, and the other part to all the earls. The English, observing this, divided their army in a similar manner.

This can hardly mean that the Danes divided their army into two squares or wedges, separate from one another, one under the kings and the other under the earls ; for in that case one of the two could not conceivably be the " middle " part. It also does not mean that there was a centre under the kings and wings under the earls, for then there must have been three bodies, not two. What Asser was told by Alfred is more likely to have been that there was an advanced " boar's-head-array," a wedge formed of the comitatus of the two kings ; and that this was followed at a short distance by an extended line commanded by the earls. The comitatus would then quite truly be " the middle part " to the eye of the English fighting-man ; and yet there would only be two bodies. The tactical purpose would be the old and familiar one of using the boar's-head-array as a spear-head to break the English, leaving the work to be finished by the men of the second line.

The English drew up in similar formation. Now, there were two English, as there were two Danish kings, (Aethilred and Alfred on one hand ; Halfdan and Baskegg on the other), but the command on the English side was differently distributed. Aethilred was to command the boar's-head-array and lead it against the Danish kings, while Alfred led the second line against the earls. But if this were so (and Asser distinctly states

that it was so) there must have been some novel and
unexpected element in the English plan of attack ; and
the probability is that Alfred was to push on past the
battle of the kings, and fall upon the Danish second line
in order to prevent it from intervening.

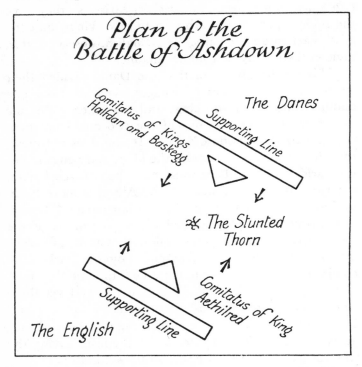

The hosts were ready marshalled. The West Saxon
comitatus was waiting in full force upon the field, ready
to move as soon as King Aethilred arrived. But King
Aethilred did not arrive. He was engaged in hearing
Mass in his tent. Alfred sent a message ; but the King,
in the spirit of Francis Drake, with less than Drake's
acumen, thought that there was time to hear Mass out
to the end and drub the Danes as well. The Danes

seized the opportunity to take the initiative. They had the higher ground ; and they began to come down-hill with the impetus it gave them. Alfred had therefore to decide on the spot whether to withdraw, since the plan arranged was already impracticable, or to take over the sole command and carry matters through as best he could. He had not a minute in which to decide : he scarcely had seconds.

It is not likely that he sent another message to Aethilred, for no such message could have reached the King, and been answered, before the Danes arrived.[1] Confronted with this emergency, he seems to have taken the king's place in the royal comitatus, and to have ordered a charge *up-hill* in order to gather way. It was a step which only a man in direct succession to the throne dared have taken ; for to give orders to the king's comitatus was beyond the power of any other man, and would have been, in fact, high treason. Even in this case it was, strictly speaking, high treason : but it was a treason which everyone seems to have endorsed !

The English plan was therefore, at the last moment, carried out, with the difference that Alfred and not Aethilred commanded the boar's-head-array. It may have been a very great difference indeed.

Asser tells us that he had actually himself seen the famous stunted thorn-tree round which the contact of the two spear-heads took place. To judge by its after fame, the meeting was a truly Homeric one—the picked royal comitatus of Wessex against those formidable " Black Gaill " whose prowess the Irish (no mean judges on such points) so well knew. As the English plan of attack succeeded, we may deduce that the English second

[1] Aethilred showed no cowardice or incompetence. His fault was only in declining to interrupt Mass *before* the Danes had moved. He hoped, doubtless, that they would not move—and, as Asser duly remarks, it was certainly unlucky for them that they did !

line broke and dispersed the Danish, and thus isolated the Danish comitatus, which, already fully occupied with the English comitatus, had to turn and cut its way out of an impossible situation.

The Danish losses were very heavy—the greater part of their army, Asser says. One king and five earls fell on the field. The pursuit lasted all night and even into the next day, and did not stop until the Danes reached " the stronghold from which they had sallied "—which (since it lasted so long) necessarily means not their camp, but their great fortress between Thames and Kennet, on " the right-hand side of Reading."

CHAPTER VIII

THE RESISTANCE OF WESSEX

I

IN spite of the great victory at Ashdown, the English retreat continued. This campaign—the first of its kind ever fought by Englishmen—illustrates admirably the rule that the English are never more deadly than in retreat. A fortnight later, they stood again at Basingstoke, half way to Winchester, when victory was with the Danes. Two months passed before another pitched battle was fought. The combatants were probably glad of a respite to fill up their ranks and replenish their supplies. Then at Marden the third struggle of the campaign took place. The English were at first victorious, but the Danes recovered, and an indecisive battle ended with honours rather on the Danish side. It is possible that King Aethilred was wounded in this battle, for he died soon after Easter, and Alfred, the last of the sons of Aethilwulf, succeeded him. Alfred was twenty-two years old when he became king; a frail and delicate young man on whose health the fate of England and the destiny of Europe depended.

The accession of Alfred appears to have made an immediate change in the conduct of the war, though whether this was due to his own initiative or to the exhaustion of the Danes is not quite clear. Both causes may have co-operated. It seems certain that Winchester fell. No struggle in its defence is recorded; and the probability is that the destruction of Winchester was a minor incident in a general evacuation and retreat westward. Throughout the summer there was skirmishing and fighting as the Danes spread slowly into Wessex.

They got little farther south, so they began to feel their way westward on the skirts of Alfred's retreat. They certainly got as far as Wilton, west of Salisbury. But in spite of strong reinforcements which poured in through Reading during the early summer, they made no substantial headway.

If we understand the facts to imply that Alfred's policy was to empty the country of its inhabitants and to retire westward leaving a desert behind him, much that is mysterious about this campaign is fully explained. Such tactics, which made it difficult for the Danes to live on the country, would have rendered the reinforcements only an additional trouble to feed. Nine pitched battles and many small fights, omitting all count of mere raids, were fought this year. Besides King Baskegg, who fell at Ashdown, nine earls fell on the Danish side. At last Halfdan withdrew. It had become clear that to force a way into Wessex by this road and by these means was not a project likely to be crowned with any kind of profitable success.

Some kind of armistice was arranged, under cover of which Halfdan evacuated Wessex and retreated upon London—no doubt falling back from Basingstoke and Staines along the great Roman road.

II

For two years following the campaign in Wessex there were no serious hostilities. Both sides were preparing to renew the struggle, and the interval was occupied with events which cast much light upon the military side of the contest.

The policy of King Buhred of Mercia was entirely opposed to that of the kings of Wessex. Buhred systematically attempted to deal with the Danes by means of peaceful negotiation. The result of his endeavours illustrates the comparative value of the two methods—at any rate, in the circumstances of the ninth century. The Danes took up winter quarters in London during the autumn of 872. Buhred was compelled to feed and supply this great host, which otherwise would have lived on the countryside in a less economical manner. Halfdan moved north in 873, fixing his headquarters at Torksey in Lindsey. Buhred continued his negotiations, and received fresh assurances and undertakings. He was, however, in an impossible position. Halfdan was planning a new set of operations which involved the use of Mercia ; and although it was useful to keep King Buhred hopeful until all the arrangements were made, the fate of Mercia was nevertheless sealed.

The stroke was not very long in coming. The next year, Halfdan began to move, and advanced to Repton. King Buhred had to flee. The collapse of Mercia, the ancient kingdom of the terrible Penda and the mighty Offa, was swift, utter, and ignominious. Buhred left England and retired to Rome. The Danes set up a native king of their own, one Ceolwulf, who entered into terms of allegiance with them that read like feudal homage. Perhaps, for the cultivator of the soil and the peaceful merchant, this fate was the happiest that could have befallen Mercia. But it implied her complete and permanent abdication of any power to control the destinies of Englishmen.

The Danes were now free to deal with other matters. There was a re-arrangement of the commands. Halfdan took the northern section, and established himself upon the Tyne, while King Guthorm, with Asketil and Hamund as his colleagues, occupied Cambridge with the main body of the Danish army. Halfdan made it his business to continue the conquest of Strathclyde and the Lothians, which Hingwar had begun in 870 ; he sought to re-establish the ancient bounds of Northumbria, as they had existed in the days of the great Bernician kings. During 876 he reorganized and settled the Danish conquests, evidently on the assumption that they were permanent acquisitions, and that he was competent to convey a legal title to property. Guthorm was preparing the campaign against Wessex. The ships were refitted. Small squadrons prospected along the south coast, where Alfred was on the watch for them with a fleet of his own. The attitude of the Danes showed a confidence in the immediate future that was not altogether unjustified.

III

The war was re-opened in 876. King Guthorm's methods were widely different from those of Halfdan. He did not propose to batter a way into Wessex by brute force. His first movement was a fleet movement, difficult to anticipate and impossible to prevent. The Danes entered Poole harbour and occupied Wareham. Alfred at once invested Wareham ; but as the garrison could not be dislodged, it was necessary to parley. They undertook to evacuate Wareham and leave the kingdom —supporting their undertaking by a solemn oath upon the Holy Bracelet " which they would not hitherto swear to any nation." [1] Alfred accepted this, as nothing better could be obtained in the way of guarantees.

Early in spring, 877, however, a mobile column of mounted infantry left Wareham by night and carried out a rapid march upon Exeter. The king pursued with all speed, but could not overtake them. He blockaded them in Exeter, and brought his own ships

---

[1] This " Holy Bracelet " was no doubt a forgery, and the oath therefore null.

round to hold the mouth of the Exe. The next step was for the Danish commander to shift his fleet round from Poole, and raise the blockade—a movement which, owing to the advantages which would be given to the Danes in fleet-fighting by the broad estuary of the Exe, might be calculated upon as almost certain to be successful. The catastrophe which followed was peculiar, and formed the first example of King Alfred's luck. One hundred and twenty ships were wrecked off Swanage. The surviving Danes fell into the hands of the English, who treated them as men convicted of piracy on the high seas.[1]

The disaster at Swanage had far-reaching effects. The expected relief of Exeter did not take place. The Danes were constrained to make fresh—and this time somewhat more serious—overtures. They delivered all the hostages that Alfred demanded, and took all the oaths they knew. Alfred had few means of taking a fortified town, and to starve out a garrison was an expensive proceeding. Once more he accepted the Danish undertakings. The army was allowed to withdraw to Gloucester, within the Mercian border. It entered Mercia at harvest-tide ; which would fall, in south-western England, round about the second week of September. From Alfred's point of view everything had gone off very well.

[1] Swanage is sufficiently close to Poole to make it unlikely that the weather would change to any serious extent after a fleet had left Poole, yet before it had passed Swanage. The wreck of a whole fleet between Poole and Swanage is a fact that needs a good deal of explanation in view of the reputation of the Danes in all ages as seamen. The most probable solution is that the relief of Exeter was urgent, and that the fleet commanders were taking risks under the pressure of necessity. If Alfred were close behind the Danes when they rode into Exeter, it is easy to understand that they might find themselves very badly provisioned for a long stay.

IV

We must remind ourselves, at this point, of one fact very relevant to the subsequent events. The distinction between Christian and heathen ethics was deep and real; it went down to the very foundations of human conduct. No one was more acutely aware of the distinction than Alfred himself. Nevertheless, at this particular moment he forgot it. He had all the less excuse for his forgetfulness, in that he had just experienced a typical instance of heathen ethics in the oath at Wareham. If the Danes had sworn their oath on a genuine sacred ring, they would doubtless have observed it with scrupulous care. But their moral philosophy allowed them to regard as null an oath sworn on a false sacred ring that was not what it purported to be. From the Christian point of view, such an oath was a dishonourable trick. But from the heathen point of view the trick was perfectly legitimate.

King Alfred evidently considered that he had made a binding general agreement at Exeter. But he had not bound King Guthorm, who was not a party to it. There is no reason to suppose that Guthorm himself had been personally in command of the expedition which ended so disastrously for his men at Exeter. He is not named as being there; and the strong probability is that he was not present. It is certain that many or all of the Danes who were allowed to retreat from Exeter kept their oaths. They took up land in Mercia and settled down. But if all this were so, Guthorm might hold himself free from the terms of capitulation; and the events of the succeeding winter would be explained.

Not the army which retreated from Exeter, but a new army, under Guthorm himself, passed through Chippenham early in the New Year and rode straight into the heart of Wessex. The advent of this army seems to have been unexpected. It met with no resistance, but spread itself throughout Wessex and secured itself with fortified posts. Without a serious blow, the country which had hitherto seemed impregnable to all the Danish armies had fallen into their hands ! Many people fled overseas. But Alfred was made of tougher material than King Buhred. He took to the woods and moors with his own house-thanes. Wessex was not to be conquered while he lived.

On his success, Guthorm was to be joined according to plan by King Hubba, the son of Ragnar and the brother of Hingwar, one of the inner circle of Danish leaders, and Hingwar's colleague during the campaign of 870. Hubba entered the Severn early in the year with a squadron of twenty-three ships, to witness and confirm the subjugation of England, and probably to superintend a general reorganization such as Halfdan had carried out in Northumbria. The final passage of England into the possession of the Danes was too important an occasion, and meant too much for the future, to be treated as an episode. It was a solemn occasion which marked the completion of one half of the great design of Ragnar, with every prospect that in due time the whole design would be complete.

V

The events of the year had so far been very distinctly to Alfred's discredit : he had allowed himself to be caught off his guard, and had been outwitted—as grave a fault in a commander as sleeping on sentry-duty is to a soldier. But Alfred was now thoroughly alive to the situation. Instead of walking into a subjugated Wessex, Hubba landed into the arms of Odda and his men.[1]

Any blame that attaches to Alfred for his earlier negligence is amply atoned by the crucial importance of

[1] If, as would seem to be the case, Alfred was down by Athelney in Somerset, he would have little difficulty in watching the Bristol Channel, and in concentrating a sufficient force at any required spot on the coast.

his promptitude now. No reliable details have come down to us of that Homeric battle ; we know only the bare outline of the result. Odda, doubtless, had some of Alfred's own personal followers to rely upon, and such reinforcements as he could gather. Hubba would not have been Hubba if he had not been surrounded by the most formidable picked champions of the Black Gaill. Hubba himself fell : the famous " Land Ravager," the standard of Ragnar, was captured : forty of Hubba's own comitatus fell round their lord, and eight hundred other Danes. Alfred had fought, and was yet to fight, bigger battles than this ; but for the fighting quality of the men he defeated, this must have been the greatest battle of all. When he heard that Hubba, the butcher of Saint Edmund, was dead, and held the Raven banner in his own hands, he must have known that the Lord still had need of him.

VI

The death of Hubba, following upon the disaster at Swanage, cannot have failed to produce considerable moral effect upon the Danes. They seemed to be weighted and oppressed. Something was fighting for Alfred—something like the Fortune of Sulla or the Star of Napoleon —a power more than mere ability or energy. No conviction was more firmly rooted in men's minds during the early days of kingship than the belief that kings carried a magical and miraculous luck with them. If this faith were a delusion, it was by no means a groundless one. Alfred certainly shared in that quality which in modern times has given " Queen's weather " a wide, and not altogether an imaginary, repute. A gift which can exalt the courage and confidence of common men is indeed a royal gift. The West Saxons rallied to Alfred as promptly as he called.

From Alfred's own actions the elements of romance and sentiment were conspicuously absent. His military operations were of the most practical nature. By Easter he had built a fortified post at Athelney, from which he began to harass the Danes. His object was to induce them to concentrate their forces, and in this he was amply successful. He gradually attracted the Danish forces to the siege of Athelney. Seven weeks after Easter he was ready to strike.

Setting out on a rapid tour, he was everywhere received with enthusiasm, and his army grew as if his footsteps were springing to life behind him. This in itself brought the last of the Danes into the field, partly drawn and partly driven by Alfred's advance. At Heddington he made contact with Guthorm, defeated him, and pursued him to Chippenham, where he caught the whole of the Danes together in a difficult military position. Hemmed in, and unable effectively either to fight or to retreat, they came to terms. They once more gave hostages and swore oaths to depart : but this time they did something more important and more significant. They notified Alfred that King Guthorm would be baptized and would become a Christian.

Three weeks later Alfred's triumph took place. Attended by thirty of his chief men, King Guthorm was baptized at Aller, with Alfred as his sponsor. At Wedmore, deep in the marsh, with the Mendips bounding the northern horizon, and Glastonbury raising its high tor over the flats, they celebrated the feast for twelve nights. England was not yet stripped of her wealth. Alfred could still find rich gifts to give, and he heaped them upon Guthorm and his friends. It was a great, a strange and a wonderful victory ! Hubba was dead, and Guthorm was a Christian !

VII

Guthorm moved his host back to East Anglia during the following year, in accordance with the undertakings into which he had entered with Alfred. Those who elected to go overseas went into camp at Fulham, whence they subsequently left for the Continent. They had a reason for choosing this destination. Guthorm settled down in East Anglia, where he dwelt for the rest of his life—a sober, capable, and successful ruler, on a smaller scale than he had at one time hoped.

Alfred, for his own part, flung himself into the urgent work of strengthening his position. He had held his ground, but he needed now to maintain it. The tide of war which had flowed over Wessex had left destruction which must be rebuilt and bettered. The next blow was impending. The failure of the Danes in England to complete their conquest left affairs in some confusion, but the stroke which was to follow the conquest of England could not be put off. Two years after the surrender of Guthorm, King Sigfrith Snake-Eye made his landing in France.

Sigfrith was one of the most important members of Ragnar's family, who had succeeded to his father's claims in Denmark itself. In so far as any man was the head of the Danish empire of Ragnar, he was that man. His assault was the main assault.

At Ghent he picked up the army from Fulham—not so large nor so victorious as it might have been, but still strong enough to be a respectable addition to his host. One battle, or even two, were not likely to dispose of Sigfrith. From all quarters the Danes concentrated to join him.

The prospects of success were very different from those that would have existed had Hubba been holding a

united and Danish England under his hand ; but they
had not disappeared. It remained to be seen whether
Sigfrith could not make good the failure of other men.
Divisions quite as serious as any that dissipated the
strength of England were rending the states of western
Europe and crippling their energies ; nor, so far, was
any state emerging, as Wessex had emerged in England,
to stand the brunt. The most stable and solid of the
western powers was Germany. France had suffered the
disastrous drain of civil war and the ravages of incessant
raids, from both of which Germany had been free.

The rule nevertheless held good. With Alfred's
Wessex still holding out, Sigfrith's luck south of the
Rhine was paralysed. The Franks beat him at Saucourt
in the first great battle he fought. He turned his march
north, and ravaged the Meuse valley with fire and sword
till he came to Aachen, the ancient capital of Charles the
Great. It was a wonderful change of times and days
when the very capital of Charles fell to a Danish army ;
and if moral impressiveness were all that counted,
Sigfrith had more than carried out the vengeance
promised eighty years earlier by Guthfrith the Proud.
The tomb of Charles perished in the fire. But Sigfrith
came too late. The romance of revenge was not reinforced by any substantial advantage. Aachen was no
longer anything more than a splendid memory, without
contemporary significance in politics and war.

VIII

Sigfrith left his armies to mark time while he organized
a fresh stroke. During the interval they maintained
themselves in the Scheldt and Somme valleys, while
the men from Fulham returned to Rochester, which they
besieged, shutting in their lines with an outer ring of

earthworks. Alfred had the opportunity of testing the new army he had trained. He relieved Rochester, and drove the Danes to their ships ; whereupon they returned to the Continent. Alfred suspected some connivance on the part of the East Anglian Danes. Although Guthorm was perhaps not personally involved, a fresh treaty was negotiated, under which the frontiers were redrawn. The south-western portions of Guthorm's kingdom, which were not settled by Danes, passed into Alfred's hands.[1] London, hitherto a Mercian town, became definitely attached to the kingdom of Wessex.

The modern greatness of London has its foundation in the acute intelligence of Alfred. The city had hitherto been of only moderate importance. Alfred transformed it into a fortified bridge-head on the continental model, of which Paris was the type—at once barring passage up the Thames to the road-junctions, and giving him free access to the northern bank of the river. This was a measure which put the keystone into the strategical system by which Wessex was both guarded from attack, and turned into an aggressive power.

The significance of Alfred's step with regard to London was illustrated in that very year. London and Paris entered upon the first step of their future careers together. King Sigfrith returned with strong reinforcements early in 885 ; and his aim this time was the Paris from which Ragnar had retreated forty years earlier.

The siege of Paris was desperate. Every known device of military engineering was employed by the Danes ; every resource of courage, vigour, and ingenuity was employed by Count Eudes, who defended it. So much did the siege of Paris (like the siege of Verdun

---

[1] Including all Middlesex and Buckinghamshire, with half the counties of Hertfordshire and Bedfordshire (Collingwood, *Scandinavian Britain*, p. 101) and the south-western half of Mercia (*ibid.*, p. 108).

many centuries later) come to represent a kind of critical point in the whole contest, that the Germans took the unusual course of marching to its aid. A vast army, commanded by the emperor Charles the Fat, came slowly to Paris, and confronted the Danes.

The power and the weakness of Sigfrith were admirably illustrated by the situation at Paris. Had Charles the Fat been a different man, the fate of the Danish army would have been certain. Nothing but prompt retreat could have saved it from the German host. But Sigfrith did not retreat. He kept his hand on Paris and his eyes on the Germans.

Charles the Fat was never a wise man, and he was moreover a sick man. Sigfrith was successful in bluffing him. After long negotiations, instead of fighting, it was agreed that the siege should be raised, but that the Germans should pay a sum of 700 lbs. of silver bullion, and should raise no objection to the Danes entering Burgundy.

This extraordinary treaty was deeply to the discredit of Charles ; but the poor man died a year or two later, and his proceedings have never been held to impair the honour due to Count Eudes and the defenders of Paris.

IX

Nothing could be more evident than that the military position of Sigfrith was a very delicate one. It depended almost wholly upon the ingenuity, skill, and audacity with which an essentially weak hand could be played against an essentially strong one. Skill of this kind plays so large a part in shaping human destiny that the failure of Sigfrith was by no means a foregone conclusion. He might pull the game round in spite of all the difficulties that confronted him.

These difficulties were serious. After two campaigns the situation was in no way advanced. The Danes were still in the heart of France, still ravaging the land and living upon it ; but no tangible advantage of a military nature had yet fallen to their share. The methods of defence which had been adopted seemed to make any decisive result more and more unlikely. France was dividing herself into a multitude of petty lordships which carried on the struggle on their own account. The local counts, ensconced in their new stone-built castles, were turning their fiefs into little hereditary sovereignties, and never ceased to harry the Danes who harried them. The struggle was turning itself into a question of how long the peasant could hold out against methods of persistent devastation. He had no longer to depend solely upon a distant royal army which arrived too late. The defenders of France were dispersing themselves over the country, equipped with legal powers to govern as well as to defend. These methods were to take on strange and unexpected political significance in days to come ; but their first and original intention was military.

It was therefore much more to Sigfrith's profit to seek a decision where a decision could be gained. The Germans presented a power which could be struck at and destroyed ; better still, they presented (as he had found at Paris) a power which could be divided and weakened in preparation for its destruction. Undiscouraged by two failures, he planned a third stroke. He turned north. Luck was still against him. Even before the death of Charles the Fat, power had been snatched out of the emperor's hands by his illegitimate nephew Arnulf, who assumed the crown that he was better qualified to wear. Arnulf was not a great man, but he was a bold and capable one. In his hands the German power suddenly became a weapon which could be used.

At Louvain, in 891, the last great battle was fought. The Danes had raised a fortified camp, powerfully entrenched against attack. Before their concentration was complete, Arnulf led the Germans to one of those mass assaults which in all ages have been a favourite German method. The Danish defences were forced ; the camp stormed. King Sigfrith himself fell, together with (so one of the later sagas tells us) a hundred thousand Danes—a figure which may be taken as representing the moral impression made upon the Danish imagination rather than as a figure literally true in point of fact.

X

The German sledge-hammer at Louvain gave the finishing blow to the dreams of Ragnar and the plans of Ragnar's sons.

Famine followed—the Nemesis of the frightful de-vastation wrought by ten years of war. The remains of the great army, forced off the Continent, were brought to England by King Biorn Ironside and his brilliant captain Hastein, where they took refuge in the river Limen. Alfred parleyed. He could not force the Danes of East Anglia and Northumbria to refuse help to their kinsmen ; and Hastein, though he was willing to let his sons be baptized, could not give any undertaking to quit the country. But it was a new and different England to which Hastein had come : one in which King Alfred was master.

When spring came, Hastein tried to march round the forest of Anderida to the fordable reaches of the Thames, and so gain East Anglia ; but Alfred drove him into Thorney near Bosham. The East Anglians and Northum-brians were stirred to send help. King Jorik despatched a fleet of one hundred ships to Exeter, while the

Northumbrians sent forty to attack northern Devon. The diversion was successful, and Hastein got his men safely away over the Thames. The garrison of London, reinforced with additional fighting men from the west, drove him first out of Benfleet and then out of Shoebury. He made for Wales ; but the Somerset and Gloucester levy intercepted him at Buttington on the Severn. Starved out, the Danes fought, were defeated, and retreated back to Essex. They could not feed themselves there, so, after committing their wives and children to the care of their East Anglian friends, marching by day and night they made for Chester, which they safely reached. They could not find food, nor penetrate into Wales, so they returned by a circuitous route through Northumbria to Essex. Finally, unable to find rest for their feet or food for their stomachs, they brought their ships round to the Lea below London, and built a camp, whence they could forage in the richest part of England. Alfred blockaded them ; so they broke out and rode to the Severn. Here they gave up the game. Some settled in East Anglia and Northumbria ; most followed Hastein back to France, where he took service under the French king and settled near Chartres. What became of King Biorn Ironside we are not told.

Such was the end of the vast hosts which Ragnar and his sons had hurled against Christendom. Their career had not been without fruit. Great changes had been wrought. The kingdoms of Dublin, York, and East Anglia, and the Duchy of Normandy were among the results of that great movement. But the main results were definite. The heathen reaction against the European polity of Charles the Great had been successfully resisted. It had been decided that Europe should be Christian. Perhaps the Danish wars of the ninth century were the determining factor in ensuring that Europe should become a group of national states, and not a Romano-Frankish empire. The national independence of England and France were made certain in those years of strife and disaster and victory.

In the determination of these results, King Alfred had borne no small share. The whole course of events might have been changed if the battle of Ashdown and the campaign of Athelney had gone another way : if Alfred had been a weaker man, and the West Saxons poorer fighting men. England had been the barrier which broke the flood.

And it was on England that the main brunt had fallen. When, in 899,[1] King Alfred died, he left behind him a tradition bred into the bone of his children. England must be reconquered, and must once more be purely and entirely English. In his life and his death, Alfred stood unbending for the principle that England must be English.

---

[1] October 26th, 899. (See M. L. R. Beaven, *Regnal Dates of Alfred*, etc., in *Eng. Hist. Rev.*, xxxii, p. 517 *et seq.*)

CHAPTER IX

THE CREATIVE WORK OF ALFRED

I

Kᴵɴɢ Alfred lived for seven years after the expulsion of Hastein and the end of the Danish wars. They were years of peace. We have, in our own days, seen the end of a great European war, and we realize to some extent the confusion and the changes, the process of restoring old institutions and of improvising new, which follows such a war. It is probable that the damage inflicted upon Europe during the years 1914–1918 was a small thing compared with that which was done in the century between the sack of Lindisfarne in 793 and the battle of Louvain in 891. The uprooting and the destruction of populations was vast and calamitous. War had gone through western Europe like some tropical hurricane. It left behind it a wreck to which no modern experience affords any parallel.

Every age has its own particular advantages. The mere material mass of modern civilization makes it a difficult thing to destroy, even with modern weapons. The reserve of wealth which it possesses makes restoration possible and swift. Civilization in the ninth century had the advantages of the resistant quality which belongs to all primitive organisms. It was extraordinarily hard to kill. The last drop of life could never be wrung out of it. It revived and spread again as promptly as a weed. In a few years, the rough huts of the agriculturist were rebuilt, and a rough primitive life had returned to its low normal.

But all that was higher than this took much more trouble to restore than it would take to-day. The reserve of wealth was far smaller. Alfred's own testimony is worth repeating.

" It has come very often into my mind," he wrote, " what wise counsellors there were of old throughout England, both spiritual and lay ; and how happy were those times then throughout England ; and how the kings who had authority over the folk obeyed God and His messengers, and both maintained peace, and morals and authority within their kingdom, and also extended their borders . . . and also the spiritual orders, how eager they were both in teaching and learning ; and how strangers came hither to this land in search of wisdom and learning, and how we must now get these things from abroad if we are to have them."

This view of the earlier age of England might be supposed to be a little rose-coloured, if we had not the evidence of Baeda, and of the still earlier English poems of Caedmon, to bear it out. Especially in Northumbria, the advances in at least the main elements of civilization had been very considerable. But in Alfred's later years " So utterly was learning fallen off in England that there were very few on this side of the Humber who could understand their Service books in English, or translate even a letter from Latin into English : and I think that there were not many beyond the Humber. So few were there of them that I cannot remember even a single one south of the Thames when I succeeded to the kingdom." He had himself seen, he tells us, " before it was all harried and burnt up," the treasures and books that filled the churches of England. His own record on this matter is confirmed by the state of English literature during and immediately after his own age. Practically all the work done was due to his own personal inspiration.

II

It was fortunate for England that her destinies were guided by such a man as Alfred. It is easy to sentimentalize over him ; but he was undoubtedly the kind of man who emerges all the more human and admirable for a little searching dryness in the light by which we see him. A man who is engaged on the task of upholding and restoring civilization is the better for a certain simplicity in his point of view ; and Alfred went to the root of things with a directness which a more sophisticated man would have missed. He was a man " cut in the large," and he was quick to see the large lines and main principles of the things he met. We can detect this gift in his military strategy, as well as in his civil policy. It perhaps deceives us a little into thinking his problems and his actions simpler than they really were.

In at least this early twentieth century, there seems to be a generally felt difficulty in bringing the religious and the secular worlds into a common focus. It is impossible to get a stereoscopic view either of the facts of human life or the reality of human character, unless we see them with this double vision. On the whole, looking at the subject historically, the religious temperament has been a hard and practical one. The difficulty is that it usually operates at two or three removes from its material objective. This distance from its objective has succeeded in convincing many people that it has no objective. But few truths are better attested by historical study than the realism of the religious attitude. Even considered as a form of drug, it has respectable claims to produce the effects not so much of cocaine as of bhang.

Alfred had a good deal of the temperament which makes the evangelist. His biographer has noted his zeal—his daily attendance at Mass, and other services ;

his private devotions ; his personal participation in worship. In a man of action, these are not the signs of weakness but of strength. There can be no doubt that he classes with that type of man which includes such exemplars as Cromwell, General Gordon, and Livingstone, to whom religion was the discipline of an active life. It is hardly an exaggeration to call Alfred the first great example in history of the northern European under the influence of Christianity. He had absorbed the religious influence in a way that no earlier king had succeeded in achieving ; he reflected it, not, like the Northumbrian churchmen, as a close copy of the Roman model, but as something strongly coloured by a new type of individuality. The morals of Charles the Great will not bear a moment's inspection. Those of Alfred will bear all the inspection we can give them. A strain of tenderness and domesticity runs through his character. His children, Asser tells us, were carefully educated ; and their careers show as much. His daughter Aethilgifa became a nun. His religion was in fact not an aesthetic but a political activity. It was a method of controlling the passions, prejudices, and weaknesses of human nature, and of stimulating its powers and idealisms towards the common wealth and prosperity of the English people, of whom he himself was the first.

He himself acknowledged this. His own words can be quoted.[1] " Our forefathers, who held these places before us, loved wisdom, and through wisdom they got wealth, and left it to us. Here their track may still be seen, but we cannot follow it up, and so we have lost both the wealth and the wisdom, because we would not bend our minds to following the track." This is a distinctly

---

[1] Letter on the state of learning in England. It is given in full by Mr. Chambers, *England before the Norman Conquest*, pp. 222–4. This particular passage is dramatically placed in the mouth of churchmen : but it is Alfred's theory.

and definitely moralistic philosophy, expressing the sound
and healthy doctrine that wisdom is a good business
investment, and that those who seek first the Kingdom of
God will have all these things added unto them. It is
a philosophy which nowadays is emphatically not
accepted as a matter of course. But probably it was not
by any means a matter of course in Alfred's own days.
If the pragmatic test is valid, Alfred perhaps came as
near to proving his doctrine as most men ever come.

III

It is, therefore, very necessary to remember that
instead of being a self-contained, self-sufficient philosophy, Alfred's religion was a guide and an index to a
whirlwind of practical activities, and that he stands or
falls by the secular standard of solid success. It is a
dangerous test by which to be judged ; for, as the famous
quotation from Addison reminds us, " 'tis not in mortals
to command success "—and it is slightly ambitious even
to try to deserve it. An individual man controls few of
the elements which create success or failure. Nevertheless, there is a form in which the test is a sound and
reasonable one. What an individual man cannot control,
may be controllable by a series of men. It may be unjust
to try one man by his power to control a situation for
which he is but partly responsible : but it may be just
to try a dynasty or a state for its power to control a situation six-tenths of which it has itself gradually created by
the cumulative effect of its own policy.

Alfred was not an isolated individual. He received
his kingship from a long line of predecessors ; and he was
careful to record them. He ruled a land with a long
history and a definite tradition ; and he took care that
they were not forgotten. He proposed to hand them all

on—kingship and custom and tradition—to a long line of descendants. His consciousness of intermediacy, of being one link in a chain, is visible in much that he did and said. We must not underrate this element, which he stressed. Even though he may be the supreme representative of the royal house of Wessex, we must take seriously the importance of the tradition which he made greater than it had ever been before. He only concentrated, into an unusually definite shape, ideas and characteristics which had been pretty generally diffused in a less marked form throughout the West Saxon royal house.

The circumstances with which Alfred dealt were thus the accumulated product of minds very like his own. When Halfdan's host crossed the Thames to the invasion of Wessex, that with which Aethilbert and Alfred met them was something that had been in process of creation over centuries of time—a temper, a training in the leaders, a loyalty and valour in the led, a social system, a military force, which stood or fell by its ability to make good against the corresponding Danish system. It did make good. When all England north of the Thames had been overwhelmed—when even Wessex itself had been juggled and hoodwinked by the Danish war-wizards, and Alfred was a fugitive in Athelney—he stood the greatest practical test that a man can stand : he won when all but hope was lost.

In this form, perhaps the test of success is the only valid one. A long period of political evolution had been tested, and by its product was known.

IV

He made few changes in the old system. The changes which gradually came about in the old English system

M

were most of them made much later than Alfred. His work was in restoring and reforming. His sense of being but one link in a chain made him conservative. It was on the side of administration and education that he concentrated his main efforts. During and after his reign the power of the king, while it may have remained unchanged in theory, became much more effective in practice, and was exerted with greater vigour.

Alfred's interests were more extensive and more complex than we are in the habit of supposing. He lived a life of incessant activity, in which there can have been little leisure, and little privacy. He was in touch with all the Europe of his day. It is well known that at least two northern sea-captains, Ottarr of Halogaland and Wulfstan, were in close relation with him.[1] It is in the highest degree unlikely that his connection with them was purely scientific. They were members of an Intelligence Department which kept him in touch with a wider world than Wessex. Ottarr furnished him with detailed descriptions of the far north—and, no doubt, of the contemporary events there. It is a great loss to us that Alfred never recorded these latter in writing. Wulfstan's voyages to the Baltic can hardly have been fruitless in respect of information other than geographical. While Wulfstan was at work around the Danish Isles and Wendland, as far as Russia, political events of the utmost importance, only imperfectly known to us, were taking place. Fleets were being fitted out, plans being prepared for vast sea-campaigns, kings were coming and going— the dynasty of Ragnar was toppling to its catastrophe on the Dyle in 891, which saw King Gorm come into power with new policies and new methods. Alfred

---

[1] He has given extracts from their reports in his *Orosius*. Translations into modern English will be found among the earlier extracts printed by Hakluyt in his *Voyages*, a book nowadays easily accessible.

almost certainly knew more of these events than we ourselves do. There is every sign that he possessed information which led him to make the most determined efforts to be ready for the advent of the fleet which ultimately Hastein brought over in 892.

Exactly how much more he may have known from the reports of other agents, whose names have not come down to us, it is now difficult to guess. We have the explicit support of Asser in attributing to Alfred the possession of a far-reaching system of acquiring information. The old bishop assures us that Alfred was in regular communication with foreign powers as far away as Jerusalem and Ireland. The mere complimentary letters which formed the credentials of these envoys are hardly likely to have been the whole of the messages they brought. In the ninth century, even more than in the nineteenth, it would have been the private communications of the ambassadors over the dinner-table—longer and more detailed than any letter—that formed the real substance of the embassy : and what they took back would have been conversation of a type that even to-day diplomatists do not usually put into writing without necessity.

There were Franks, Frisians, Gauls, Northmen, Welshmen, Scots, and Armorican Bretons at Alfred's court, Asser tells us, in more or less permanent relations with the king, and certainly in his pay. Two of the Northmen we know already. The Frisians had much to do with Alfred's ship-building, and his naval policy. The *Chronicle* mentions some of them by name—Wulfheard, Ebbo, and Aethilhere—evidently members of the king's comitatus. We have the same sort of account of Alfred from Bishop Asser as the Icelandic poets later on gave of King Knut the Great—a genial, affable, accessible man, rich and freehanded—paying well for service or for information.

V

The Frankish element was not the least important. Frankish influence was growing. It would seem certain that Alfred knew and appreciated the new methods of defence introduced first by Charles the Great, but developed and systematically applied by Charles the Bald and his advisers. Alfred's anxiety to adopt a policy of castle-building is explicitly stated by Asser. He met with opposition and passive resistance ; but even those who opposed him came, after experience, to regret their action. The king's anxiety to acquire London, his success in doing so and the use to which he put the city when he got it, all clearly hint at an extensive acquaintance with the latest continental ideas. He passed this policy on to his son. Edward the Elder's subsequent reconquest of England was, as we shall see, largely carried out by a bold policy of castle-building.

More obscure to us is King Alfred's attitude towards the political developments which accompanied these ideas in France. It was the military defence of France against the Danes which caused the rise of feudalism that we first detect in the ninth century. Each step in the one was paralleled by a corresponding step in the other. The military principles of the fortified bridge-head and the self-contained castle had their counterpart in the rise of a hereditary class of fighting seigneurs governing their territories by a net-work of special rights, liabilities, privileges, responsibilities, and immunities, at first forced upon them by necessity, and then accepted as insignia of honour, isolating them from the common herd into an almost regal dignity. The loss of power by the French crown dates from these days.

It would be worth while to know precisely what view Alfred took of the political trend amongst the Franks.

Kings in England have not usually smiled upon the conception of the haughty vassal. Alfred himself, typically English as he was in his humanity, his almost suburban spirit, his respect for the moral simplicities, showed also a typically English respect for central government. He increased rather than lessened the royal authority in England. Some of his views may perhaps be read indirectly in the policy he bequeathed to his son Edward, who distinctly checked the growth of great vassal fiefs in England. But Alfred did undoubtedly follow, to some extent, the natural trend of his age. It was a trend determined by practical necessity—which no statesman can escape—and its pitfalls were not yet glaringly evident. Great earldoms began to shape themselves soon after Alfred's day, and although the earls were held in strong control by the vigorous English kings of the tenth century, they constituted a power which, under some circumstances, might be a threat to the authority of the crown, and might throw England back into the condition of local separatism from which the royal policy of unification had rescued her.

Alfred himself expressed, in his preamble to his Laws, the conservative spirit which he showed in his actions. " I did not venture to set in writing much of my own, as it was unknown to me how much of it would seem good to those who will come after us." This is the phrase of a man who was determined to maintain a tradition. His judgment was sound. In after years many a Frenchman must have regretted that this principle did not check the growth of the system which grew up in France.

VI

A sense of continuity has all the advantages of a sense of principle without the necessity of defining the principle :

and the advantage of keeping clear of definitions is that a living principle in course of active development is a particularly difficult thing to define. Definitions come when a thing is dead and done with.

Alfred's educational activities had a meaning that was quite in keeping with the main tradition he followed : and one that was none the less real because he could not adequately have described it. To think that he sought to decorate the human soul with a few petty accomplishments is certainly not an adequate description of it. He sought as far as was practicable to *diffuse* knowledge. In this he followed a tradition expressly English. He did not create closed colleges of priests treasuring a secret knowledge hidden from the vulgar ; closed colleges that some astute Hengist could wipe out at a blow. The diffusion, the spread of knowledge was essential to his policy. He never defined such an objective ; and in fact he could not have defined an objective of which he was unconscious. He could only follow the logic of a tradition which led him on by natural steps towards such an objective, even though he could not foresee it.

Knowledge can exist in many forms, and be preserved and used according to a large variety of systems. But there is a profound and radical difference between a society in which it is diffused, and one in which it is concentrated and concealed. The former is the more stable system. If any man is building towards an immense society, which shall defy assault and last impregnable over great periods of time, the earlier steps of that society which he guides must be ruled by the logic of its development, the ultimate meaning of which is not known to him. It is a logic, because the successive steps are causally connected, and long afterwards, in the light of actual consequences, the rationality of the process may be pointed out ; and yet often enough it is only by

the results that we can see a development to have been
rational at all.

Such a concealed rationality, such a logical causation,
ran through the policies which, to Alfred, were traditional,
and, as such, only partly and with difficulty capable of
rational explanation. The civilization which, after the
fall of the Roman empire, grew up in western Europe
under the protection of the kings, varied a great deal,
from place to place. Its most distinctively English
manifestation lay in an emphasis on the power of the
crown. Alfred showed no intention of creating, or even
of tolerating, any power which should be independent
of the royal authority, or should share its supremacy,
or command as a rival the allegiance of his subjects.
He made no such mistake as that which saddled the
Frankish emperors with a papacy which held their crown
in its gift. This question of education, though the most
fundamental one, is not the only point on which he
showed the hand he held. The bishops were his friends
and helpers ; they were not rival powers. He wished for
himself, and intended for his children and for all men
who could avail themselves of it, a knowledge of all that
was necessary to human life.

He encouraged, therefore, no closed college of priests,
no privileged order of landholders ; no body of any sort
which could claim a status independent of the crown.
Even the council which in later ages exercised some
restraint on the king had not in his time acquired more
than an advisory function. It would be difficult to bring
against the West Saxon kings the charge that they were
autocrats or tyrants. All the impression we receive from
their history is that of men singularly moderate in their
use of power. This impression is probably accurate.
It sprang partly from their family temperament ; but
partly from the extent to which they were guided by

tradition—a law unwritten, because no one could have
defined it with sufficient clearness to put it into words.
While their rule lasted they preserved something that
was to prove of unique importance in the later ages of
England—the supreme authority of the crown.

VII

Alfred was no Lycurgus. His Laws are not of the
importance in the history of England that we might
expect from his reputation as a statesman. Ina, long
before him, and Edgar, long after him, have greater
names as legislators. The whole trend of his policy was
antipathetic to those great systems of rigid external law
of which the codes of Draco and Lycurgus are types. It
is conceivable that he and his predecessors were influenced
by the Christian conception that the Mosaic Law had
been superseded by an age of Grace in which the will of
a supreme being was communicated direct to an individual human conscience. An equally strong influence
may have been exerted by the persistence of old tribal
customary law which, now that the tribes were broken
up, survived partly as a habit of conducting life on a
traditional basis which allowed of a considerable amount
of convenient elasticity in the memories of those who
remembered and declared the law. When we add to
this the absolute authority of the king over his own
companions—his comitatus—it is clear that a tradition
including all these elements did not tend towards the
creation of a rigid code, but rather towards a system of
voluntary contract and mutual agreement.

The significance of this lies in the strong bias it gave
at an early stage to the type of relationship between men
which would be evolved later on. Civilization cannot
easily be conducted without written law and coherent

systems of jurisprudence based upon rational principles. Mediaeval law, when it in due time appeared, did not err upon the side of vagueness. But when it did appear, it had already been given—at least in England—a quality which prevented it from becoming rigid.

Alfred contributed his full share towards creating this quality. Such evidence as survives does agree in depicting him as a man who believed in a good deal of personal interference with the world around him. He was indefatigable in revising and adjusting and modifying the natural relationships of men. His interest in the poor, and his anxiety to see justice done them ; his assiduity in hearing appeals, all alike hint at a faith in a dispensing and discretionary power which could be exerted in the cause of equity. We can, on the other hand, detect very little sign that he regarded law, as the Romans did, in the light of a power which over-rode all individual discretion. This attitude gave rise, later on, to two distinct streams of tendency—that is to say, to the theory of regal absolutism, and to the habit of statutory legislation. The time had not arrived when such questions could have any practical meaning ; but the tradition which we see Alfred expressing unmistakably implies a view that law was intended for the convenience and benefit of man, and should be adjusted to this purpose.

We get, from Asser (confirmed from other quite accidental sources [1]), a striking picture of a people who had not the gift of trusting one another, but who trusted Alfred. They could not agree together ; but the king managed to make them agree with him. They depended upon him as their point of unity. And (as was the case with Knut, later) there was nothing physical about his dominance. The big-heads and the small-heads, the

---

[1] See the very graphic picture of Alfred, Birch, *Cart. Sax.*, No. 236, translated in Chambers, *England before the Norman Conquest*, p. 229.

feminine bishops like Asser and the brawny fighting
thanes of Wessex, all alike hung on the words and
decisions of this delicate, frail-bodied, calm, intelligent
man, who never lost his temper, but, with something of
the childlike seriousness of Nelson, reasoned with their
unreasonableness and uttered the magical phrases which
touched their emotions to zeal or shame.

VIII

Alfred resembled Nelson in a good many ways. He
had a similar gift for leadership, and it was a gift of very
nearly the same sort. Alfred's charge at the battle of
Ashdown has much in common with Nelson's " blind
eye " at Copenhagen. Even the campaign which ended
at Athelney has a resemblance to the campaign which
ended at Trafalgar ; both involved the idea of driving
an elusive enemy to a spot where a decision could be
reached under the most advantageous conditions. And
both men suffered the same ill-health, and seem to have
shared the same frailness of body. The West Saxon
fighting men, like the seamen of Nelson's fleets, doubtless
saw to it that their leader came to no more harm than
they could help. But Alfred, whether by breeding or by
fortune, was a more scholarly man, and perhaps a less
vain one. No tragic scandal marred his life. He never
needed to fall gloriously to maintain his fame. He died
in his bed, as good kings and successful commanders ought
to do. His task was not to die for his country but to live
for her.

CHAPTER X

EDWARD THE ELDER AND THE RECONQUEST OF ENGLAND

I

THE death of Alfred was instantly followed by a test of the work he had done. Much of his power seemed to be due so exclusively to the personal ascendancy he had exercised, that it still remained to be proved whether the new organization which he had created was strong enough to hold its own when he himself was gone. But Alfred had been no wayward genius. He was as successful as a father as he had been as a king. He left a kingdom, and he left a king to rule it after him. His son Edward succeeded him almost as a matter of course. But Alfred had been a younger son, and there was at least one man descended from an elder brother of Alfred who might show an abstract claim greater than any Edward could prefer. The aethiling Aethilbald shut himself up in Wimborne, and was understood to imply that he would live or die there in defiance of Edward.

We know singularly little of King Edward as a person. Able as he proved himself to be, he can have had nothing of the charm of his father. All his proceedings seem cool, official, and impersonal. He was as impersonal as his great grandfather Egbert—and he was quite as swift. He was promptly at Wimborne with an army ; and Aethilbald, for all his valiant assertions, thought it the wisest plan to make for Northumbria. Thither he rode, with Edward's emissaries hard on his heels. The Danes of Northumbria did not fail to receive him with honour, and to acknowledge him as king. An ambitious fool is always useful.

II

The cold and impersonal Edward was now undisputed king of Wessex. He represented the convergence of several claims which, in their totality, greatly enhanced the strength and prestige of the kingship. He was the son of the last reigning king ; he had stepped into control of the organization created by Alfred ; he stood for the same policy of West Saxon supremacy in England which Alfred had made the foundation of all his work. Aethilbald was not likely to increase his own popularity in Wessex by accepting Danish support. No king put forward with Danish support was likely to be more than a dupe and a tool of the Danes.

There were very few arguments of Aethilbald's side of the case that were not double-edged. Primogeniture was hardly yet a fixed rule of succession. But this, which made Edward's descent from Alfred of less importance, made Aethilbald's seniority of descent equally unimportant. Aethilbald, similarly, would not have been the first West Saxon king to take refuge among foreigners, and to return to claim the crown. But the foreigners to whom Egbert fled were not enemies settled on the soil of England ; they had been only Franks, neutral in English quarrels and but mildly interested in England. Aethilbald was an example of a type of man who upholds a purely theoretical claim in the face of substantial facts. There was no room, there was no sympathy for a romantic pretender who had nothing but his own graces to offer to a world which had its living to make. In Edward, Wessex had a king with an acceptable policy, and with power and will to carry out that policy.

While Aethilbald lived, Edward proceeded with caution. The Danes had no hesitation in using the pretender as a pawn in the game. They sent him abroad to gather help. They understood their own position. The accession of Edward brought them face to face with the prospect of an aggressive war, the loss of which would involve the loss of the privileged position given them by the treaty of Wedmore, and might even involve the actual loss of the lands they had won by the sword.

There were very serious reasons why they should view with apprehension the likelihood of war. Their conquest of England had depended to a large extent upon the advantages given them by greater unity. This advantage had now crossed over to the English. When Hingwar landed in Thanet, he had opposed a single flexible power to a confused and divided one. But Hingwar and his brothers had founded no dynasty, and had organized no unified nation : Danish Northumbria, Danish East Anglia, and the Five Boroughs of the Midlands were separate powers with no common government. It was now the Danes who were divided into petty states ; and it was the power of Wessex which was united and flexible. Wessex had conquered England once. She could do it again. Like Egbert, Edward awaited his chance.

III

Aethilbald was away for three years. In A.D. 903 he returned with a somewhat scratch fleet, and was welcomed in Essex. The next year hostilities began. The Danes themselves took the offensive. King Guthorm was dead, and his successor, Jorik, represented a reaction to a heathen policy.

Jorik and Aethilbald marched west, crossed the Thames at Cricklade, and drove an expedition into the heart of Wessex. Edward's answer reveals his readiness and his talent for war. He held all the lower fords of the Thames and London with its bridge. He instantly crossed the rear of the Danes, marching as far as the fens. Jorik returned in haste. Edward retreated. A decisive battle was forced sooner than he had designed. The Kentish contingent, contrary to express and repeated orders, allowed themselves to lag behind, and Jorik caught them. The fight that followed was memorable. Two aldermen, an abbot, and many thanes of high rank on the English side were slain ; but Jorik himself, Aethilbald and several of the leading Danes of East Anglia fell with them. Alfred's royal luck had descended to Edward, who had every reason to thank the Kentish men for a disobedience which had considerably clarified the situation.

Guthorm II, who succeeded to the East Anglian kingdom, was a man possibly less able than either Guthorm I or Jorik ; he certainly showed a consciousness of weakness which may have been only a more acute sense of reality than Jorik had possessed. He entered into amicable negotiations with Edward. The terms, which included the provision that the East Anglian Danes should abjure heathenism, show that Edward was now the real master of the situation. The new king returned to the more prudent Christian policy of Jorik's predecessor. He also agreed to a series of provisions under which offenders against the law should be judged by the law of their own nation. From Guthorm's point of view such an agreement could be justified only by its necessity, since it extended English law over a kingdom theoretically Danish. The reconquest of England was beginning.

IV

The Danish conquest had differed radically in character from that by which the English had established themselves in Britain. It had been rapid, and it had some touch of the superficiality which is apt to attach to rapid military conquests ; whereas the English conquest had been slow, and very thorough. But a deeper distinction than this lay in the fact that while the English settlement of Britain had been exclusively rural, the Danish settlement was much more urban in character. The policy of Alfred towards the Danes, developed by Edward, had been founded on this urban nature of the Danish settlements. Alfred had got back into his own hands those portions of both East Anglia and Mercia, which, being mainly rural, had not received Danish colonists ; and they formed a starting point for further advance.

The East Anglian Danes were grouped chiefly round Colchester, Maldon, and Cambridge ; the Mercian Danes round the famous " Five Boroughs " of Lincoln, Stamford, Leicester, Derby, and Nottingham, where they commanded the great Roman highways. These towns owe their subsequent importance to the Danes, who first carried out the policy later on adopted by Henry the Fowler in Germany, of making fortified towns the centre of agricultural districts portioned out among the townsmen who formed its military garrison. The Danes did not evolve this method of organization out of their own inner consciousness. It was, if anything, an older plan than that adopted by the English. The great city-states of classical antiquity had been formed on just such a model, which had probably descended with unbroken tradition from the Bronze Age. The English system was destined to prevail as the typical institution of the Middle Ages— the mediaeval " Manor "—but the influence of the Danish system was never to die out. It imported a fresh element which was a distinct enrichment of the national life. The Danes gave an impulse to urban life in England which was largely responsible for the power and prestige of the English mediaeval town.[1]

[1] Alfred seems to have created boroughs in Wessex on the Danish model. Corbett, *Camb. Med. Hist.*, iii, p. 357.

The immediate result, however, was to concentrate the Danish settlers in certain definite districts of strategical importance. The element of weakness in the plan was that although it would have enabled the Danes to repeat, at any time, the methods of Hingwar, it was not equally advantageous when the tables were turned, and Wessex became the aggressor. It presented Edward with fixed and definite objectives of which he was not slow to take advantage. Alfred, by his negotiations in 885, had acquired the south-eastern portion of Mercia. Now Alderman Aethilred, who had married Edward's sister Aethilfleda, seized and refortified the derelict Roman city of Chester, and the Danish position began to be turned (906).

The leading fact of the situation, which with every step taken came more clearly to light, was that the English had a prudent and skilful leader, while the Danes possessed no adequate central direction at all. When, three years after the seizure of Chester, Aethilfleda built a fortress at Bramsbury, there was desultory frontier fighting. Next year came an attempt to destroy the strangle-hold which was tightening upon the Danes. Edward was collecting a fleet from the Kentish ports— with what precise object was uncertain, but it could only have been against either Northumbria or East Anglia. The two Northumbrian kings, Jogisl and Halfdan, seized what they thought to be the double opportunity, and struck a blow at Mercia. They were, however, expected. Contrary to all that they had counted upon, strong forces closed upon them both from Mercia and from Wessex. Their march was not pushed far ; it rapidly became a retreat. Their rear-guard was overtaken by the English at Wednesfield near Wolverhampton ; and in the decisive battle which followed both Jogisl and Halfdan were slain, together with two earls and eight of the leading Northumbrian Danes (910).

V

This was severe punishment—and it put the Danes of Northumbria out of the contest for many years to come. Edward could accordingly turn his attention to East Anglia. He was a careful man who left little to chance. Alderman Aethilred died in the year following the battle of Wednesfield, whereupon Edward tightened his grip over the kingdom by taking the southern portion of Mercia, including Oxford and London, into his own direct control, leaving the widowed Aethilfleda the northern part. Aethilfleda had enough to occupy her. She continued Aethilred's work by building fortresses at Shergate and Bridgnorth during the year. In 912 Edward built a fortress at Hertford, and then proceeded to Maldon in Essex, where he built the fortress of Witham. All along the border, from Maldon, Hertford, and Bedford to Northampton, many men submitted to him and abandoned the Danish allegiance. Aethilfleda meanwhile was continuing the great chain of fortresses at Tamworth and Stafford ; in 914 she built two more at Eddesbury and Warwick ; in 915, others at Chirbury, Warburton, and Runcorn, shutting against the Danes of the " Five Boroughs " a fortified frontier that stretched from Maldon to the Mersey.

These methods were effective. When, in the succeeding year, the Danes sent out columns to test this line, one was routed and its baggage captured.

But the deadly method of the fortified frontier was founded on something still more dangerous—the political power of the West Saxon kingship. It was this centralized and unified authority that was reconquering England.

If the Danes were not to succumb before the slow, irresistible advance of Wessex, it could only be through help from abroad. They must already have been in

N

treaty with Ragnvald O'Ivar, the great-grandson of Ragnar Lothbrok. Events of some magnitude were on foot in Ireland, where a fresh generation of youthful leaders was coming to the front. Ragnvald, with a great and growing reputation, joined the wickings of Waterford during the very year in which Aethilfleda was fortifying Cherbury and Runcorn. His brother Sigtrygg Gale O'Ivar became King of Dublin in 916. They were not ready to move yet, but in 917 a strong fleet of the Brittany Danes crossed the Channel to make a diversion. They entered the Severn mouth, and landed in Wales, but were defeated at Urchingfield in Hereford, and were compelled to give an undertaking to leave the kingdom. Edward drew a line of posts across the country, from Wales to the Avon mouth.

The invaders did not seem anxious to fulfil the terms of their undertaking : very possibly they had not sufficient supplies to take them home. After being repulsed from Watchet and Porlock—whither they can scarcely have gone to find gold—they took refuge on Flat Holm, one of the islands that lie out in the Bristol Channel. There they sat and starved until they managed to get away to Ireland.

The interlude did not disturb Edward's plans, which went steadily forward. He built a fortified bridge at Buckingham. Thorketil Jarl, and most of the principal Danes of Bedford, together with many who owed allegiance to Northampton, saw that it was time to come to terms. They offered to accept Edward, who next year entered Bedford without a blow. Aethilfleda had already seized Derby during the previous summer. Leicester surrendered to her. Maldon was occupied and re-fortified. Edward assisted Thorketil and his followers to cross over to France (919).

VI

It must have been obvious that the Danes were falling piecemeal into Edward's hands. When in 920 Edward built a fortress at Towcester, they aroused themselves for a last effort. The men of Northampton and Leicester laid siege to Towcester while the East Anglian Danes built a vast fortress at Tempsford as a base for further operations. Towcester held out, so the Danes threw up the siege and marched south by the Icknield Way. Meanwhile the Danes from Tempsford advanced upon Bedford, where they were repulsed.

Edward's preparations were more thorough. It was summer before he advanced. Then he unemotionally met force with force. He besieged the fortress at Tempsford and took it by storm, slaying most of the defenders, including King Guthorm II. Colchester was his next objective. It also was stormed, most of the garrison put to the sword, and the town sacked. The Danes had not finished. They were busy raising fresh forces, including all the wandering wickings they could gather ; and this motley host now marched on Maldon in a desperate effort to retrieve the fortunes of the war. They could not take the town. Edward's army of relief was soon at hand ; the siege was raised ; and the relieving force, joined by the garrison of Maldon, fought a pitched battle with complete success.

Edward returned to Towcester, and not only saw that the fortress was repaired, but surrounded it with a stone wall. The Danes of Northampton gave up the struggle. Thorfrith Jarl and his men submitted, and took Edward as their lord and protector. Edward repaired Huntingdon and rebuilt Colchester, which had suffered severely. He received the submission of the entire body of East Anglian Danes, who swore that they " would will what he willed, and protect all that he protected, whether by sea or by land." Cambridge made a separate peace on its own account.

The rest of the Five Boroughs fell without fighting. Edward marched on Stamford, built a fortress there, and received the submission of all who belonged to the town. While he was there, Aethilfleda died at Tamworth, "twelve nights before midsummer." She had lived just long enough to see the great work, in which she had helped her father, her husband, and her brother, brought to a successful conclusion.

Edward at once rode to Tamworth, where the careful king saw that all the allegiance owed to Aethilfleda was duly transferred to himself. Later on in the year, about the beginning of December, he removed Aelfwina, the daughter of Aethilfleda and Alderman Aethilred, from Mercia, and had her taken into Wessex. Precisely what reason he had for this step, we are not told ; but it is very clear that Edward was not anxious to see great feudatories growing up in England, which might compete with the royal power. In this, he was, as usual, entirely right and wise. Aelfwina was, moreover, a granddaughter of Alfred, and might transmit a claim to the crown. Prudence demanded that he should keep her close under his own eye.

From Tamworth he went to Nottingham, which his army had entered during his absence in Mercia. With the submission of Nottingham in 921 four out of the Five Boroughs passed into his hands. Lincoln was perhaps included in the general surrender at Bakewell in the year following. In any case, Edward did not waste his time in Lincolnshire, where the Humber presented a wide barrier to any advance northward. He built his next fortress at Manchester, just within the western boundaries of Northumbria across the Mersey, and garrisoned it (922).

EDWARD'S
RECONQUEST
OF ENGLAND

SCALE.

YORK

NORTH
SEA

Manchester
Rumcorn
Chester
906
922
Bakewell
923
Lincoln
915
Stafford
Derby
Nottingham
THE
FIVE BORO'S
921
Chirbury
Tamworth
Leicester
Stamford
Bridgnorth
Huntingdon
Towcester
Bedford
Cambridge
Tempsford
920
Colchester
Recovered
by Alfred
in A.D. 885
Hertford
Witham
Maldon
LONDON

LINE OF 912

W E S S E X

ENGLISH
CHANNEL

Here Edward came into touch with a new situation which was to mean much, and that of a very serious nature, to his successors.

VII

Whether or not the invasion of the Brittany Danes in 917 had been designed in co-operation with the Irish wickings and the English Danes, it is clear that their leader, with the remnant of his men who escaped from Flat Holm, sailed to Ireland and joined Ragnvald O'Ivar, with whom, in the year 918, he landed in Cumberland. Crossing eastward, the host fought a battle at Tynemoor, near Corbridge, with the united hosts of Constantine, king of Scots, and the Bernician English who still dwelt under their own old hereditary rulers in the midst of the Danish kingdom of Northumbria. Ragnvald is reputed to have won this battle ; but it seems clear that neither Strathclyde nor Northumberland fell into his hands. He did not, therefore, secure the kingdom of Northumbria. All he secured was a drawn battle which gave him sufficient freedom of action to enable him to turn southward upon York. He took York the next year, in time to prevent its surrender to Aethilfleda. In 921 he died, and was succeeded by his brother Sigtrygg Gale O'Ivar. This was the situation with which Edward was confronted when he built his fortress at Manchester.

We cannot tell whether the diplomacy of Edward had taken any part in the events which thus checked Ragnvald and isolated him ; but the course of events makes the supposition a probable one. His neglect of Lincoln, and his move westward to the Mersey, bears every resemblance to a deliberate design of checking Sigtrygg upon the south, as the Scots and Bernicians had checked Ragnvald upon the north. Aethilfleda's seizure of Runcorn had been a far-sighted measure. It had closed the Mersey to the Dublin Danes, and driven Ragnvald to make his landing in Cumberland.[1]

The Norse were settling Cumbria during the earlier years of the tenth century, and formed a connecting link between Dublin and York which made communication comparatively easy. Sigtrygg, however, was not in a particularly strong position. He had not the full resources of the Northumbrian kingdom behind him, and he was none too secure of what he had. He needed to walk warily to avoid a fall. When, in 923, Edward threw a fortified bridge over the Trent at Nottingham, and built an advanced fortress at Bakewell in Derbyshire, half-way between Nottingham and Manchester, Sigtrygg was among the rulers of the north who bowed before the supreme power of Wessex, and accepted Edward as king of all the English.

VIII

The proceedings at Bakewell, important as they were, have been very imperfectly recorded. We are reaching a period when English power was rising again, greater than it had ever been before. The strategy of the Danes under Hingwar and Halfdan had been no greater than the sure and inevitable steps by which Edward, castle-building and bridge-building, had advanced from the Thames to the Humber. There never had been a time before when such methods were even possible. When, at Bakewell, they reached their culmination, and it was clear that neither Sigtrygg nor any other

[1] Presumably in the Solway ; conceivably at Whitehaven ; whence he would without serious difficulty cross the comparatively short stretch to the Tyne valley. It is hard to see how any port between the Mersey and Whitehaven would have been suitable for him. To conduct an army over Pen-y-gwent or Whernside, or the Cumbrian mountains, may be taken as too difficult to be practicable. The seizure of Chester and Runcorn meant, therefore, either the Severn or the Solway for Ragnvald's landing-place.

Dane could break the strangle-hold, the whole of the north surrendered without a further struggle. Edward received, apparently by deputy, the submission of Constantine king of Scots, Edred and Uhtred, the English aldermen of Bernicia, Sigtrygg king of York, " and all that dwell in Northumbria, both English and Danish, both Northmen and others." This detailed and explicit list makes it probable that the Cumbrian Norse also gave in their allegiance.

By the surrender at Bakewell, therefore, Edward was advanced to a position such as Egbert had occupied. His power stretched from the English Channel to Strathclyde. It was a larger England than the Norman and Plantagenet kings controlled. Not even Egbert had held it so securely. The under-kings were vanishing. Only Constantine and Sigtrygg remained. South of the Humber the aldermen were appearing. Edward was become, not merely the supreme English king, but the only English king.

Yet in spite of this, the record becomes more and more fragmentary and uncertain, as if the kings of England had grown disinclined to take the world into their confidence. The silence which surrounded Egbert begins once more to prevail. It may have been wise. There are times when silence is the condition of success.

IX

The work was now complete. England was reconquered by the English, and the son of the fugitive of Athelney ruled over a reunified kingdom. Edward's task, extending over twenty-five years of constant strain and activity, was done. He died at Farndon in Mercia on July 17, 925, and was soon followed by his son Alfward. Their bodies were buried at Winchester.

Of all the kings of England, Edward was one of the most able and efficient, and one of the most enigmatic. Of his personality—his virtues, his faults, his foibles (if he had any)—we know nothing at all. No betrayal of human weakness or human charm disturbs the cold adequacy of his career. He must have been a typical Englishman.

NOTE

THE KINGS OF KENT AND THE KINGS OF WESSEX

Edward the Elder was the first English king to be crowned at Kingston-on-Thames. This fact is the outstanding feature of a historical puzzle. Why he was crowned there, in particular, and why he, in particular, should be the first to be crowned there, are complete mysteries.

The following explanation seems a probable, if not a certain solution.

Sir Charles Oman has pointed out that Ealhmund, the father of King Egbert of Wessex, and a West Saxon of the royal blood, probably obtained the kingdom of Kent through his mother or his wife. Now Egbert is a Kentish name. There was a Kentish King Egbert (*Chron.*, s.a. 664, 669 : Baeda, *Hist. Eccl.*, iv, 1, and iv, 5, where he dies in 673), and the Father Egbert to whom Baeda refers in such favourable terms (*Hist. Eccl.*, v, 9 and 22) is shown as interested in the Continent ; while there was a well-known Frank, Count Egbert (*Annales Einhardi*, s.a. 809, 811) contemporary with Egbert of Wessex. In the light of the connections known to have existed between early Kent and the Rhineland, we may infer that the royal house of Kent had given this name to the Franks, got it from them, or shared it with them. It is highly probable, therefore, that King Egbert of Wessex was named after his ancestor on the mother's (or grandmother's) side : the Kentish side. He united the claims of the Kentish and West Saxon houses.

Egbert called his son " Aethilwulf," which is not an especially West Saxon name : but Aethilwulf, who was (as we have reason to think) king of Kent under his father, called his sons by the names of Aethilstan, Aethilbald, Aethilbert, Aethilred and Aelfred—and even the latter may be a variant of " Aethilfrith." Of these names, Aethilbert is unmistakably Kentish, and is a reminiscence not only of the great Aethilbert who received Augustine and his companions, but of the other King Aethilbert who died in 760, a grandson of King Egbert. The whole West Saxon family after Ealhmund was Cantwarianized. Aethilwulf shows signs of having felt himself more a Kentish than a West Saxon king ; for if Mr. Stevenson is right, Aethilwulf was content to retain Kent while giving up Wessex to Aethilbald. But it is Aethilstan who deserves our attention.

Some doubt exists whether Aethilstan, the sub-king of Kent (slain by the Danes in 851) was Aethilwulf's son or brother. Either event will suit this argument. " Aethilstan " is a very curious name. " Aethil " implies origin from a privileged caste : *adel*, high-born, *gentil*, noble. " Aethilbald," " Aethilbert," and " Aethilred " we can understand, and " Aethilfrith " too : for the courage, or the glory, or the counsel, or the peace of the high-born are conceivable ideas, but pray what is an Aethil Stan ?—a stone of the high-born ? The answer is, it was the stone at Kingston. But why the stone at Kingston ? Let us consider.

It was pointed out (*supra*, p. 62) that the Thames valley beyond Kingston formed in ancient times a kind of bottleneck between Kent and the west, which was easily defended and hard to force. Surrey was a district which came into separate existence quite late in the day. It was not a kingdom in its own right. The original boundary between the kingdom of Kent and the kingdom of Wessex must have fallen at Kingston ; for when, in 568, Ceawlin notified King Aethilbert of Kent to keep his claws off Wessex, the battle took place at Wibbandune, which despairing antiquaries have made out to be Wimbledon—and have left it at that. But if Wimbledon were the place where a battle would take place between Kentish men and West Saxons, it is obvious that Kingston might well be the border town. It would not be surprising to hear that a holy and inviolable boundary stone stood at Kingston. And if any one disbelieves that some sacred stone did stand at Kingston, let him go to Kingston. It is there now !

The explanation that this stone at Kingston was a boundary stone will admirably fit the facts. The name " Aethilstan " commemorated the union of Wessex and Kent—the person who, like the stone, faced and touched both kingdoms.

Some importance, not immediately clear to us, attached to the first Aethilstan. Though dead, he was not forgotten. Alfred came to the throne in the midst of a war—and he had the memory (though a mistaken one) of his sacring at Rome to satisfy him. His son Edward, however, was crowned on that noble stone at Kingston, and called his son—Alfred's favourite grandchild—Aethilstan. And until Edward the Confessor all the English kings save Edgar were crowned at Kingston.

There is no reason, except the foregoing, why they should have been crowned at Kingston. The acquisition of Kent was the corner-stone of West Saxon supremacy, and the means by which Wessex made sure of her command of England. The ceremony of crowning on the stone at Kingston symbolized the achievement of her victory.

CHAPTER XI

AETHILSTAN AND THE FOREIGN POLICY OF THE ENGLISH KINGS

I

THE unknown man who stepped into the shoes of Edward was his son Aethilstan, named in memory of King Aethilwulf's eldest son, the king of Kent, who was slain by the Danes in 851, and who never reigned over England. He had not been forgotten. In the person of his grand-nephew the name of Aethilstan came at last to the throne of England.

Edward left his successor a task widely different from his own. That which had been won by the silent and enigmatic soldier who had reconquered Britain, Aethilstan needed to organize and to guard. The whole tenor of Aethilstan's reign was therefore in striking contrast with that of his father and grandfather. He fought little ; he negotiated much. His life was one prolonged story of arrangements and designs by which he isolated and checkmated his enemies, and by which he avoided those grand tests of strength which Alfred and Edward had sought. The silence which had gradually fallen upon the actions of Edward fell with tenfold profundity over the diplomacies of his son.[1] And yet the more we study the history of early England, the more our attention drifts to the reign of Aethilstan : for all the signs point to this

---

[1] But it was not peculiar to England : Mr. Reginald Lane Poole says : " I doubt whether a single word of history, beyond the briefest entries on Easter Tables, was written in France or Germany between 906 and 940 " (*Chronicles and Annals*, p. 38).

reign as the time when all that was to be fertile in the future was first planned—the remodelling of the local government on Frankish lines, and the invention of those foreign policies which went far to determine the fate of England for a century and a half to come.

II

That Aethilstan realized the nature of his position and the problems it involved, and took up the task with energy, we can see by his first actions as king, which broke new ground. He married one of his sisters to Sigtrygg Gale O'Ivar, king of York, and another to Otto, the son of Henry the Fowler, the new and powerful king whom Saxony had given the Germans. The meaning of these two diplomatic steps we may consider in turn.

Ragnvald O'Ivar, king of York, had died in 921, soon after his successful attempt to snatch York out of the hands of the English. His brother Sigtrygg, king of Dublin (who had been driven out of his realm by Guthfrith, the third brother), accordingly came to England and was accepted by the Northumbrian Danes as king of York.

As far as we can now make out, this family of Danish kings of Dublin, who fought and reigned in Ireland, were the direct descendants of Hingwar, Ragnar's son. The battle of Louvain, which for a full century broke Danish power, had on one hand left Denmark struggling with domestic dissensions and on the other had left the kings of Dublin in isolated glory, but still a power not to be despised. Their strength, if concentrated, might still have been formidable. But some lack of intelligence or of moral power seemed to prevent them from organizing their realm to a degree which would do justice to the potentialities of Ireland. They spent much of their time in civil contests which diverted and wasted their strength.

THE HOUSE OF ALFRED

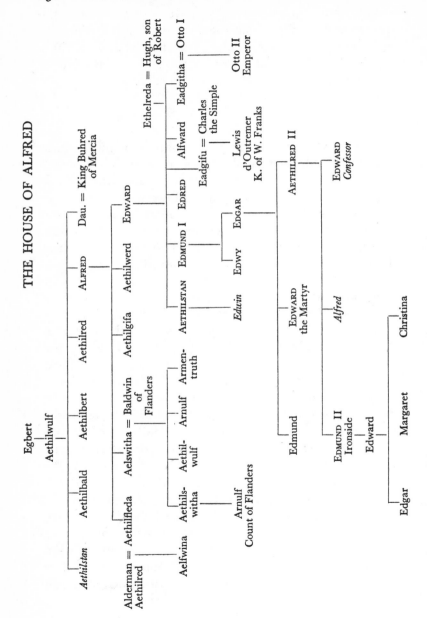

The task of Aethilstan was therefore to ensure that it should be diverted as much as possible, and wasted to the utmost extent.

He did not quarrel with the presence of Sigtrygg in York. Sigtrygg himself, like Ragnvald before him, was none too certain of his foothold in York, and had scarcely the resources necessary to meet Aethilstan upon equal terms. The two kings came to an accommodation profitable to both parties. Sigtrygg was baptized, married Aethilstan's sister, and held York as an under-king, securely allied by marriage with Aethilstan, and by his baptism safely parted from his Irish kinsmen.

The security which this alliance gave Sigtrygg was no doubt worth the price ; but in addition to tranquillity in Northumbria, the marriage certainly gave Aethilstan, both as suzerain and as brother-in-law, a right to intervene if occasion should demand it. Occasion did demand it. Sigtrygg lasted but a year after his marriage. Upon his death, Aethilstan promptly occupied Northumbria.

The results of his action fully justified it. Sigtrygg's sons, Guthfrith and Olaf Kuaran, made an attempt to seize their father's kingdom. They had not, however, offered any guarantee such as would have induced Aethilstan to accept them as under-kings of his. He drove them out of Northumbria, and henceforth retained the kingdom of York in his own hand. The disappointed candidates took refuge with Constantine, the king of Scots. By the Treaty of Emmet between the English king, the king of Scots, the Northumbrians, and the Welsh, the occupation of Northumbria was ratified and made secure. Aethilstan handed the direct administration over to Edred, the representative of the old royal house of Bernicia, the house of Ida the Flamebearer ; and so, after nearly sixty years of Danish rule, Northumbria once more came definitely under English government, and again became a part of the realm of England.

III

For some seven years, Aethilstan successfully maintained the state of affairs established at Emmet. He had achieved it with the minimum of military exertion, and he proceeded to keep it by the same means.

His action was not likely to remain permanently unchallenged. From Denmark itself there was now no direct threat. Gorm the Old was busy in reviving its strength and consolidating its power, not now as a sea-empire in rivalry with the Romano-Frankish land-empire, but as a national state among those that were beginning to appear throughout Europe. The centre of danger lay in the kingdom of Dublin, which had not dropped its ambitions with respect to Northumbria. The danger had been stayed, but it was far from having been removed. The kings of Dublin, however, would not act alone. In the contest between Dublin and Winchester for supremacy in the British Isles, the strength of the antagonists was too evenly matched. Success would lie with that side which could command the most important allies. The struggle to isolate the kingdom of Dublin occupied the whole of the remaining years of Aethilstan's reign.

The growing purpose, as well as the power and dignity [1] of the English kings is visible in the marriages made by the daughters of the royal family. As the national

---

[1] Aethilstan was the first to assert clearly the supremacy and the absolute sovereignty of the English kings. From this time onward their style was " Rex (or Basileus) Anglorum," and the title " Rex Anglorum " remained the official style till long after the Norman Conquest. The title " basileus " was a claim to complete independence. (Stevenson, *Asser's Life of Alfred*, note to Ch. i., p. 147 *et seq.* ; Freeman, *Norman Conquest*, vol. i, p. 145 *et seq.*, and App. C.) Mr. Wickham Legg (*The Sacring of the English Kings*, p. 15) quotes the salutation of Pope Urban II to St. Anselm, archbishop of Canterbury in later times : " Papa alterius orbis ! " Aethilstan was the first definitely to set up the banner of this " other world," entirely separate from the Roman jurisdiction.

states, under the guidance of the kingships, slowly acquired form, the change presaged in the days of Aethilwulf and Charles the Bald became gradually an accomplished fact. The royal families were becoming an international caste, and such uncrowned junior branches as the Northumbrian and the Mercian were being excluded from the conception of royalty. The process was the natural continuation of one that had long been in operation ; but it was becoming clearly visible. King Alfred had given one of his daughters to Baldwin, Count of Flanders. Three daughters of Edward the Elder married kings. Eadgifu had married Charles the Simple in 920, before the accession of Aethilstan. Their son, Lewis IV, spent some years of his boyhood at the court of Aethilstan, and from that fact gained his name of " d'Outremer." He left Aethilstan in 936 in order to be crowned at Rheims. For a great part of his reign, therefore (with an intermission of seven years between 929 and 936), Aethilstan was either brother-in-law or uncle of the French king. While the latter had no longer the imperial power which his ancestors had wielded, the alliance was doubtless sufficient to give Aethilstan assurance of support across the Channel. Another sister was married to a greater man than Charles or Lewis : namely, to the powerful feudal count Hugh the Great, ancestor of the Capetian kings of France. Aethilstan's cousins were already the ruling family of Flanders. Finally, as we have seen, he connected himself, through the marriage of his sister Eadgitha to Otto, the son of Henry the Fowler, with the Saxon dynasty of Germany, which was soon to produce the mighty line of Saxon emperors : an alliance of especial importance, because it safeguarded him on the side of Denmark. There was little love lost between the Danes and the Germans. This alliance, which was not forgotten during the seventy years following Aethilstan,[1] aimed at preventing Denmark from exerting any considerable influence upon either German or English affairs : a purpose which it seems to have fulfilled.

The circuit of alliances thus covered all the adjoining lands of continental Europe which shared with England a common preoccupation with the Danish question. As long as they continued, Aethilstan could count upon as much assistance as he could expect to obtain in the work of preventing Danish help from being given to the kings of Dublin.

IV

But the Dublin kings were not exclusively Danish in their interests. The Norwegian element in the western seas was large and influential. Nothing could be more suitable for the purpose of Aethilstan than a friendly relationship with Norway. The Norwegian kings held their realm under the shadow of Danish claims and Danish power, the reality of which the course of events was destined to show. To gain them over would achieve two ends : Denmark would be still further restrained, and the Dublin Norsemen, most of them old foes of Harald Fairhair, would receive no help from Norway. It was, of course, little likely that Harald, now nearly eighty, would take any active side. He had once brought his fleet as far west as the Orkneys. He would not repeat that sea campaign. But his influence could do very much towards stopping that drain of private help which was almost as dangerous as royal assistance.

Many traces survive of Aethilstan's relations with Norway—the strangest, most puzzling, yet (next to his relations with Germany) the most important of all his diplomacies. No English king before him had ever

---

[1] See Aethilweard's *Chronicle*, Introd.

exercised any influence upon Norway, and for him to do so was a remarkable testimony to the growing power of the English kingship.

William of Malmesbury tells us that the envoys of Harald came to Aethilstan at York ; which points to the years 926 or 927, when we know that Aethilstan was in the north. It cannot have been 925, for Sigtrygg was in possession of York in that year, and went to Aethilstan at Tamworth. In 929 Harald abdicated ; so that the available years are 926, 927, and 928, with the greatest likelihood for one of the first two.

The envoys, according to William, were Helgrim and Asfrith ; and he draws a glowing picture of the splendour of their ships and the magnificence of their reception. We may believe his account on that score, for both kings were exerting themselves to impress one another with their importance and power. Harald sent, as a present, a ship with a gilded beak and a purple sail, fenced with a bulwark of gilded shields.

The account given us by Snorri Sturlusson, the Icelandic historian, tells us nothing of any such details, but gives us an entirely fresh set of statements covering different ground. According to his version, Harald sent his youngest son, Hakon, with the envoys. Hakon must have been about seven years old in 926 and eight in 927 —an age which perfectly fits the story. The envoys put Hakon on Aethilstan's knee, and invited him to accept the boy as his foster-son. Since a fosterer was regarded as of rank inferior to the man whose child he fostered, this was perhaps a dexterous way of turning a hostage into a diplomatic advantage. Aethilstan (so Snorri tells us) accepted the boy.

If we are to judge by the large family circle in which, as far as we can see, he dwelt with little friction and no overt trouble, and by the protection he extended to

Lewis d'Outremer, Aethilstan must have been a man of domestic tastes who took up a benevolent attitude towards children : and that he adopted young Hakon would be quite in keeping with the rest of his character. But even if it had been otherwise, the point might have been worth conceding in view of possible advantages of a more serious nature in the future. The friendship of Harald would add Norway to the circle of support with which Aethilstan had surrounded himself ; but the possession of young Hakon might have a future importance over and above this. Harald—like Henry VIII of England— had a prestige in the eyes of his subjects which owed a great deal to admiration, but even more to fear. He was not a popular king. He had over-ridden too many old vested interests, and too many independent powers for that. Eirik Bloodaxe, who took over Norway upon Harald's abdication in 929, was neither admired nor feared to the same degree. His marriage had been a Danish alliance, little liked in Norway—or, we may guess, in England either.

V

The chroniclers agree as to the personality of Hakon. Theodoric [1] says " Hic fuit aspectu pulcher, viribus corporis robustus, animi virtute praestans, omni populo gratissimus "—and Snorri, in the vernacular, is definite and crisp in the same sense. Such a child as Hakon might be invaluable to a shrewd intriguer, especially if Norway, under Eirik, showed any sign of weakening in its friendly attitude. Harald, in sending him, had taken a step which has its puzzling side. He certainly went back upon the policy he had pursued in respect of Eirik's marriage. It is hard to believe that the action was performed in ignorance of its possible results.

[1] *Hist. de Antiq. Reg. Norweg.*, iv.

The subsequent career of Hakon illustrates the kind of education he received at Aethilstan's court. He was a Christian, who adhered to his faith throughout life, though not to the point of martyrdom. He suffered humiliation, but he was perhaps too much of a practical man to avoid it at the cost of his life. He was an excellent statesman, who introduced the first systematic principles of national law into Norway. The Laws of Hakon the Good were to Norway what the Laws of Edgar became to the English. If he did not invent he seems to have reorganized on a national scale the defences of Norway against raiders. He attempted to introduce Christianity. Not a word is breathed against his private character. All this says much for the court at which he was educated and for the era and country in which another great statesman also, Saint Dunstan, was born. In Lewis d'Outremer that court sent to France, moreover, a young king who, though less successful than Hakon, was an honest, able, and upright man.

Hakon had certainly acquired larger views than most of his Norwegian contemporaries ; and if he could think more easily in national terms than they could, it was no doubt partly because he had lived in a land where ideas of national width had for a hundred years past been familiar to men. He contrasts favourably with his brothers, who had nothing like his moral training nor his political education.

The political tradition in which Hakon was trained was the English tradition of the West Saxon kings. He took to Norway not the political ideas of Charles the Great and the Frankish emperors, nor those that were arising in the new Saxon house, but the strictly national ideas which had grown up in England. Of this tradition, Christianity was an essential element. The task of Aethilstan's predecessors, and of the kings who followed him, was to break up the small local interests which held men back from whole-hearted association upon a national scale : and local religion—heathenism, as we call it— was a serious factor in binding together those interests and giving them a coherence they would not otherwise have possessed. If Harald Fairhair could have seen the type of statesman turned out by the English court, he might have come over to the view that national states were incompatible with the heathen religion.

It was this view, slowly sinking into the minds of the men of the north, that had the most weight in pushing forward Christianity. We can, in the case of Norway, see the process passing from the mild tolerance of Hakon, through the blind zeal of Olaf Tryggwi's son, to the un- bending determination of Olaf the Holy. Their conscious- ness of Christianity as a philosophical doctrine may have been feeble ; but their consciousness of it as a political factor was acute. It meant a great deal for the future that Christianity should come to Norway allied rather with the English view of the national state than with the Roman imperial idea. We must therefore look upon Hakon's religion as a part of his political training ; not that it did not affect his moral quality as a man, but that it was most significant as influencing his actions as a king.

VI

Harald Fairhair died in 932, three years after his abdication, and Norway passed entirely into the hands of Eirik. This was the first breach in the diplomatic defences of Aethilstan. It was followed by the defection of the Scots. Now, if ever, was the time to use the power given him by the possession of an heir to Norway. He doubtless paved the way by inquiries and negotiations : but Snorri's explicit tale is that Aethilstan fitted Hakon out with ships and money, and despatched him to Norway. Hakon, significantly enough, was received with friendliness by the powerful earl Sigurd of Ladi, who had once named the child after his own father Hakon : and with Sigurd's help he established himself firmly in Norway. Eirik lingered a year or two, but at last gave up as hopeless any attempt to recover the crown. He left the country to Hakon, and went to look for a new kingdom across the seas.

In the same year Aethilstan struck his blow at the Scots by sea and land, and, as the *Chronicle* tells us, laid waste a great part of their country. These measures, like the action of Drake against Cadiz, had their effect. They postponed for some years the trouble that was brewing in the Irish Sea.

Snorri's narrative then takes a turn that is interesting. Eirik, he tells us, went to Scotland, and was invited by Aethilstan to take land under him. It would indeed have been a master-stroke to provide Eirik with a new kingdom that would prevent him from returning to Norway to trouble Hakon : and at the same time to withdraw Eirik from association with the Scots. Aethilstan recalled his friendship with Eirik's father—a delicate way of directing Eirik upon the right path—and promised him Northumbria.

We have no means of judging whether this story is true. We do not meet with Eirik in the English annals until 948 ; but the account is explicit, and contains nothing inconsistent with the rest of the story. It is possible that Eirik received some place in Northumbria,[1] which Aethilstan was retaining in his own hands. Eirik's possession of the kingdom of York was to come later on in the tale.

---

[1] According to Snorri (Hakon's Saga, iii) he held it on terms of feudal service. This would be about 936 or 937.

VII

Howsoever much Aethilstan fenced himself round, and howsoever far he deferred the evil day, the crisis had to come, sooner or later. After many delays, at last, in 937, the storm broke. An immense fleet, which it must have taken years to prepare, landed Olaf the Red, king of Dublin, and a great host, which effected a junction with the forces of Constantine king of Scots, with those of Eugenius of Strathclyde and with the Cumbrian Norse. The place of their landing and the site of the battle have not been recorded, but they were probably near Carlisle.[1]

The onslaught of the Irish Danes was no trifling affair : it deserves to rank with the great historic invasions of England. Some suggestion of the acute tension of the years while England was awaiting this Armada has crept even into the bare annals of the English *Chronicle*. They grow shorter and shorter and less and less important until suddenly they explode into the paean of the battle of Brunanburgh. We know little of the battle except that it was a complete triumph for Aethilstan. It was fought from dawn to sunset. Five kings and seven earls fell on the field ; Olaf and Constantine escaped with their lives. The great host of the Dublin kings was dispersed and destroyed.

Aethilstan must have owed much of his success to his careful diplomacy during the preceding years. Throughout, Northumbria remained quiet ; the Welsh took no part in the contest. There is strong reason to think that Northumbrian Danes fought on the English side. If so, it is the first sign that the Danish settlers were

[1] Dr. Hodgkin (*Political History of England*, vol. i, pp. 334–5) voted for Burnswark, and this is a very probable site : it involves a landing in the Solway. For a detailed discussion see the essay by Mr. George Neilson in *The Scottish Historical Review*, vol. vii, p. 37 (Oct. 1909).

beginning to be absorbed into the nationality of their new home, and we must carry back to Aethilstan's reign the policy of racial unification which we see in operation later on, in the reign of Edgar.

Aethilstan remained at peace for the brief remnant of his reign. He died at Gloucester on October 27, in the year 939.

VIII

The battle of Brunanburgh was the last of the great series of battles in which England was conquered by the Danes, freed again by Alfred and his son Edward, and finally confirmed in her national unity and independence by Alfred's grandson, Aethilstan. The kings of Dublin were never again the great power they had been. They declined more and more, as the native Irish kings began to revive. Sixty-five years later, King Brian of the Dalg Cais broke them for ever at Clontarf, and the Danes began to be absorbed into the fabric of Irish life. But the battle of Brunanburgh was the critical point at which their advance was given pause. It was the effective blow which finally destroyed the sea-empire of Ragnar.

We know almost more of Aethilstan from the northern point of view than from the English. From English sources we see a strangely vague and incalculable figure, hard to quicken into humanity. But to the Danes and Northmen " Adalstein " was a vast figure of power, mighty and august, somewhat remote, but very great. He was the first English king whose foreign policy extended over Europe and affected its history. That policy was destined to continue long, and to influence later events to an extent almost beyond calculation. It was to form the foundation of the policy of Saint Dunstan and the Church party. It was not to prove perfect or eternal ; and, having in its youth gone whither it would, it had in its age to go whither it would not, to unexpected ends, as we shall see ; but with all its faults it was the first definite scheme of relations between England and the surrounding lands, and not the least effective of those that have been in various ages designed to that end.

It certainly secured for England a period of fifty years of peace and reorganization. While the Saxon emperors were lifting Germany to the supremacy of Europe, and while Hakon remained king of Norway, England could rest secure from foreign foes, and could rebuild the power that once, while Alfred lurked in Athelney, had seemed destroyed for ever.

IX

Aethilstan's only son, Edwin, had died before his father : Aethilstan, therefore, was succeeded by his brother Edmund. Only with the death of Aethilstan do we begin distinctly to be aware of the fatal flaw that was to destroy the royal house of the West Saxons. Its men were dying early, and in spite of their intelligence and ability were beginning to show the lack of stamina which afterwards marked them.

The fact that Aethilstan died at Gloucester is not without meaning in view of the events which immediately followed his death. The revolt of Northumbria followed almost at once, and the election of Olaf the Red at York.[1] Olaf had been replaced at Dublin by his brother Blakari after the defeat at Brunanburgh : he had therefore gone to Northumbria—and what he could not do with an immense fleet and all the wickings of the western seas while Aethilstan was alive, he apparently had no

[1] According to Snorri (Hakon's Saga, iv), Eirik understood himself not to be *persona grata* with Edmund, and retired from Northumbria. In any case, as he held by oath under Aethilstan, he had no rights that survived the latter's death.

difficulty in doing, without their help, when Aethilstan was dead. The firm old northern doctrine, that oaths are dissolved by the death of one of the parties, played its part. Olaf carried with him not only Northumbria, but the Five Boroughs as well. He could claim their allegiance as soon as their oaths to Aethilstan were voided by the king's death. For some time it seemed as if the work of King Edward had been undone at a stroke. The Welsh, with whom Aethilstan had probably been negotiating at the time of his death, were uncertain. Their defection would probably have hurled everything into anarchy. But the dead Aethilstan's last diplomatic measures held things together. The Welsh remained neutral, and the contest was localized.

Edmund advanced into the midlands and put down the revolt of the Five Boroughs. The year following, Olaf and the main forces of Northumbria came to the help of their allies, marching south-west towards the Welsh border. They stormed Tamworth ; but Edmund forced them to retreat upon Leicester. Only a night march enabled them to escape being caught there and captured. After this, Edmund and Olaf came to an accommodation. Olaf was baptized, as also was his brother Ragnvald : but Olaf died during the year.

Edmund now entered Northumbria and drove out Ragnvald. Cumbria was next visited, and was handed over to Malcolm, the king of Scots, as the price of an alliance. At the moment when Edmund had completely restored the work of Aethilstan, he was assassinated at Pucklechurch.[1]

---

[1] Dr. Hodgkin (*op. cit.*, p. 339), gives the details. They would not satisfy a modern coroner, who would have adjourned the case for further evidence.

X

The murder of Edmund was a new and startling note in English history : and it portended and heralded changes which, though natural, and indeed inevitable in view of the work of his father and brother, seem at first to be retrogressions. Not since the disturbed days of the eighth century had a political murder broken the calm orderliness of the English royal house. But those who inspired the crime gained very little from it. Edred, a second brother, who succeeded him, completed the work of reducing Northumbria. He received the oaths of the Scots, confirming the treaty with them. The allegiance of Northumbria also was solemnly confirmed.

This did not last long : and now at length Eirik appears recognizably upon the scene. He was elected king of Northumbria the very year after the oaths of allegiance had been sworn. This, however, was a very different matter from the election of Olaf the Red. It involved the deliberate violation of oaths and the transfer of allegiance : in effect, it was a Danish rebellion against English rule. Edred instantly invaded Northumbria : whereupon the Northumbrians came to terms, and Eirik was deposed. No sooner had Edred returned home, than Olaf Kuaran came forward and was elected. This time Edred held off and waited upon events.

He had not long to wait, for Eirik had only gone to gather help. Two years after the election of Olaf Kuaran the latter had to bolt before Eirik's return. Several of his friends—among whom was Wulfstan, archbishop of York—prudently followed his example. Edred promptly arrested the archbishop. Wulfstan had been deeply implicated in the proceedings in Northumbria, and he paid for it now by a period of imprisonment, from which his rank did not save him. Eirik held his ground in York for two years more. Then Olaf returned with a suitable party of kindred spirits, and they fought their fight out at Stainmoor, on the great Roman road that brought Olaf down from Carlisle. It was a Homeric struggle. Eirik seems to have been the victor ; but he, and four kings with him, fell.

Edred stepped in and took Northumbria quietly into his own hands. Archbishop Wulfstan was released and transferred to the see of Sherborne. Northumbria was once more put under the control of the Bernician aldermen. This was the end of the struggle of the Danes. Edred died in the following year.

XI

So far, the luck of the Wessex kings had not failed them. At this point it began to flicker. Edred was the last of the fighting men of his house. By the barest margin he had accomplished the task which Alfred had set his successors. He left his crown to two boys, Edwi and Edgar, of eleven and twelve years old. There were no other heirs.

Such a fact was by itself a revolution. The kingship was not constructed to endure a minority. It depended so exclusively upon the personal bond between the king and his guild of companions—a bond which could only with the utmost difficulty survive when a boy came to the throne—that the very foundations of the English nation were now put in peril at the very moment when its reunion had been achieved. The national organization had, up to this point, no existence apart from the king, without whom it would dissolve into a series of disconnected local organizations without any national meaning. Hence, there was no impersonal system of government which could continue to run on of itself. Even if the military guild, the companion-group, could be held together, its power would be paralysed. The system would not work without the presence of a strong and mature man at the head of affairs.

A system which could be wrecked by an accident of this sort had obvious weaknesses which disqualified it from being a permanent form of government. It was bound, sooner or later, to meet with some disaster which would throw matters back to the starting-point ; and if England could produce nothing better, she was doomed to go on struggling forward towards an aim which she would repeatedly miss. Either the effort to unify the nation, and to hold it unified, was a mere dream which would be achieved and lost again without any permanently secured progress, or else an organization must be created apart from the kingship, to embody and retain the progress made.

The experiences of five centuries had, of course, not failed to show the difficulty that was involved in a minority. It had shown many difficulties, which had been met in a variety of ways. In earlier times, kingships had simply risen and fallen, and there was an end of the matter. But a world which intended to evolve a civilization could not rest content with a negation so simple. Difficulties must be solved, not accepted. The Merovingian Frankish minorities had been dealt with by putting the crown into tutelage under the Arnulfing Mayors of the Palace, from whom a new royal dynasty was evolved. But this was no solution, since the Arnulfings in due time met the difficulty afresh, and no advance had been made. If anything, Frankish kingship had fallen into decay ; great vassals had arisen who in practical power were equal or superior to the crown, and a process of segregation and disunion had begun. The election of Hugh Capet as king of the French was bought at the price of emptying the French crown of all its practical power.

To whatsoever aspect of the problem we turn, there was no clear way of solving it save by the creation of a secondary organism which would remain when the kingship lapsed, and which would give a quality of permanence and stability to the progress made by the kings. But precisely what this body should be, and how it should be created, remained to be seen.

XII

The man who came to the rescue was the remarkable man whom we know as Saint Dunstan, archbishop of Canterbury. He took over the guardianship of the young kings and set out to solve the problem they presented.

The mere fact that a subject, who was not a member of the royal house, could command the co-operation of the various elements of the nation shows that great strides had been made in some of the processes of social life. He was, of course, under disadvantages. As a churchman, he was excluded from some forms of action which are very convenient to secular rulers. He had not the full authority which a parent would have possessed. In Edwi he had somewhat intractable material to deal with : and he had, at the same time, to struggle for possession of the young kings' minds with rivals whose purposes were not necessarily disinterested. He could not issue unquestionable commands. He could only get people to meet together, and persuade them to act in concert. Even the kings' authority suffered from the common knowledge that their words were usually the words of Dunstan. But these limitations, this necessity for gathering the leading men, the great aldermen, abbots, and bishops, together in council, and organizing their agreement, created precisely the instrument that was wanted—a general council of the realm.

While it was not in Dunstan's power to create at one stroke institutions which needed the experience and struggle of five hundred years to build them up, he certainly opened a new chapter in English conceptions of policy. We owe to him the first idea of a consultative body sitting more or less regularly to express the mind of the nation, and to advise the crown.[1] The idea was not originally adopted because of its abstract beauty, but for reasons of practical necessity. Its development was destined, at a later stage, to render possible expedients which revolutionized the social structure of English life, and changed the methods of monarchy.

Dunstan was the first minister who ever governed on behalf of an English king. His position and his policy were signals for the appearance of parties in the state. The new council was the field of contest between the churchmen who held the Roman tradition of unity and collegiate government, and the aldermen who represented the secular forces of local separatism and personal rule.

The death of Edwi after a short reign relieved Dunstan of some of the worst of his difficulties. When Edgar became sole king, the archbishop found a pupil who was amenable to instruction, and who followed dutifully, throughout his reign, the guidance of the strong man who stood at his elbow. The government of Edgar was the government of Dunstan, and the fame which Edgar has ever since enjoyed is a fame which Dunstan gave him.

Some of the difficulties with which Dunstan had to struggle were begun before the death of Edred. The fall of Eirik Bloodaxe had results of a very serious nature.

---

[1] There never had been a time without a council. The very idea of a comitatus involved frequent meetings and consultations. But this was a different thing from such a conference of various territorial rulers as began about this time to arise : though no doubt the new form of council grew directly from the old.

It sent his sons back to Denmark with a claim to the rule of Norway. Gorm the Old was dead, and Harald Bluetooth was the Danish king. Disputes had already arisen between Harald and King Hakon of Norway. The return of the sons of Eirik shortly after 954 put into the hands of Harald Bluetooth just the weapon he needed.

XIII

The period between 954 and 961 was therefore the most active time of Hakon's reign. He repelled two invasions of the sons of Eirik from their base in Denmark shortly after 954. They waited seven years in order to strengthen their position, and then they made a third attempt. Hakon was surprised by much greater forces, and though he is said to have won the battle of Stord, he bled to death of the wounds he received.

The importance of this event became visible only by degrees. Hakon was succeeded by the joint government of Eirik's five younger sons, of whom Harald Graycloak, the senior king, gave his name to the reign. As their mother, Gunnhild, struck the public eye as chairman of the board, they went down to history as " the Sons of Gunnhild " rather than of Eirik.

Dunstan had neither the power nor the opportunity to prevent this destruction of the great achievement of Aethilstan. It resulted in a considerable extension of Danish prestige and ambition at a moment particularly inconvenient to England. The whole policy to which the archbishop guided Edgar was one of conciliation and peace, the unification of the country, and the blending into one nation of Englishman and Dane. Any factor which induced the English Danes to look overseas damaged this policy.

How far it was successful is a point on which it is hard

P

to pronounce without more complete information than we possess. Edgar had a remarkably firm possession of England. Perhaps none of his predecessors, and certainly none of his successors until William Rufus, wielded so undisputed a sway. He owed this to Dunstan. The legend that he was rowed upon the River Dee by six tributary kings is well known. He certainly met six kings at Chester, and received their covenants of allegiance and good faith. Dunstan himself was sufficiently powerful to gain the acceptance of an advanced ecclesiastical policy. We begin to hear once more of the building of churches, and the refounding of those which an earlier age had destroyed : of the displacement of secular canons by regular monks, the re-issue of charters, and the re-organization of endowments.

But there are signs that Dunstan's policy did not meet with unqualified appreciation.[1] It resulted in the division of England into parties, one of which looked with little enthusiasm upon a revival of ecclesiastical power, while the other has left on record scathing references to immoral men and detestable aliens, which probably found their billet at the time, though they are spent shafts by now. Dunstan undoubtedly kept the king under a control which, howsoever justifiable, was hard to justify. It was only in 973, when Edgar was twenty-nine, that the archbishop was at last forced to crown him and to grant him some measure of independence.

The edifice was cracking at its foundations just as it reached its perfection. Edgar's policy, as soon as he was freed from the control of the archbishop, showed the distinctly greater influence of the Danish element, which was thrown upon the side of the aldermen who held what were growing to be perilously like the great fiefs of France.

---

[1] For some of the arguments involved see Oman, *England before the Norman Conquest*, pp. 379–80.

And he had not that power which had made his predecessors the masters of the aldermen. He had never had—
and it was the essential weakness of the archbishop's
position that Dunstan could never give him—the opportunity of establishing that web of personal relationship
with the best men which created an effective comitatus.
It is doubtful even if he had the strength to create one.
He confronted the secular powers of England with nothing
but the prestige of his rank and the moral influence it
had derived from his predecessors. It was like confronting
a bull with the picture of a pole-axe.

CHAPTER XII

THE RESULTS OF THE GREAT FAMINE OF 976

I

WHAT might have been the future of Edgar—whether he would have triumphed over his enemies or fallen before them—we shall never know. He did not live long enough to prove the native stuff of which he was made. He died in 975 at the height of his fame, with a power and repute which he had not himself earned, and which he had not had time to tarnish.

His reign was marked by those omens which we despise when the annalists earnestly relate them. Pestilence swept England in 961, the year of Hakon's death : and St. Paul's Minster was burned to the ground. But Edgar died one year before a catastrophe vaster and more terrible, which was to change the face of Europe—the great famine of 976. The famine was universal. The crops failed throughout Europe. Not only so, but even the herring fishery failed, and the shoals did not arrive in Norway, where it was noted that snow lay on the ground in Halogaland throughout the summer, as if the arctic circle had drifted south.

The sons of Eirik had ruled, not very well, in Norway for fifteen years. The famine ended their rule there. They had slain the great Sigurd, earl of Ladi, and alienated his son, earl Hakon. The same year saw the famine, the invasion of Denmark by the Germans, the discrediting of Harald Bluetooth, the entrapping and death of Harald Graycloak, and the rise of Hakon of Ladi and Swein Forkbeard. The pendulum was swinging : and it had already swung so that one of the most important points of Aethilstan's policy was undone ; while instead of restraining the Danes, the Germans had merely provoked the rise of a new generation of vigorous and determined leaders ; and finally, a heathen reaction was on foot, which aimed at confronting the new Saxon empire with a new Danish empire. Earl Hakon in Norway and King Swein in Denmark were the leaders of a heathen party which saw in the Christian faith, perhaps, a hostile philosophy, but certainly a hostile political propaganda inspired from German and English sources.

And at this very time, as we have seen, an increasing cleavage was parting the Church and the feudal aldermen in England. Young Edward, the son of Edgar, who continued the policy of Dunstan, was assassinated in 978 ; his brother, Aethilred, a child of ten, was placed upon a throne on which he was isolated and helpless. In 980 the Danes reappeared in the western seas. A new era had begun, fraught with momentous possibilities for the future.

II

The kingship of Alfred had no adequate champions at this juncture save the churchmen. Its battle was fought by saintly bishops and unworldly monks. To gain a better idea of the opponents against which they conducted their crusade, we had better, at this point, survey the circumstances in which the new Danish empire arose.

One of the chief trade routes of the north lay through the valley of the Oder, and gave access to that region which in all ages has been of especial importance as a commanding centre to Europe. It is now known as Czecho-Slovakia, though not so long ago it still bore the more august name of Bohemia. In the island of Wollin, at the mouth of the Oder, stood the town of Julin, which by its relation to the rest of the Baltic lands formed the natural mart through which the currents of trade flowed between Scandinavia and Central Europe. In the tenth century, Julin was the medium of a rich commerce between the Baltic and the eastern Mediterranean. The monies of England, Frisia, Lorraine, Bavaria, Constantinople, and the Moslem kingdoms were current in its market. There were large revenues to be gained by the power which held Julin ; and there at Jomsborg, sometime in the tenth century, the Danish king, Harald Bluetooth, planted a military garrison, to protect and control this gateway of trade.

This garrison became the most formidable military force that Europe had known since the dissolution of the Praetorians. Its only rival was the Varangian guard of the emperors at Constantinople, which never exercised anything like the same political power. It was a guild, corporation or community, systematically organized and governed by definite statutes. No one under eighteen or over fifty years of age was admitted into its ranks. Personal qualities alone were the ground of admission ; and the tests on this head were severe enough to exact the highest possible standard. Discipline was as rigid as in a modern guard-corps. And as the possessor of Julin was rich, he could pay high for the best human material. On this comitatus the new Danish empire was built.

III

The first chief—*Maior Palatii*, the Franks would have called him—of the Jomsborg wickings was Palnatoki, a Dane belonging to the principal family in Funen. Under Palnatoki the Jomsborgers soon became a political force able to exert a controlling influence upon the state of affairs in Denmark. His intervention was the decisive factor which removed old King Harald Bluetooth, and placed Swein upon the Danish throne. Very soon after Swein's accession, Palnatoki was succeeded as earl of the Jomsborgers by Sigwaldi, the son of Strut-Harald, earl of Skane.

Sigwaldi was an even more dangerous servant than Palnatoki. It would almost seem as if King Swein (who had a peculiar gift for surviving the intentions of both his enemies and his friends) had marked the history of the Frankish *maiorès* ; and possibly earl Sigwaldi also had marked it. Accordingly the earl lost no time in opening negotiations with King Burislaf of Wendland. He pointed out the value of the Jomsborg guild, which formed a closed door to Burislaf's kingdom : and he gave Burislaf the choice of a marriage alliance, or of seeing Jomsborg abandoned and the guild dissolved.

The alternative may have been bluff ; but Burislaf took it seriously. His decision was soon made. He promised Sigwaldi the hand of his daughter Astrid if the earl would bring King Swein so far into his power, that binding terms could be extracted from him. Sigwaldi agreed.

According to the story handed down to us, Swein shortly afterwards received the startling news that Sigwaldi was dying, and had an urgent message to give the king, on which his life and realm might depend. Swein hurried to the spot where three Jomsborg ships lay off shore, stem to stern. With thirty men, Swein went on board the innermost ship, and was directed to the earl, who lay under the awning of the outermost. " He went and raised the curtain, and asked if the earl were able to speak. The earl answered in a very low voice that he was able to speak, but had very little strength. Then the king asked him : ' What are the tidings of which you sent me word, all-important for me to know?' And the earl answered: 'Lean down over me, so that you may hear what I say, for my voice is very weak.' As the king bent down over him, quite low, the earl seized him with both arms and held him as tight as he could, showing very little signs of weakness now. Then he called out to his men and bade them row all the ships to sea as hard as they could. This was done; and they rowed away, having the king with them and the thirty men who had accompanied him on board. All the rest of the king's men were left standing on the shore, as there were no ships near at hand in which they could follow." [1]

The polite reassurances of Sigwaldi, and his expressions of loyalty and welcome, did very little to hide the fact that King Swein was a prisoner in Jomsborg. Little by little the scheme was revealed. Sigwaldi had arranged that while he married Astrid, the king was to marry her sister Gunnhild. There was a condition attached to the marriage—to wit, that Swein should set Burislaf free from tribute; and if this condition were not accepted, then Sigwaldi regretted that it would be his duty to surrender Swein into the hands of the Wends. Swein appreciated well enough what, in that case, his fate would be. He accepted the terms. The kingdom of Burislaf was set free from all liabilities towards Denmark. Swein promised his sister Thyri to Burislaf and himself married Gunnhild, Burislaf's daughter, who became the mother of Knut the Great. The treaty included a mutual peace and amnesty between all the parties to the arrangement.

[1] Great Olaf Trygwisson Saga, c. 85 (Rev. J. Sephton's translation). Snorri prudently omits some of these graphic details. Saxo's account is a variant; but all agree that King Swein was kidnapped by the Jomsborgers.

IV

Sigwaldi's *coup d'état* had been remarkably successful ;
but it was not destined to be the end of the story. King
Swein settled down again in Denmark, and in the general
peace and amnesty all ill-feeling was wiped out. Swein
was careful to invite the Jomsborgers to the celebration
of his father's memorial feast. As Strut-Harald, Sigwaldi's
father, was recently dead, the king proposed to honour
his friend by holding the memorial feasts jointly. Willing
to underline the amicable state of their relations with the
king, the Jomsborgers accepted. Forty ships carried a
full force of the leading men of the guild : twenty more
brought Sigwaldi's kinsmen from Skane. With a force
so strong there was little fear of treachery : nor was any
treachery intended. Something subtler was hatching in
the fertile mind of Swein.

On the first day of the feast, before occupying the
high seat of his father, King Swein drank to his memory,
and made the solemn vow that before three years were
over he would be in England, and would either slay
King Aethilred or drive him oversea. The vow was
greatly applauded : the Jomsborgers asked nothing better.
The largest horns were filled with the strongest drink for
them, and the toast was honoured. So large were the
horns, apparently, and so strong the drink, that even
the Jomsborgers were not proof against a certain surge
of enthusiasm. Swein suggested that it was now their
turn.

Sigwaldi accordingly drank the memorial toast to
Strut-Harald, and vowed that within three years he
would be in Norway, having slain earl Hakon or driven
him overseas. The other Jomsborgers added their vows.
Wagn Akasson's vow seems to have been particularly
noted at the time ; for he vowed not to return from

Norway until he had slain Thorkel Leira and taken his daughter against the will of her men. They made a night of it with great good-fellowship, and the morning after was a time of slow realization and awakening to the heroes of Jomsborg. They had been trapped !

Serious conferences put no better face upon the situation. King Swein's vow was harmless enough : King Aethilred would never hear of it, and it would not much matter if he did : but the vow concerning earl Hakon was a very serious business. It would soon come to his ears : and the longer the execution of the vow was postponed, the less chance there would be of ever successfully carrying it out. It could not be laughed away. The credit of Jomsborg had been staked. The leaders finally agreed that the best thing to do was to carry out the vow at once. The ships were made ready for sea as soon as the feast was concluded.

They were not misled. The news was swiftly conveyed to earl Eirik Hakon's son in Norway, and word was at once sent out to raise the levy of ships and men. The Jomsborgers slipped through Limfirth into the North Sea, to avoid the sea-borne traffic of the Skager Rack, and then sailed north. Even if their general destination were known, it would be impossible to predict the exact point of their descent upon the Norwegian coast. They touched at Agdir, and during a night descent at Jadar their identity was recognized. Word was sent north. While the military gentlemen from Julin were looking for earl Hakon, the fleet of the latter, crowded to the gunwales with hard-bitten farmers, sealers, and grab-what-you-cansters from Throndham, Halogaland, and the western coast—heathen to a man—moved slowly southwards, searching every inlet. At Hiorunga Bay the Jomsborgers found it. There was nothing to wait for. The two fleets closed, and the battle was fought.

V

The battle of Hiorunga Bay belongs to the world of epic and legend : to the kind of war men could wage before the complex motives and inhibitions of Christianity had laid their restraint upon them. If the saga-men told the truth, half the picked war-beasts of Norway were there.[1] The Jomsborgers had the bigger ships, but the Northmen had the larger number.[2] In the preliminary exchange of shot-weapons the Jomsborgers showed their strength. Wagn Akasson broke the line opposite him, but before he could scatter the ships, earl Eirik came and restored the struggle. Eirik returned to his own wing to find it giving way before the ships of Bui the Stout. Then earl Hakon, finding all he could do vain against the Jomsborg centre, made the fierce and dramatic gesture which lingered in the memories of men. He returned on shore, and solemnly offered up in sacrifice his young son Erling, aged seven years.

He was not like Abraham. If the saga-men told the truth, no angel stayed his hand. In whatsoever ways such things may work, they worked now. As Hakon rejoined his fleet a storm of hail came, terrible and torrential, beating in the faces of the Jomsborgers : and earl Eirik cast off the grapplings of his ships and went for them hand-to-hand. Sigwaldi was the first to cut free and run for the open. Thirty-five ships of the Jomsborgers followed him. Twenty-five remained, locked in ferocious death grapple. Bui the Stout sprang overboard. Wagn's ship was cleared. Thirty prisoners were

[1] Wigfus the famous son of Slaying-Glum and the famous Sigmund Brestisson of the Faroes fought under Earl Eirik. The reader must pay these names the same kind of respect he would pay to those of Tom Sayers or Jem Mace. They were unbeaten champions in their day.

[2] Snorri gives them 180 ships against the Jomsborgers' 60 (*Heimskr.* O.T., c. xliii).

collected from amongst the slain—all that fell alive into
the hands of the Norsemen. Of them, Wagn was one.

VI

The battle of Hiorunga Bay is imperfect without the
episode which followed it. The thirty prisoners were
tied to a log by a rope twisted round their ankles, but
otherwise left free. Then Thorkel Leira, axe in hand,
interviewed them. He said, with ponderous humour :
" You made a vow, Wagn, to slay me. I think it more
likely that I shall slay you." (We may safely insert, at
this point, *Guffaws from the surrounding Northmen.*) He
accordingly proceeded down the line, beheading one
man after another. The Jomsborgers took it coolly.
One metaphysical speculator said to another : " Look
at this cloak pin in my hand. If I know anything after
my head is off, I will stick it into the ground." When
his head came off, the pin fell out of his hand, so his
subsequent experience has not survived to enlighten us
upon the subject. When eighteen had fallen to Thorkel's
axe, the nineteenth, a young man with beautiful hair,
said : " Do not defile my hair with blood." So one of
earl Hakon's men obligingly held the hair out ; whereupon at the critical moment the Jomsborger jerked his
head back, and it was the wrists of the Norseman that
received the stroke. This seems to have been the occasion
necessary to rouse earl Eirik to action.

After a brief colloquy the amused earl offered the
prisoners quarter ; and with a still briefer formal protest,
they accepted it.

Thorkel Leira said : " At any rate, Wagn Akasson
shall not get off." But as he rushed at Wagn one of the
Jomsborgers, Biorn the Bretlander,[1] flung himself at

---

[1] Evidently a Norseman from the settlements on the north Cornish
coast—one of those Hawkes, Hawkens, and Hubbers who still flourish.
Snorri, however, gives his name as Scardi, or Scarth, as we should now say.

Thorkel's ankles. Thorkel fell, and lost the axe, which Wagn seized ; and that was the end of Thorkel Leira.

The humour of this episode thawed earl Eirik into geniality. To his inquiry whether Wagn accepted quarter, Wagn replied that he would do so if he were allowed to fulfil the rest of his vow. So he was duly married to Thorkel Leira's daughter, and was sent home in a good ship with his bride ; and according to the saga-men everyone lived happily ever after.

Now, these were the men whom the churchmen of England were preparing to meet with the meek and holy weapons of their cloth. These weapons can seldom have had a more searching test to endure.

VII

It is uncertain whether King Swein ever heard these romantic details. He may or may not have shared earl Eirik's sense of humour ; but more important to him were the practical consequences of the battle. Without open hostility King Swein had tamed the dangerous power that once had seemed his master. The Jomsborg guild, just sufficiently damaged in prestige, in *personnel*, and in pride, returned to its original function of serving the Danish king by guarding the trade route along the valley of the Oder.

Swein had lost nothing. Although he might have had no objection to the possession of Norway, he was content to see it isolated in the hands of earl Hakon, whose position was too delicate to permit him the luxury of an aggressive policy. Swein's successful resistance to the attempt of the Germans to reimpose upon Denmark the policy of the Kaiser Otto, was a triumph that still further strengthened his hands.

The whole drift of events began therefore to set steadily in one direction. The famine had damaged the prosperity of many men, who were not willing to sit down quietly under their reverses ; the whole interests of the Jomsborgers lay in war ; and a southern war would suit the policy of everyone concerned. Four years from the fall of Harald Graycloak the wicking ships reappeared in British waters after the interval of nearly a century. They came to gather funds and information for King Swein. Irish gold had financed Ragnar's designs. English gold now financed Swein and the heathen reaction.

The English war, prepared for during the preceding years, began in A.D. 991. During the struggle with the Germans, young Olaf Tryggwi's son, who was in the service of King Burislaf, had worked with Swein. This partnership was destined to have historic results. Olaf, when he left the Wendish service, threw in his lot with Swein. In the campaigns of the next few years, Olaf apparently provided the expert direction, and Swein the capital and organization. His fleet crossed to British waters by the regular route from Denmark, past Frisia to the Scheldt mouth, and thence to Sandwich. The expedition was a reconnaissance in force. He sailed up the east coast, sacking Ipswich on his way ; and he passed round Scotland to the Hebrides, Man, and Ireland.

It is improbable that the advent of this fleet was altogether a surprise to Aethilred's government. Even in the tenth century the preparation and movement of great bodies of men could not be concealed. Aethilred seems to have entertained some doubt whether it were desirable to fight : for he bought off Olaf's fleet for 10,000 pounds [1]—the first gafol ever paid as ransom to the Danes.[2]

---

[1] Reckoning in lbs. of silver bullion.
[2] The special tax by which it was raised was called the " Danegeld " : when being paid to the Danes, it was called a " gafol."

The payment of such a sum raises many historical problems. What was the real meaning of this entirely new departure? It was warranted by nothing obvious to us in the state of England. In the light of subsequent events we can see the possibility that Olaf professed (not altogether untruly) to be merely after money, and that he offered to leave England if he had a lump sum down. But this is unlikely to be the full explanation. Archbishop Sigeric is credited with responsibility for advising the policy, and the identity of its sponsor points to the churchmen as the originators of the plan.

Throughout the next few years, the churchmen never hid their firm conviction that the aldermen were both incompetent and disloyal ; and it is possible enough that they wished to avoid a war which, in the circumstances, would probably add to the importance of the secular magnates. Olaf was indeed after funds for his own purposes ; but during the next year he spent this first ample instalment in fitting out a still larger fleet in Irish ports.

VIII

The policy of paying ransom was not yet accepted as final. The aldermen seem to have preferred more active methods of resistance. But when, in the following year, alderman Aelfric, the commander of the king's fleet, met with disaster and was all but captured, he scarcely demonstrated the superior merits of either their theory or their practice. A fresh opportunity of testing the alternatives arose in 993. The loss of Aelfric's fleet left the coast open, and Olaf Tryggwi's son appeared at Sandwich with a fleet of ninety-three ships, while a Danish fleet entered the Humber. The latter went up to Lindsey and ravaged Northumbria, incidentally burning Bamborough, the old stronghold of Aelle. Olaf's operations were more serious. After a feint against Ipswich he slipped southward and landed at Maldon. Now Maldon is the sea-gate of one road to London, as Sandwich is of another. But Olaf got no farther. He was met by alderman Brihtnoth and the Essex levy, and a fierce battle ended in divided honours. Brithnoth was slain; but the Norsemen were in no position to follow up their success.

All this was preliminary. The year after the Battle of Maldon, King Swein arrived in person with the main Danish fleet. He and Olaf proceeded up the Thames to London. Alfred's fortress resisted all assault, and held out while Essex, Kent, Sussex, and Hampshire were devastated around it, and King Aethilred lay idle at Winchester. The churchmen now came back into power. The aldermen had done nothing.

Unable to take London, Swein and Olaf listened to proposals for peace : though Swein, at any rate, was little likely to regard such a peace as more than temporary. Someone on the English side was evidently very well informed as to the identity of Olaf Tryggwi's son. That identity was interesting. He was the son of Tryggwi, who had been an under king of Hakon the Good ; and he was a direct descendant of Harald Fairhair, and the heir to the Norwegian crown.

To anyone who was acquainted with the old policy of Aethilstan, these facts suggested the possibility of driving a wedge between the Norse and the Danish interests among the invaders. The men entrusted with the task were Alphege,[1] bishop of Winchester, and alderman Aethilweard.

---

[1] Alfheah ; but his church, on the site of his martyrdom at Greenwich, preserves his name in a familiar modern form as " Alphege." He was a favourite pupil of Dunstan, and therefore high in the councils of the Church party. Aethilweard is generally supposed to have been the chronicler of that name. If so, he was a descendant of King Aethilwulf, a kinsman of the king, and probably a supporter of the churchmen.

Olaf evidently listened. Nothing in the experience of modern men would lead them to credit the idea, implied by his biographer, that Olaf Tryggwi's son returned suddenly and impulsively to Norway in the romantic hope of being accepted as king by a nation which admired his beauty and prowess. Nor does the known character of Olaf encourage any such belief. Revolutions and *coups d'état* need more careful preparation. The hints in the English *Chronicle* are far more likely to be the truth. Bishop Alphege and alderman Aethilweard were commissioned to propose to him the idea of breaking with Swein and recovering the crown of Norway. That Olaf was in communication with his own party at home, and was already building up funds for such an enterprise, is suggested both by his conduct and by our knowledge of the usual methods of political intrigue. His chief consideration in coming to a decision would be the amount of help he could expect from Aethilred.

The assurances he received were evidently satisfactory. He accepted hostages, and went in person to visit King Aethilred at Andover. There he was solemnly confirmed, and entered the circle of Christian sovereigns—an indispensable necessity before any serious support could be given him. Aethilred's presents to him are said to have been rich. Olaf had received 10,000 pounds in 991. He was now about to share a gafol of 16,000 pounds with Swein. Much of this would, of course, be absorbed in paying off his fleet. The gifts of King Aethilred would represent the balance necessary to enable him to make, with some real prospect of success, his claim to the crown of Norway.

We need not be surprised at having to read closely between the lines to detect the evidence of this transaction. Olaf would never have left Southampton had King Swein known his purpose ; nor would he afterwards be especially eager to admit that English gold, and not his own native virtues, had made him king in Norway. He gave Aethilred the solemn undertaking that he would never again levy war on England—a promise which he kept. Undertakings of such a type are not made idly ; they imply serious agreements and substantial considerations.

Olaf returned to Ireland, paid off his fleet, and sailed to Norway at the beginning of summer. His adherents had already paved the way for him. He overthrew earl Hakon with an ease which is surprising after Hakon's long and, on the whole, successful rule. A Christian king once more ruled in Norway. That the treaty of Southampton was a real and effective victory for the churchmen we can judge by its results. In spite of minor raids, no further serious effort was made until the year 1001, after Olaf Tryggwi's son's death ; while King Swein never returned to England until 1003, a period of nine years.

IX

After the defection of Olaf Tryggwi's son, King Swein placed no further reliance on heroic strategy. His method was to wear down the English power by steady attrition, until the time came for the final blow. The history of the remainder of Aethildred's reign bears witness to the nature of Swein's plans. The Danes shifted their fleets from point to point, and, when circumstances were suitable, mounted themselves for rapid land raiding. The devastation became so serious that measures had to be taken to deal with it. The English fleet was reorganized. The chronicler—a churchman—records with sardonic contempt the inefficiency of the organization and the negative nature of the results.

A tenth-century invading fleet, striking in succession

at the west, south, and south-east coasts of England, could
have its base only in the Irish sea, either in the Irish ports,
or the Isle of Man, or Cumbria. Aethilred's council
determined, since Ireland was inaccessible, to strike at
Cumbria. A land-force and sea-fleet were despatched
for the purpose, and carried out systematic reprisals on
the north-west coast. Meanwhile the Danish fleet had
run into Norman ports—a move which shows that it had
not come from Denmark, but was composed of auxiliaries
who were keeping the war alive for Swein. Having
refitted, it stood across the Channel, and in the absence
of the English army and fleet it raided Hampshire as
far north as Alton. It then returned westward, and
devasted the Devon coast. It finally came to rest at the
Isle of Wight.

These events are carefully narrated, in more detail
than usual, in the English *Chronicle*, and they were doubtless made much of at the time, because they reflected
very seriously on the ability of the aldermen to defend
England. They were followed, significantly enough, by
a return to the churchmen's policy. The Danish fleet
asked for supplies, and for 24,000 pounds. Meanwhile,
Aethilred hastened to make overtures to Normandy, and
married Emma, sister of Duke Richard.

The struggle in the king's council became severe, and
his policy fluctuated. Had Aethilred been a strong king,
he might have adopted one policy or the other and stuck
to it ; but he had not the personal power necessary to
make trenchant decisions in the teeth of opposition.
King Swein's plan of systematic raiding now began to
yield its fruit. Signs of doubt and stress began to appear
on the English side—accusations of treachery, suspicion
of plots. The flaw in the churchmen's policy was that
while admirably suited to far-off ultimate issues, it provided no method of meeting the actual immediate issue,

the invasions and devastations. The alderman, on the other hand, had no adequate means of fighting : and the old royal comitatus which won the battle of Ashdown was no longer in being. Moreover, King Swein never gave any opening for a decisive battle. The hour was not yet come.

X

The upshot of such a war could only be the downfall of England. In such circumstances prudent men hasten to make friends with the Mammon of Unrighteousness, especially if it chances to be not altogether remote in point of race and language. Exactly how far Swein may actually have tampered with the English-born Danes we have no means of knowing ; but we do know from modern experience that such methods of propaganda are a natural resort in war. That some men, English as well as Danes, had begun to provide against the day of a Danish king in England is clear from the freely uttered accusations that have come down to us.

The reports which came to the king involved the English Danes. A plot against his life was alleged to be contemplated. When we remember the fate of his brother, King Edward, and the assassination of his grandfather, King Edmund, it must be admitted that he was not without cause for apprehension. The details of the plot —if there were a plot—are obscure. The evidence was never known to anyone save the king and his advisers. We only know that Aethilred issued orders for a counter-plot. On Saint Brice's day a simultaneous attack on the Danes took place throughout England. A large number— how many we cannot guess—were slain.

The massacre of Saint Brice's day created a sensation throughout Europe, and it was long remembered. The Icelandic tradition is that the men at whom Aethilred struck were King Swein's " Thingmen." But the Thing-men—that is, the Jomsborgers—did not arrive in England until seven years later. The only Danes in England at this time—apart from hostile raiders—were English sub-jects who had taken the oath of allegiance either per-sonally, or through their natural chiefs. It is said that Gunnhilda, King Swein's sister, was among the slain. As King Swein himself was in England shortly afterwards, under peculiar circumstances, it is difficult to avoid the conclusion that some kind of plot did exist. He came, after nine years' absence, with a small force. His visit almost bears the marks of a private journey. We find him with a squadron in the Isle of Wight, as if he had come to witness the final scene of some conspiracy. If so, he was disappointed.

He sacked and burned Wilton and Sarum before he withdrew. Alderman Aelfric, with the Wiltshire and Hampshire levy, refused to take any steps against him. The accusation of treason against Aelfric in the English *Chronicle* is open and unmistakable. The events of the year before, the sudden appearance of Swein, and the peculiar conduct of Aelfric, all taken together, certainly give colour to the allegation that a real plot had existed.

XI

East Anglia was the next point of attack. By the year 1005 the devastation of England had been carried from the mouth of the Severn round to East Anglia, and the result was a famine so serious that even the Danish fleet went home. Despair began to grow in England. It seemed impossible to deal with the problem. The king and the council decided that they must buy a respite. Negotiations were opened. The sum agreed upon was thirty thousand pounds, and the respite was obtained.

It was meant to be used. Several changes of some importance were made. Edric Streona became alderman of the Mercians. Archbishop Alphege, appointed to Canterbury two years before, went to Rome to receive his pall and regularize his position. Preparations were pushed feverishly forward. Schemes were evolved for the reorganization of the defences of England. Ships were to be built, and a revised system of military service was prepared. The gathering of a fleet was hastened. There was need for haste. The designs of Swein were probably known. The hour was at last come ! Thorkel's fleet was even now fitting-out in Denmark, and was intended for Sandwich. With it was to come a fleet of Jomsborg wickings. The English fleet was the most numerous ever known in England. It was concentrated at Sandwich in the spring of the year A.D. 1009, while Thorkel, having dropped down past the Frisian coast, was overhauling in the Scheldt mouth. The king was present at Sandwich in person.

The English fleet never met the Danes. Strange events began to shape themselves. Alderman Brihtric, brother of alderman Edric, denounced one Wulfnoth to the king : and Wulfnoth fled with part of the fleet. Brihtric followed with another squadron, was caught in a storm, and lost it. The king returned to London with the rest of the fleet, as if all were lost.

All was indeed lost. At Lammas-tide, early in August, Sandwich Haven was filled with ships. Thorkel had arrived !

CHAPTER XIII

THE RISE OF KNUT THE GREAT

I

THE army of Thorkel, after accepting a ransom from Canterbury, made a wide sweep along the south coast as far as the Isle of Wight. Thorkel fulfilled two purposes by this preliminary operation—he gathered supplies, and he prevented them from being utilized by King Aethilred. Hampshire, Sussex, and Berkshire were devastated ; after which Thorkel fortified a camp at Greenwich upon the Thames, blockaded London, and proceeded to isolate the city by surrounding it with a vast belt of desolation.

Thorkel's army was triple. He, though the senior in command, had two colleagues—his brother Heming, and Olaf Haraldsson, afterwards King of Norway, known to later history as Saint Olaf, Olaf Helge, Olaf the Holy. Earl Thorkel himself commanded forty-five ships of Jomsborg wickings, the finest military corps in Europe. Heming possibly had charge of the rest of the Danes. Olaf led a body of men whose numbers and character are not positively known ; probably most, if not all, were Northmen ; but his contingent was numerous enough, and sufficiently distinct in character, to cause him to be named by the English chroniclers as one of the host-leaders.[1] Over all these elements Earl Thorkel exercised a general command.

Olaf brought with him some reputation as a skilful engineer. He undertook operations against London

[1] E.g. Fl. Worc., Roger Hoveden, Peter Langtoft.

during the autumn, while Thorkel was fortifying Green-wich. The chief objective was the fortified bridge which barred progress up the river. Olaf's ships rowed up under cover of wicker awnings, fixed ropes to the wooden piles, and by hard rowing sought to dislodge the piles and break down the bridge. He is said to have succeeded in causing part of the bridge to collapse ; but he could not capture it.[1] By the end of the autumn Thorkel had collected horses, and the direct operations against London were apparently abandoned.

At midwinter the Danes made a raid in force through the Chilterns to Oxford, which they burned ; recrossed the river at Staines, to avoid an English army which waited for them, and returned to Greenwich by the following spring, devastating all the country they passed through. They then completed the belt of desolation by sailing round to Ipswich and beginning a fresh land-campaign from East Anglia.

II

Wolfketel Snilling had collected the levy of East Anglia, and the first serious battle which had been fought since Maldon, seventeen years before, took place at Rondham Heath, near Thetford.[2] Wolfketel was so decisively defeated that the Danes met with no further resistance. They spent three months in carefully de-vastating East Anglia. Thetford and Cambridge were burned, and a vast ellipse of desolation was cut from Essex to Oxfordshire, back to Buckingham, Bedford, Tempsford and so to Greenwich again. The plunder

[1] Snorri, *Olaf the Holy*, xi, xii. Snorri says that Olaf took Southwark, but his quotations do not bear him out. The English writers explicitly deny that London was taken, and the subsequent course of events proves them to be right.

[2] Fl. Worc. ; Snorri, *Olaf the Holy*, xiii. See Mr. W. H. Stevenson, " The Battle of Ringmere," in *Engl. Hist. Rev.*, xv, p. 301.

was heavy. Northampton also was burned, and the district plundered.

Before this systematic campaign and its consequences the English national defence collapsed like a house of cards. Chaos followed. Only one resort was possible : the enemy must be bought off.

Thorkel was willing to negotiate, and a gafol was accordingly arranged, pending which the Danish army was to refrain from plundering, and was to be kept at King Aethilred's expense. The terms were not, apparently, very well kept, for the Danes continued to harry in a more or less casual and unofficial way. Thorkel was probably in no haste. He was well acquainted with King Swein's intentions, and knew that a gafol more or less was of little importance. If any of the leaders were anxious to receive his share of the money at the earliest date it would, by all the circumstances of the case, be Olaf. It was, at any rate, Olaf who was responsible for the tragic chain of events which ensued.

Canterbury had ransomed itself two years before for a sum of 3,000 pounds. The town and its district remained, therefore, untouched amid all the ravages that had devastated the richest part of England—a tempting prize, if it could be assumed that much was left after the ransom had been paid. Olaf laid siege to Canterbury, took the town by storm, and sacked it.[1] The archbishop fell into his hands as a prisoner.

To capture an archbishop of Canterbury was a truly

[1] Fl. Worc., *Chron.* s.a. 1011. Snorri, *Olaf the Holy*, xiv, quoting Ottar the Black. There seems to have been a conviction that much was left at Canterbury after the ransom had been paid. Osbern, the archbishop's biographer, makes the strange and (as far as we know) groundless assertion that Edric Streona led the Danes thither. The truth may be that Edric dropped hints adverse to the Archbishop's good faith. This would explain why attempts were made to torture the citizens into revealing hidden hoards. The whole episode was a very black one. Vigfusson's text of Ottar and Sigvat will be found in *C.P.B.*, ii, 153–4 and 126. They leave no doubt as to the identity of the man who sacked Canterbury.

remarkable feat, which probably remains as unique as it was at the time. But in the person of Alphege, Olaf had caught a tartar of the first rank, and long before Alphege's death he must have realized to the full the mistake he had made. The people of Canterbury were no doubt sold off to the slave dealers. Alphege could not be disposed of so easily. As a chattel in the market he was worth nothing ; but as archbishop he was worth a vast ransom. This aspect of the case was one which the archbishop perfectly realized, and proceeded to exploit. As a man of God, he could not fight with carnal weapons, but the whole range of passive resistance was freely open to him without blame. The armies of England, her king and her great men, had failed to deal with the Danes. Alphege set up a banner of a different kind, and became the heroic representative of English resistance. He refused to pay any ransom.

He was accordingly deported to Greenwich, there to remain in custody until he took another view of the fitness of things. The faint echoes of the chronicles, and the blank silence of the northern sources, are significant of the thrill which passed through England, and the storm of controversy which broke out, over the captivity and martyrdom of the archbishop.

III

The situation at Greenwich was thus a very unusual one. The head of the English Church, the leader of the churchmen in the king's council, was a prisoner in the camp of the Danes, and was prepared to carry his policy to its bitter end. No one can have been ignorant that it might be a very bitter end indeed. More than this : Alphege, as we know, had a history. He was the man who, as bishop of Winchester, had carried out the negotiations with Olaf Tryggwi's son in the year 994. Several very interesting coincidences were thus brought to pass. Here again was Alphege; and here was another Olaf, the son of Harald the Grenlander, who was also the nearest heir to the kingdom of Norway, as Olaf Tryggwi's son had been. All that remained to be seen was whether Alphege could again break up the combination that confronted him, and could send this other Olaf likewise back to Norway, a Christian, to reconquer the realm in the interests of the Christian faith and the English monarchy. This was the battle fought out, during nearly twelve months, in the camp at Greenwich.

We can only discover what took place by observing the results. It is certain that the archbishop held his ground with unflinching courage. No ransom was ever paid by him; and he forbade that any should be paid by his friends on his behalf. Before Easter, in the year 1012, there was a full assembly of the king's council in London, and the great gafol of 48,000 pounds was delivered to the Danes. On the Saturday after Easter " the army was much stirred against the bishop." Time was slipping by. If he paid no ransom now it was fairly certain that none would ever be paid. The day was the eve of their dispersal, and they had been enjoying a breaking-up feast, during which the wine flowed freely, and they had become roaring drunk. By a general consensus the archbishop was brought before some kind of semi-official court, similar to the court of Judge Lynch in another age and another continent: he persisted in his refusal to pay a ransom, and was partly battered to death by the brutal, half-jocular old game of bone-throwing, from which he was rescued by the merciful axe-blow of a man named Thrym.

IV

This is the brief outline we gather from the *Chronicle* and Florence of Worcester ; but by piecing together trifles from other sources much more, of a highly interesting sort, becomes visible. Florence of Worcester makes the assertion that the man " Thrym " had been confirmed by Alphege the day before. Now " Thrym " is a name much more Norse than Danish. Snorri records a battle between Olaf and the Thingmen which can be placed at no other time than this. It is certain, if Snorri possesses any authority on the subject at all, that Olaf left England immediately afterwards, and went south.

The only intelligible meaning which can be placed on these scraps of evidence is that archbishop Alphege had been successful in impressing Olaf Harald's son just as he had formerly impressed Olaf Tryggwi's son : that he had so established his influence among Olaf and his Norsemen, that a vigorous effort was made to save him from the hands of the Danes, resulting at least in the merciful axe-blow which put him beyond the reach of his tormentors : that Olaf Harald's son fought a battle with the Jomsborgers before he left England : and that Olaf's fierce zeal for Christianity originated, like that of Olaf Tryggwi's son, in his conversations with Alphege. It can have originated at no other time.

It may be borne in mind, in this connection, that Alphege, however deservedly a saint and martyr, was by no means a simple and unsophisticated man, but a diplomatist and a politician who had learned in the school of Dunstan, his master. Nor was either of the Olafs a man likely to be converted by the simpler emotional methods. Both of them were astute statesmen not overburdened with the softer sort of feeling. What Alphege had to say to them was without doubt more closely

interwoven with politics than with metaphysics. It is
certain enough that Olaf Harald's son, like Olaf
Tryggwi's son, became an uncompromising champion of
Christianity ; and it is hard to see whence he derived
his peculiar lucidity and determination on the subject, if
not from archbishop Alphege during that memorable
year at Greenwich.

V

After the martyrdom of Alphege, the Danish army
broke up. Olaf left England in late spring or early
summer, and disappeared southward, taking with him
his share of the gafol. Thorkel and the Jomsborg Thingmen entered the service of Aethilred. The body of
Alphege was borne to London by bishops Ednoth and
Elfhun, and deposited in Saint Paul's. He was soon
working miracles. Whosoever had failed, Alphege had
not failed. He had stood his ground to the death ; and
the story was not to conclude until the last of the results,
in the due course of time, became visible to all.

The peculiar feature of 1012 was the conduct of
Thorkel.[1] What he meant by entering the service of
King Aethilred is a riddle unsolved to this day. Why
Aethilred accepted him is equally difficult to guess.
Thorkel was King Swein's man, and a man of established
position and well-known repute. He was no wandering
wicking, open to engagement by any paymaster, nor was
he heir to any lost kingdom. King Swein was coming ;
and when he arrived not even the head of the Jomsborgers would be able to deny the prior claims to his
allegiance possessed by the Danish king. Why then did
Thorkel assume a position which both he and Aethilred
must have known to be a mere pretence ? The best we

[1] It must be remembered that Thorkel was own brother to earl Sigwaldi :
and Sigwaldi's repute for honesty was well below zero.

can say of Thorkel is that he may not have intended flat treachery. But who can say anything at all in favour of the English king whose first attempt at creating a comitatus consisted of bringing forty-five ship-crews of Jomsborgers into the most important fortress of his dominions? The victory of King Swein was assured when Thorkel landed in London.

VI

Sixteen months after the death of Alphege the Danish king touched at Sandwich harbour. His actions reveal plainly that his campaign was designed to fit in with the previous work of Thorkel. Coasting up past East Anglia to the Humber, he sailed into the Trent and fixed his headquarters at Gainsborough. Here he received the submission of the Northumbrian earl Ughtred and the people of Lindsey : the Danes of the Five Boroughs followed : and then all those north of Watling Street. Swein took hostages as a guarantee.

Then, leaving young Knut to command the fleet, he struck south, and began to sweep the country. Oxford easily fell to him : but Winchester was his objective. After taking hostages for the reality of the submission of Winchester, he moved upon London. Here he met his first check. London was not to be taken by assault. Moreover, Thorkel was there. Swein did not take the check seriously. He at once withdrew to Wallingford and then to Bath, where he received the submission of all the west of England, and again took hostages. He finally returned to his base at Gainsborough, having demonstrated beyond doubt that the whole surviving part of England was ready to receive him as king. He did not enter any of the districts swept by Thorkel's operations in 1009 and 1010.

In the face of this convincing proof, Aethilred could
not continue to hold out. London decided to give up
the struggle. Aethilred lingered at Greenwich with
Thorkel for a short while ; but the case was hopeless,
as Thorkel probably pointed out. He sent Emma on
to her brother Richard in Normandy, to prepare for his
own arrival ; the aethilings Edward and Alfred followed,
and last of all Aethilred himself reluctantly, near the
end of the year, left for the Isle of Wight, on the way to
Normandy.

Thorkel does not appear to have been at all em-
barrassed at meeting King Swein again ; nor does the
interlude seem to have disturbed their amicable relations
and perfect understanding.

VII

It is impossible now to ascertain where Olaf Harald's
son had really been during the years 1012–1013, but it is
clear that he was in Normandy over the winter of 1013–
1014. He reappears on the scene a changed man, fully
resolved to make a bid for the crown of Norway. As he
had, during his absence, reached the age of eighteen, no
obstacle stood in his way. The only difficulty was to
discover the best means of carrying out the project. He
probably met Aethilred at Rouen, and the two kings
came to an agreement which would be mutually advantageous. Olaf's chief adviser, Rani, was already in
England in order to report on the situation there. He
seems to have employed his time to good purpose. The
chance, with a truly royal fortune, came precisely at the
moment when it could best be seized. King Swein died
at Candlemas, 1014. The news cannot have taken long
to reach Normandy.

Every incident of these years has its obscurity and its

problem, and the death of Swein is no exception to the rule. The Danish king came of a family liable to sudden strokes ; but the occasion of the seizure which removed Swein in the very hour of his victory was in some way—imperfectly recorded by the chroniclers—mixed up with the religious question. The legend that Saint Edmund of East Anglia slew him in a dream is no doubt a case of association of ideas rather than a historical fact ; but that Swein was about to take some step highly obnoxious to the churchmen would seem fairly certain. Whatsoever it may have been, it was never carried out. Swein died suddenly, leaving English affairs in hopeless confusion.

The fleet chose young Knut without dissent. The English magnates lost no time in sending Aethilred an invitation to return, combining a little healthy criticism with their apology, by explaining that no man was dearer to them than their rightful lord if he would but govern them a little better. Aethilred might fairly have replied that the genius of kings is to some extent conditioned by the ability of those they govern ; but there was no necessity to discuss this controversial point, for now a stronger and more virile hand seized the control of affairs. Olaf Harald's son crossed to England with young Edward (afterwards the Confessor) leaving the king himself to follow during Lent.

Olaf probably landed at a western port, possibly Charmouth, where the roads, avoiding London, ran straight north-east. Knut was at Gainsborough until Easter, gathering up the threads left by King Swein, and arranging with the Lindsey men for horses and a joint advance. Olaf's blow was rapid, sudden, and unexpected. He was up in Lindsey before Knut could move. Completely out-generalled, Knut was forced to his ships. A complete evacuation of England was now the only prudent course. Coasting back to Sandwich, Knut landed the hostages which his father had gathered, cut off their hands, noses, and ears, and sailed away to the Scheldt mouth to refit and prepare for a new campaign.

Unlike Thorkel, Olaf had fulfilled his part of the bargain with Aethilred. He now took his reward. Proceeding on into Northumbria, he paid off his army and with three ships and his comitatus of two hundred picked men he set sail for Norway.

The first part of Alphege's work was accomplished.

Aethilred was joyfully received back into an England almost miraculously cleared of Danes. There was loyal enthusiasm on the one hand and earnest promise of reform and improvement upon the other. Every Danish king was declared outside the law, and incapable of receiving English allegiance, so that all oaths made to Swein, and any oaths sworn to Knut, should be null and void. This heroic gesture was a little spoiled by the necessity of remembering that Thorkel was still at Greenwich. A gafol of 21,000 pounds was paid him. If Thorkel had left memoirs, the part of them which dealt with the year 1014 would be particularly interesting reading.

VIII

The restoration of Aethilred and the retreat of Knut exercised a dangerously intoxicating effect in some quarters. The conviction that the Danes had gone for good, and would never be seen again in England, was at the best a groundless belief; at the worst it was a dangerous fantasy which drove its deluded victims to their own destruction.

The aldermen began by a success the consequences of which were enough to prevent any further steps in the same direction. They advised the king to remove Sigfrith and Morcar, the leading Danish lawmen of the

Five Boroughs, which had taken a prominent part in the submission to Swein in 1013. Alderman Edric undertook the task. During a council at Oxford, the two lawmen were invited to Edric's lodging, were separated from their men, and murdered. Their retainers, on discovering what had happened, died in a desperate attempt to avenge their lords. Sigfrith's widow Aldgytha was secured and sent to Malmesbury abbey, while the whole property of the dead men was forfeited to the king.

Such an action as this may have been a wise precaution, but it was much more probably a madness which immediately divided England into two hostile camps, and undid all the work of unification which had gone far to blend the English Danes into the fabric of the nation. It had at least one vigorous opponent who was entitled to speak with authority—the aethiling Edmund, the future King Edmund Ironside. The murder of Sigfrith and Morcar brought him for the first time into active politics.

Edmund's answer was immediate. He went to Malmesbury, took Aldgytha out of the custody of the abbey, and married her. He then went north to the Five Boroughs and seized Sigfrith's property. As he was acting against his father's wishes, and apparently in antagonism to Edric Streona, Edmund must have had the definite intention of conciliating the English Danes and preventing the alienation of Sigfrith's lands and goods from Aldgytha. With the status of a husband, he would have the legal right to act on her behalf, and to assert any claim she was entitled to make. The Danes of the Five Boroughs accepted him without demur.

Those who thought that Knut had abandoned the designs of King Swein were awakened from their dream to face a divided England and a new invader. Knut's fleet returned to Sandwich and coasted south. For his

own reasons he was evidently exploring the route which
Olaf had used so effectively the year before, for he
followed it across Wessex and up to the crossing of the
Avon. Under this accumulated weight of misfortune
and disappointment, Aethilred broke down. He was
not an old man, as the moderns count age ; he was only
forty-seven years old. But men matured early and died
soon in the eleventh century, and Aethilred had suffered
more worry than most kings.

There was some reason for despair. The very act by
which Edmund had so effectively conciliated the English
Danes had torn a fresh rift in the ranks of the English
themselves. Knut had taken care to avoid the Humber.
He had struck at Wessex, trusting, no doubt, to restore
his prestige by a series of victories there, before he asked
the north for support. Edric raised the Wessex levy,
while Edmund, with a strong army of reinforcement from
the north, marched to join him.

Edmund was a very different man from his father—
a good soldier, and a man of vigour and decision. When
he reached Wessex, it rapidly became evident that he and
Edric could not get on together. One of them would
have to go ; and Edric elected to be that one. He went
over to Knut. What is more, he induced Thorkel to go
too. Thorkel would have to drop the mask sometime or
other : and perhaps this was as good an occasion on
which to do so as he could reasonably expect.

IX

The defection of Edric must have been a sensational
event at the time ; and it probably had a retrospective
effect upon his reputation. All those who had differed
from him in opinion, or who for any other reason had
suspected his good faith, were now amply confirmed in

their opinions, and read his past actions by the light of his present treason. But Edric had more motives than one. The time was at hand when men must begin to think clearly of the future. It is likely enough that Edric had no use for an England in which he was not a great and powerful person—and if that be treason, he was a traitor. He had quarrelled with the aethiling ; the king was sick, and perhaps dying. The best course might be to make terms with the enemy whose triumph was imminent, while there was yet time for Edric to reap the credit of making it certain. With Edric, Wessex submitted.

Knut and Edric were, however, reckoning without one man—and that man Edmund. Councils and deliberations had little further part in events. Edmund fought the rest of the war to all intents and purposes on his own responsibility. He hurried north. Affairs were too disorganized and too paradoxical to be immediately easy, even for Edmund. He was attempting to raise an army against Edric in Edric's own country, whilst Edric was taking Edmund's hereditary kingdom of Wessex over to Knut. Men hesitated. Ultimately they declined to fight unless the king were present to authorize their actions, and unless London approved.

Knut had already crossed the upper Thames in force. Urgent messages were therefore sent to the king : the orders for the levy were issued, and Aethilred, to do him justice, crawled from his deathbed to lead it. His presence imported all the old troubles. He was soon convinced that his life was threatened, and he returned to London. Edmund went on to Northumbria, to engage the help of earl Ughtred. With the earl's help they raised an army with which they entered Mercia, and tried to knock a little patriotism into the Mercians. Meanwhile the army of Knut had swerved east to Bedford, and was marching by road through Northampton to strike the

great highway north. He passed through Lincoln and
pressed on to York, completely turning the position of
the English army. As soon as the news arrived, earl
Ughtred hastened home and submitted. Edmund made
for London to see his father.

Ughtred gained nothing by submission. Knut took
Edric's advice, slew Ughtred, and handed over Northumbria to earl Eirik Hakon's son, the victor of Hiorunga
Bay. He then took the western roads—the direct Fosse
Way—back to his fleet. So rapid was his march that by
Eastertide he had his ships round to London. Before they
arrived, King Aethilred was dead. The old king had
beheld the glorious reign of Edgar, and had lived long
enough to see England in the hands of the Danes.
Edmund made for Wessex. He went no longer as
aethiling, but as king.

X

Knut made his base at Greenwich, and proceeded
with the last act of the great drama, the siege of London.
The bridge was, of course, held in force by the London
men, and could not easily be taken by ships. A ditch was
dug, and a detachment of vessels drawn through into the
upper reach. The city was then encircled with an earthwork, and the blockade closed, so that nothing could
enter or leave London. All assaults were repelled.

King Edmund lost no time. He received the submission of Wessex and rapidly organized a relieving army
to raise the siege of London. Knut was evidently well
informed as to his movements, and kept in close touch ;
for Edmund fought his first battle at Gillingham in
Dorsetshire. The southerly roads to London were so well
watched that the king fought his way north, shook off the
Danes at Sherston in Wiltshire, and took the route by

the left bank of the Thames, through Cirencester and Saint Albans to Clayhanger.[1] His arrival was unexpected,[2] and the siege of London was hastily raised. Knut retreated by the road to Southampton in order to keep his position in relation to Wessex, but King Edmund turned off south-westward, reached the Thames at Brentford, and intercepted him. The result seems to have been a drawn battle ; for although the Danes are said to have been put to flight, heavy English losses in the fighting at Brentford are hinted at,[3] and immediately afterwards the king returned to Wessex, to gather reinforcements, while the Danes resumed the siege of London.

The city resolutely held out ; and now arose the problem of supplying the Danish army. The fleet was sent round to Ipswich, whence a great foraging raid was conducted into the Mercian shires, the least damaged counties of England. Herds of cattle were driven away ; but Edmund was returning, by the same route as before, and the cattle were taken down into Essex, and shipped over into the Medway. Edmund crossed at Brentford, raised the siege of London, and drove Knut before him. Knut retreated by the south-easterly road into Kent, with Edmund in pursuit. He retreated into Sheppey, one of the old fortified Danish bases, where, with his fleet to hand, he had choice of movement.

Edric came to meet the king at Aylesford, and a reconciliation took place. The energy, ability, and success

---

[1] This route is deducible from the entry in the *Chron.*, s.a. 1016, supposing the old Roman roads to be used. The *Chronicle* certainly gives Gillingham—Sherston—" all by north of the Thames "—Clayhanger : and the inference in the text is the obvious one.

[2] Whereas Knut was in touch with him as far away as Gillingham and Sherston, no attempt was made to meet Edmund between Sherston and London.

[3] From Ottar the Black (*C.P.B.*, vol. ii, p. 155) we may infer that Knut counter-attacked at Brentford and re-took the town.

of the new king might have given pause to a less astute man than Edric. With a fair amount of luck, Edmund might yet pull his country out of the slough ; while, on the other hand, there was yet time to be of invaluable service to Knut by means of a timely betrayal. It is hard to see how Edric could have broken away from Knut without some sort of consent from that crafty statesman. Edmund's motives in accepting a reconciliation are even plainer. He was always anxious for unity ; he had everything to gain and nothing to lose by recovering the support of the Mercians ; and he had no reason for apprehension.

XI

Knut was not long in resolving upon his next move. He ferried his army over the Thames, and headed his march for Mercia. Edmund still had the advantage of position. He did not intend Knut to reach the road-junctions of the midlands, where he could begin one of those rapid and baffling marches which were so difficult to deal with. He hurried back to London, raised all the reinforcements possible, including Edric's Mercians, and struck along the roads that flank Essex. His possession of the roads enabled him to overtake Knut, who was cutting across an almost roadless country, where the few high-ways ran in directions useless to his purposes. The two armies met at Assingdon.

Knut so far had not shown to especial advantage. Faced by unexpected ability in the person of the new king, his moves had been sound enough, but not of the kind that inspire enthusiasm. Nor have we any reason to suppose that they did inspire enthusiasm. A later generation of writers, drawing their information from northern sources, were critical of Knut's abilities, while admitting his success and his firm hold on power. He had every appearance of succeeding almost by accident, or by the byplay of intrigue : and yet there are features in the case which suggest that his march to Assingdon was not without a touch of the deep reflection and subtle calculation of the chess-player. He had all the convenient ports of East Anglia at his back if he were beaten ; he had space and scope, as he had not in Kent ; he drew Edmund as far as possible from Wessex ; he had the advantage of choosing his own ground, and of meeting a not very highly trained army which had made a series of long, forced marches.

The battle of Assingdon was a decisive battle. The details of the fighting are lost ; but the allegation of treachery against Edric—or of the cowardice which is as fatal as treachery—is clearly made in the English *Chronicle*. The ultimate and irreducible fact is that " there King Knut had the victory, though all England fought against him." That the phrase " all England " was no rhetorical flourish we can see by the tale of the leaders ; alderman Godwin of Lindsey, alderman Wolfketil of East Anglia, alderman Aelfric, besides a bishop and an abbot, who fell ; Edric who fled with his Mercians, and Edmund with the host of Wessex. The whole of England was represented in the army that lost the battle of Assingdon ; and from that verdict there was no appeal.

King Edmund himself recognized the fact. He had retreated to the western border—to Gloucestershire. Knut followed. In the negotiations which ensued, Knut for the first time showed the moderation, the prudent good sense, which were to make his reign unaccountably famous, and his reputation inexplicably saintly. It was still possible for Edmund to give much trouble, and to drag out the agony of England while his life lasted. Knut cut short that possibility by agreeing to divide the kingdom : each man to be the other's heir. It is

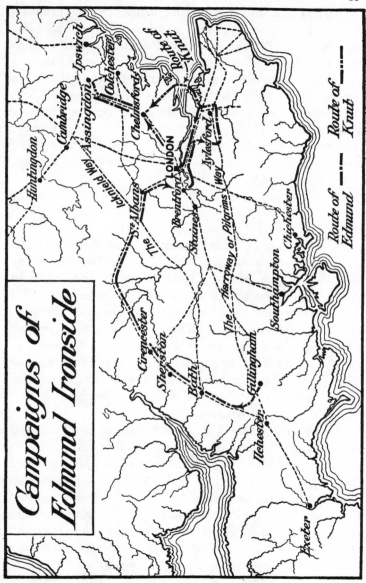

Campaigns of
Edmund Ironside

Route of
Edmund —— —— ——

Route of
Knut ——·——·——

unlikely that Edmund would have accepted the proposal had there been any chance of further resistance ; and equally unlikely that Knut would have agreed, unless he had foreseen that the whole country would fall into his hands in the end. At Olney, near Deerhurst, a peace was made between the two kings. An indemnity was part of the terms. London made a separate peace. Knut took the old Danish realm which the sons of Ragnar had won ; Edmund took the Wessex of Alfred. The work of Edward the Elder and his successors was undone, and could never be repeated.

XII

The career of King Edmund Ironside was brief, wonderful, and brilliant : it ended at Assingdon, and he did not live long after it. He died on the feast of Saint Andrew, and was buried at Glastonbury, where he could look out over the flats towards Wedmore and Athelney. Into his shoes stepped the Danish king—a figure whom we cannot call sinister only because, in spite of his ruthlessness, his rapacity, and his deep subtlety, he had generosity, common sense, and that worldly wisdom which is so wise, that we forget its worldliness and remember only its wisdom.

During the interval between the treaty of Olney and the death of Edmund, Knut had already taken possession of his own realm. London, as we have seen, had entered into a separate agreement, and paid an indemnity of its own, apart from the general indemnity. London counted nominally as a portion of Mercia, and was thus within the dominion of Knut. He transferred his headquarters thither, and settled the Danish army there for the winter —the first distinct sign that the city was destined to become the capital of England. After the death of Edmund, Knut took Wessex into his own hands. Thorkel, the commander of the Thingmen, received East Anglia ; Edric Streona, Mercia ; Eirik Hakon's son, Northumbria. But though Knut paid his debt to Edric, the latter was too dangerous a man to be tolerated. When Edric was slain by Knut's order, England recognized the justice of the deed. Edric has gone down to history as the worst and most successful traitor his country has ever produced.

XIII

Knut's policy as king was subtler and even better calculated than his policy as an invader. His executions and banishments removed all the more dangerous persons from the country. His next step was the work of reunion and reconciliation. He associated himself with the hereditary royal line of England by marrying Aethilred's widow Emma ; a step by which he gave the first sign of his future attitude. As the brother-in-law of a Norman duke, the new king of England cast in his lot with the Christian civilization of southern Europe. His calculations were justified by self-interest. If the kingship were to be preserved, a counterpoise must be found to balance the power of the local magnates ; and he turned, naturally enough, to the churchmen, who, under certain conditions, were ready to accept his rule and help to make it permanent. Knut was willing to fulfil their conditions. He had no real use now for the little gods and petty local interests of heathenism. The sovereign of the great realm he governed could be nothing but a Christian king—a believer in the God who said : " Thou shalt have none other gods but me."

With Knut's accession to the throne of England, therefore, the heathen reaction petered out to its inevitable, its perfectly natural end. The reaction was destroyed by its own results. The tide of northern conquest had stopped for ever.

CHAPTER XIV

THE LAST DAYS OF THE MILITARY GUILD

I

THE war indemnity which Knut exacted from England took two years to collect. It was the most immense sum which England had ever paid to the Danes. Into the treasury of King Knut were poured 72,000 pounds ; and London added a further amount of 10,500 pounds. It says much for the wealth of England that after so many heavy payments in the past, this crowning indemnity could be raised from a country still suffering from systematic devastation.

Knut paid off and broke up his army, which for the most part returned to Denmark. Forty ships remained. These forty were the ships of the Thingmen—Thorkel's corps of Jomsborg wickings which had come to Sandwich in 1009, and for a while had taken upon themselves the curious function of supporting—or rather watching—King Aethilred. The Thingmen were destined to play an important part in the politics of the next fifty years.

They had, of course, played a very important part already. The paralysis of the English kingship under Aethilred had been due to a set of causes concerning the identity of which there is little room for mistake. King Aethilred, coming to the throne at ten years old after the murder of his brother Edward, and the long minority of his father Edgar, was a king without a comitatus, and therefore without the machinery of authority. The local magnates had proved themselves more powerful than such a king. But Knut, with his comitatus of Jomsborg wickings, had proved that he was more powerful than such an aristocracy as they. So far, then, the problem rested there. It was not to rest there permanently, as we shall presently see.

No alderman possessed the resources from which to create such a body of men as surrounded the Danish king. Knut drew into it the cream of Scandinavian manhood. The Scandinavian visitor, calling upon Knut at Winchester, saw nothing of his subtle statesmanship or his deeply thought, far-seeing policy ; he only saw a northern king, genial, accessible, formidable, at once awe-inspiring from his power and fascinating from his incredible prodigality with those material rewards which intoxicate men by their immensity. To serve Knut was to serve a wizard who could fill one's hat with gold. He asked much in return : but men will do great deeds for great rewards, for most men are apt to be the same size as their wages. And the gold which the wizard gave by the hatful was drawn from the gafols which England paid.

II

The accession of Knut thus marked a great change in the status of the English kingship. The central power of the state once more exercised supreme and undisputed sway. Egbert had united England into one realm. After the slip which temporarily lost the north, his descendants had confirmed and made permanent the unity which he imposed. Now, after the second slip which lost the power of the central government, Knut's kingship recovered it, and carried the process further. He actually began to exercise the authority so built up, and to wield the state as one undivided whole. The success and the failure of his methods were really important, in the sense that they marked the progress of an experiment to find a system of government which might form the solid basis of an expanding national life.

It is plain enough that the powerful central authority which he gave England was indispensable to her future. More doubtful is the value of the means he employed. There were real advantages in the system of personal fealty which the Thingmen represented. They had none of the drawbacks of an hereditary aristocracy : no fool could enter their ranks merely in virtue of being the son of his father ; they were renewed from year to year as men left the service and others entered it ; they could be picked and chosen : they were a corporate body, free from local ties and local prejudices ; and from living together in close association they possessed a solidarity, a discipline, a capacity for united action and common thought, which no feudal aristocracy ever possessed. But if they were free from the disadvantages of aristocracy they also lacked its advantages. They had not a permanent interest in the soil and substance of England : they had not the peculiar spirit of understanding for it which springs from long ancestral possession ; and they were much more expensive. The Norman nobility, planted out on the land, supported themselves from local resources, and rapidly learned the art of tending the goose that lays the golden eggs. The Thingmen were from first to last a body of men outside the currents of national life.

There were also certain dangers inherent in the system. The Thingmen not unnaturally tested kings far too much by their generosity ; and it gradually grew certain, as time went on, that instead of the king being the head of the Thingmen, the head of the Thingmen would be the king. The actual narrative of events is by far the best illustration of both the strength and the weakness of the system.

At least one Englishman entered the ranks of the Thingmen. There were probably others ; but we know of one in particular—Godwin. According to the Danish tradition, Thorkel one day met the son of a swineherd, and repaid him for some very real service by taking him into the ranks and furthering his fortunes. The English tradition says that he was the son of that Wulfnoth who fled from Aethilred's fleet in 1009. He would in this case be a grand-nephew of Edric Streona, and the allegations concerning his low birth would reflect those which were spread concerning the birth of Edric. We may take it that Godwin sprang of a family which produced many aldermen in the previous generation, and although disparaged by the Danes, he rose to high rank himself.

In the process, he thoroughly adopted the ways of his new comrades, while completely preserving the principles of his ancestors. His sons were Swein, Harold, and Biorn—three Danish names never given to Englishmen—besides Leofwin and Gyrth. Even while the Thingmen brought kings back to power, a kinsman of Edric Streona inserted himself into their ranks !

III

As soon as the fleet had departed, and Knut had settled down in peace, he called a council at Oxford, at which the main lines of his policy were indicated. He went back to the laws and methods of Edgar, the great conciliator, for his model. He neither imposed a new code of laws, nor desired any duplication of codes. There was to be one English nation, of which the English Danes were indissolubly part. As with so much else, this settlement, made by Knut's strong hand, was permanent, where Edgar's was temporary. It might have been his mission in life to make good those things in which wise but weaker men had failed.

Few men (and this was perhaps one of the sources of his success and his fame) ever showed so little wish to dictate to others the details of their life and labour. Outside the circle of high politics, he was tolerant : as long as men walked with him, they might walk as they would.

He had the country so well in hand, and had so completely won the acceptance of his English subjects, that he spent the next year in Denmark. King Olaf was busy consolidating his own power in Norway, and converting his realm to Christianity by methods of active and paternal interference that were in remarkable contrast with those of Knut. Returning, Knut found England quiet enough. A few people were outlawed at the council at Cirencester ; but the England of the Danish conqueror needed far less violence to govern than the England of the Norman conqueror in later years. With all his unscrupulousness, Knut had the true kingly mind, which sees deeply and sometimes amiably into the hearts of all manner of men. He planned the building of a church upon the field of Assingdon, to commemorate those who fell there—English and Danes alike. The English—especially the churchmen—found this after their own heart. It was a further act of reconciliation which they accepted.

His attitude was confirmed by a wise and bold impartiality. He had outlawed an English alderman—Aethilweard—the year before : it was now Thorkel, the head of the Thingmen, who had to flee. The king and the earl were ultimately reconciled, and since Thorkel was perhaps too big a man to be kept in leading strings, Knut exchanged hostages with him, and gave him the rule of Denmark.

Whosoever conquers England, soon finds that the centre of his power has transferred itself thither. Knut was now almost more an English than a Danish king : and his perception that he held Denmark through England quite as much as he held England through Denmark, is shown in his action respecting Saint Alphege. The translation of Alphege was a deed which almost completely won over the English. Knut showed sympathetic imagination in grasping so accurately the degree to which Alphege had become a patriotic and inspiring symbol to all Englishmen. To carry the body of Alphege solemnly home to Canterbury, with the full pomp of archbishop and king, would be a great confession—a great reparation. And in this, Knut rightly judged.

In the presence of the king, the body of Alphege was lifted from its temporary resting place. Some tinge of excitement and sensation has crept even into the brief accounts handed down to us—an excitement which would be incomprehensible were it not for our knowledge of what Alphege had represented. Some said, that Knut with his own hands helped to raise the body. Some said, that the holy martyr was perfect and uncorrupt. It may have been so ; in which case, considering the death he died, it was a miracle indeed.

The king, with the archbishop, the diocesan bishops, the earls and a great concourse, carried the body by ship across to Southwark, whence it was borne to Rochester. There Queen Emma joined the procession, and Alphege was laid to rest on the north side of the altar of Canterbury. It is said that Knut laid his royal crown upon the shrine —a noble gesture, if it be true. When the servants of Henry VIII stripped the shrines of Canterbury, they turned out the dust of Alphege to mingle with the dust of England.

IV

So great was the moral effect of Knut's action, that when he went to Denmark to direct in person the war against Olaf of Norway, he took many Englishmen with him. The sea fight of Helge-aa belongs to Scandinavian history, but its causes and its results have reactions upon the history of England. Even when England was not only conquered, but had come to accept the Danish conqueror with loyalty, and almost—if not quite—with devotion ; even then the old policy of Aethilstan worked to the benefit of England.

Olaf of Norway remained a perpetual threat to Denmark, and to some extent constrained the policy of Knut. The Danish king had additional motives for a conciliatory attitude to his English subjects when their aid might be so useful to him. Olaf was successful, where his predecessor Olaf Tryggwi's son had failed, in making an alliance with Sweden : and against the combined Norse and Swedish fleets even the power and prestige of Knut could make no substantial headway. It was necessary to proceed in a more circuitous manner. Knut, when his interests were affected, was not above encouraging and financing the heathen party in Norway, in order to weaken his enemy. When, three years after the battle of Helge-aa, Knut sailed from England with fifty English ships to reinforce his Danish fleet, Olaf was driven to take refuge in Sweden.

Knut was now at the height of his fame, king of three great kingdoms, from the North Cape to Seelund, and from Seelund to the English Channel. He owed this mighty dominion—never owned by one man before, and never owned by one man since—to an intelligent combination of unscrupulousness and generosity. He stopped at nothing, and he paid high wages for good work.

Having supreme faith in his own worthiness to rule, he could see no reason why he should stop at any means of achieving his ends ; and on the whole, his faith in himself was not misplaced. He knew his own limitations, and therefore he made few mistakes. Knut came nearer than most men to proving the possibility of wisdom without heart.

King Olaf won his victory in another way, and with other weapons. He fell in the battle of Sticklestead during a vigorous attempt to regain his kingdom.[1] Almost at once strange rumours were afloat. His body was working miracles. Moral perfection is not indispensable to a saint, since no man can, in any case, be saved by morality ; but the miraculous power is a sure sign of saintship. One of his deadliest enemies was the first to experience it, and the testimony grew. In his death, Olaf continued his war against Knut. The Norwegians found that the hand of the Danish king was heavy : the heathen party became unpopular ; the cult of Olaf grew ; and it wanted but this to make Norway finally and for ever a nation. The battle of Sticklestead may have been, in the ordinary and human sense, a defeat for Olaf ; but if things are to be judged by their consequences, it was his complete victory. It made permanent in Norway all he had stood for, all he had hoped and meant. Knut's reparation to Alphege had no doubt been wise. But it had not saved him from the long hand of the archbishop, working through many years and across vast spaces. Space and time are nothing to the dead.

---

[1] He would probably have regained it had he been financially better supported. The narrative of Snorri is a deplorable story of brave men fighting vainly with cheap and inferior weapons that would not keep an edge.

V

Knut was the first Danish king to visit Rome. Few men have ever trodden the stones of that city save as prisoners or as vassals. He, the descendant of Ragnar and the successor of Guthfrith, carried to Rome the adhesion of the Scandinavian north. The great series of wars was over. It was perhaps not altogether chance that in 1031 he gave Sandwich haven to Christ Church, Canterbury. It would never again be the port of call for invading Danish fleets.

His journey to Rome in 1027 had particular meaning. He lent countenance and support to Conrad of Franconia, when Conrad was crowned emperor by Pope John XIX. Knut had been born not long after a very critical moment in history—the death of Aethilstan's nephew, the emperor Otto II. That death meant the accession of a minor, the freeing of Denmark from the watchful guardianship exercised upon her by the Saxon emperors, and the consequent establishment of the new Danish power. Knut saw the crowning of the first Franconian emperor, and the confirmation of all the vast changes involved.

He died at Shaftesbury after a reign of twenty years. He was not much more than forty when he died. He had given England nearly a generation of peace and order ; he had brought many things to a satisfactory end ; but he had not to any great extent built for the future. He had not been a creative statesman. He represented a somewhat strange and striking consummation of events, which had in many cases depended upon accident, and had been contrary to reasonable expectation. He had been wonderfully adequate in meeting facts and circumstances. He himself does not seem to have expected the continuance of his great sea-empire. The death of Knut meant that kind of decadence which looks like collapse and reversion,

but which is only the scramble for position and power
that goes before the advent of great new eras.

VI

The council met at Oxford shortly after Knut's death.
There was a clear division in its ranks ; but what had
once been a distinction between English and Danes was
now a distinction of party. Earl Leofric headed the
magnates from the north of the Thames, with whom the
Thingmen sided ; earl Godwin led the party of the
Wessex magnates.

The proposal before the council was the joint election
of Harald and Harthaknut, the two sons of Knut. The
plan bears obvious traces of a Danish origin. It was a bit
of the purest old North-European tradition to think of
all the sons of a king as equally royal, with equal claims
to the crown. It had also, perhaps, advantages of a
peculiar sort which did not lend themselves to public
advocacy. A divided royalty is as much easier to rule as
any other divided thing. The real desire of the northern
party was the election of Harald ; but they did not see
their way to denying the claims of Harthaknut, so they
proposed, as the readiest means of carrying the choice of
their own candidate, the election of both sons of the
late king.

To this plan Godwin led an emphatic opposition.
The party of Wessex had, no doubt, motives as mingled as
those of their rivals ; but their case was stronger. They
wished for the election of Harthaknut, who was the son
of Knut and Emma, and therefore " porphyrogenitos "
—born in the purple to a reigning king and queen. He
was, incidentally, in Denmark, and having been brought
up in that country he had a not unnatural preference for
living there : a detail not without some bearing upon the

case. In the light of subsequent events, we may imagine that Godwin did not share the belief that a divided royalty is of any service to ambitious magnates who hope to inherit its powers. It might be much less easy to control two kings than one. Moreover, Harald was not Emma's son, and did not possess the full royal descent on both sides. There seems to have been some confusion of fact on this last point. Harthaknut was certainly the son of Knut and Emma, commonly known in England as " Elfgiva," or " Elfgiva-Emma." The Elfgiva who was the mother of Harald was a quite distinct person, the daughter of alderman Elfhelm of Hampshire. This was denied, but Harald confirmed the fact. Many men were unconvinced, probably because they did not wish to admit it. The long and the short of the matter was, that the northern party had put forward a candidate brought up among themselves and in sympathy with their views, while the party of Wessex supported the candidate who was the son of Emma, and was identified with the policy of Knut.

Godwin and his party were finally overruled, and the proposal of the northern magnates was adopted. Harald and Harthaknut were elected joint kings with full equal rights, and Queen Emma was to act as regent until Harthaknut came in person to take possession of his crown. She remained at Winchester under Godwin's protection, and the two of them had effective control over Wessex, while Harald took the north. Harald put in his claim for a share in Knut's treasure, to which Godwin and Emma had no alternative but assent.

VII

How little Godwin's action was due to any loyalty to the old English ruling family can be seen by the events which followed. The aethiling Alfred, the second son of Aethilred, made an attempt to return to England and to see his mother at Winchester. Godwin took a leading part in seizing him, blinding him, and consigning him to the monastery of Ely, where he died. This deed—more akin to the crimes of Frankish history than to English manners—caused a revulsion of feeling, of which Harald took full advantage. Harthaknut was deposed on the ground of his continued absence in Denmark, and Harald expelled Emma from the kingdom. If he hoped to seize the rest of Knut's wealth, he was disappointed. Emma fled to Bruges, where Count Baldwin gave her protection.

Harthaknut still delayed his coming. At length he arrived in Bruges. He was not a man of strong character, and he was incapable of such a project as the armed invasion of England, even if he had possessed the means for it—and Emma had no intention of parting with Knut's gold. The problem was solved by Harald's death, after a reign of four years. Harthaknut was invited to England and accepted by all parties.

He proved a complete disappointment. Englishmen, of any party or degree, were not particularly interested to see the bones of Harald exhumed, and thrown into a ditch, as a mark of reprobation for his wicked conduct. But the financial demands of Harthaknut, on the other hand, were positively alarming. Knut had been content with forty crews of Thingmen, reduced, in his later years, to sixteen—a figure at which Harald had continued it. Harthaknut's establishment, in his first year, was sixty-two ships, later reduced to thirty-two ; which meant a Danegeld of 32,000 pounds. The Danegeld was resisted in Worcestershire—but without success, and it had to be paid. The king was entirely in the hands of his mother, who controlled his policy and took possession of most of his money. The seasons were bad ; corn rose to famine

prices, and there were heavy losses due to cattle disease :
so that any unnecessarily high taxation was, to say the
least, inexpedient.

Harthaknut might have excited more general and
more powerful opposition, had there been a likelihood
that his reign would continue indefinitely. But it was
recognized that he was a stop-gap, affording time for
a more careful decision in the matter of the succession.
He was about twenty-four years old ; he had no children,
and there is no record that he ever married ; he was
probably epileptic. The only resort now was to call the
last surviving son of Aethilred, a man of mature age and
steady character—Edward, whom we know as the
" Confessor." The matter seems to have been regarded
as urgent, for the unusual course was adopted of swearing
Edward in as king during the lifetime of Harthaknut.
In this way, at least, disputes concerning the succession
would be avoided. The step was taken none too soon.
Harthaknut was seized with a fit two years after he had
been consecrated, and died without speaking again.
He died as King Swein his grandfather, and King Gorm
the Old, his great-great-grandfather, had died ; and
with him perished the mighty and the famous house of
the Skioldings.

King Edward succeeded him without trouble or
opposition. He, too, was a childless and unmarried man,
fairly well on in years. He, like Harthaknut, might serve
to give men leisure to decide about the future of England.
Over him was to be played the last stage of the intrigue
for the possession of the English kingship.

VIII

Edward was consecrated with pomp and ceremony
at Winchester, on the Easter Day of 1043. The auguries

were not good. A succession of bad years was spreading disaster throughout England, and Edward possessed no money of his own. There is no getting round or over the fact of bad seasons in an agricultural community : when the peasant is hit, the lord is hit with him, and no third person exists on whom to throw the burden. The earls were not in a position to be generous to Edward. Each probably wished to gain that precedence and ascendancy which would come of securing the king's friendly gratitude. Had one of them financed the king the others, in self defence, would have been compelled to follow suit. They agreed that none of them would do so. Another expedient had to be thought of.

The queen-mother was the obvious resource. Emma had been the centre of English life for very nearly forty years, first as the wife of Aethilred, then as the wife of Knut, and finally as the mother of Harthaknut and Edward. Official hands might record the succession of Harald and Harthaknut ; but she had been the real successor of Knut the Great. She had retained at least half of the contents of his treasury ; and most of the great gafol of 1041 remained in her hands. While she held it, she was unmistakably master of the situation. There was no reason for taxing an impoverished country while that immense sum, which of right belonged to the king, was available. The only difficulty was to get it.

The earls met at Gloucester, and arranged the *coup d'état*. It is easy to understand the basis on which agreement was established. They would be providing the king with a competence, saving their own depleted pockets, and at the same time disarming a very vigorous and ambitious woman who had pulled the strings of power for more than a generation. The northern earls probably disliked the tradition she represented. She stood for that connection with Normandy and the south which was still somewhat alien to Danish sympathies. All the earls must have felt that their relations with the king would be easier when Emma was removed from the political arena. In this they were wrong. Edward had sufficient ability to be stronger without her rigid and determined mind. As for Edward himself, he owed very little to his mother. She had not helped him much in his long years of exile. She showed no great desire to help him now. She had thrown in her lot with the enemies of his dynasty, and even if he had been recalled because he was her son, he had made a bad second to Harthaknut in her regard. He agreed to give his consent to the action of the earls.

Earl Godwin, earl Leofric, and earl Siward of Northumbria left Gloucester with their retinues and made a rapid advance on Winchester. They had formed their plans so secretly, and acted so swiftly, that Emma had no time to forestall their action. The great treasure was seized. It was a huge amount—the accumulation of many years. No harm was done to the old queen. She was allowed to live on at Winchester until she died in 1052, when she must have been at least seventy—a very great age in the rough and troublous times of the eleventh century. She never figured again in politics.

That this action was well thought out beforehand can be seen from the preliminary step which perhaps made it possible. The adviser behind the old queen was Stegan, Knut's chaplain. At Edward's coronation Stegan had been promoted to a bishopric and removed out of the way. After the downfall of Emma, it was Stegan's turn. He was deprived of his bishopric, and his possessions were seized on the ground that they were royal property illegally alienated from the crown. Edward did not rest content with the movable treasure of his mother. He confiscated all her lands, and regranted them.

IX

Edward has been systematically represented by modern writers as a feeble nonentity.[1] This is far from being the truth. He was an able and prudent man, very well aware of the difficulties of his position, but not always possessed of either the means or the opportunity to deal with them. In other days he might have been just such a man as Aethilstan.

Much of the apparent weakness he showed was due to the necessity of meeting—or attempting to meet—simultaneous and incompatible demands. His situation was complicated by the very progress of England under Knut's rule. There was no longer the same clear-cut distinction between the churchmen and the secular magnates that had marked the reign of his father. Men of Scandinavian descent, who did not lose their natural instincts and sympathies by an ecclesiastical training, were coming forward in the church—men of talent, whose talent was not of precisely the same type as that of Dunstan or Alphege. The backing these men possessed was not to be despised. In the alternation of his necessities, Edward leaned now to one side, now to another, seeking to keep his grasp upon power, and to steer a devious course between the obstacles.

From the first days of his reign, he sought to fill the high offices of the church with men in sympathy with his own aims. It was the same kind of policy which would at the present day lead a statesman to seek to control the newspaper press. The church, with its vast and uniform organization, was the supreme moulder of public opinion. When, in the year following his accession, archbishop Eadsine of Canterbury resigned, the king

[1] Even as an albino—a charge effectively disproved by Professor Karl Pearson in *Eng. Hist. Rev.*, xxv, p. 517 (July 1910).

agreed with earl Godwin to " split the difference " and consecrate Siward, the abbot of Abingdon, whose name is a sufficient indication of his ancestry. On the other hand, the king secured the nomination of one of his own chaplains, Heremon, to Sherborne, of Aethilstan to the vacant abbacy of Abingdon, and of Wulfric to the abbacy of Saint Augustine, Canterbury. Dull as these details may seem when related, they represent the scoring in the concealed struggle that was on foot.

Famine was stalking through England : and it was not the only danger threatening. Magnus, the son of Olaf of Norway, had made good his claim to the crown, and was preparing to turn the tables upon Denmark—a process which would involve his conquest of the whole of Knut's empire. Swein Astrid's son, Knut's nephew, the new king of Denmark, was finding considerable difficulty in holding his own against Magnus. In these circumstances, Edward could not risk a quarrel with earl Godwin, nor even any coolness in their relationship. As the head of the Thingmen, the earl could put upon the sea a fleet far transcending any within the power of the northern earls. Such a threat as a Norwegian war meant growing importance for Godwin. He could dictate his own terms. Edward married Godwin's daughter Eadgitha early in 1044.

X

The king's marriage was a link in an interesting chain of relationships. Godwin had married a daughter of Knut, and his claim to be an heir of Knut's dominion was, therefore, not much less than that of earl Ulf, who, by a similar marriage, had transmitted to his son Swein the right to Denmark. Godwin's path had not been quite so clear. Between him and the English throne, besides Harald and Harthaknut, had stood also Alfred and Edward, the sons of Aethilred, and another Edward, the surviving son of Edmund Ironside. Harald and Harthaknut had died. Godwin had had every motive for removing Alfred—and we need not doubt that he had done so. Edward, the son of Aethilred, was childless. Edward, the son of Edmund Ironside, was in Hungary, and therefore inaccessible. The existence of this other Edward was perhaps a very fortunate circumstance for the king : for Godwin was not likely to suffer the destruction of the Edward he knew, to throw the legitimate succession into the hands of an Edward he knew not of. The earl riveted a new link into his claims by his daughter's marriage to King Edward. If there were children to continue the royal line, they would be Godwin's grandchildren : if not, he still retained as sound a claim to England as earl Ulf had possessed to Denmark. A son of Godwin would possess exactly the same claim to England as Swein Astrid's son possessed to Denmark.

The most effective rein upon Godwin was the jealousy of the northern earls, Leofric and Siward. In the meantime, since the king did not wish to make the concessions which would be necessary, policy did not allow him to call too frequently upon their aid : and the northern earls were too far away to be a quite reliable check. Edward therefore had every motive to placate Godwin. For two years in succession the fleet lay at Sandwich, ready for action. King Swein Astrid's son, however, kept Magnus busy, and no Norwegian appeared.

CHAPTER XV

THE END OF A STORY

I

EDWARD was reaching out, meanwhile, for external help, and he found it in the obvious place, in Normandy, with which, both by kinship and by policy, he had affiliations. Edward's relations with Normandy are readily explainable. He and Duke William were close kinsmen, and therefore well acquainted with one another's existence, repute, and character. In the eleventh century the profession of a monarch might be classed among the dangerous and ill-paid occupations, and the trade union feeling among sovereign persons was proportionately strong. Edward and William shared youthful memories of a not dissimilar type : memories of trouble and worry, and of being hurried away by watchful guardians from dangerous situations and deplorable catastrophes. If William's memories had later on taken a more cheering turn, it was because he grew up into a man of extraordinary astuteness and energy—not to say violence—and had battered a way by mingled craft and ferocity to a position which the milder Edward could but envy.

It was natural that two men, so placed, should both of them feel much interest in the main intellectual trend of the day—the Cluniac movement which their great contemporary, Henry the Black of Germany, did so much to foster. It represented more even than a religious philosophy—it was an organized society devoted to the achievement of certain ecclesiastical ideals : and men such as William were quick to perceive the way in which the spirit and object of the Cluniacs could be made to

lift to a higher level the whole feeling entertained by
the world at large concerning monarchy. This is perhaps
not the right place in which to describe the movement
which originated from Cluny. It is enough to mark
the degree to which the Cluniac movement suggested a
cognate philosophy ; a stimulation of thought and a
stiffening of discipline in the attitude of men towards
the state as well as towards the church. Men like
William became ardent, and men like Edward became
moderate supporters of Cluny : but all alike saw that
the principle involved was the supremacy of the head
over the parts—the supremacy of the central unifying
principle over those great local magnates who threatened
to break society up into fragments.

It is fairly certain that Edward and William corresponded and exchanged views. The duke could not fail
to watch with interest the trend of affairs in England :
and there is plenty of evidence that he did so. He was
ready to advise and to help. Among the men who began
to take a prominent part in English affairs was Robert,
a Frenchman, and Ulf, a Norman. It is safe to suppose
that recommendation from William was among the
credentials which gained them the favour of the king.

II

King Edward continued his policy of seizing important
ecclesiastical positions by promoting his chaplains into
suitable vacancies. Leofric was given the see of Credi-
ton in 1046 ; Heca the bishopric of Selsey in 1047.
When, two years later, Ednoth of Oxford died, Ulf
received the see. Robert became bishop of London.
The king could not prevent Stegan from obtaining
Winchester ; but on the whole he managed to succeed
with most of the vacancies.

If a disinterested care for righteousness in the abstract be a virtue, Edward's policy was a good one. It was at least much more than a selfish struggle for personal or party advantage. The old English world of Alfred and Edgar had fallen for ever upon the field of Assingdon, and all the conciliatory measures of Knut could not permanently conceal the fact that England had been made Danish. For all their conversion, the strong traces of heathen social tradition—that is, of localism—lingered about the English Danes, and affected even the English themselves. A converted heathen was in some respects more dangerous than an unconverted one, for he helped to slacken the energies and to dilute the zeal of the faithful. Godwin and his sons were far more Danish in tradition than they were English. Edward could call upon nothing, if not upon the spirit of the new Cluniac movement, to counteract the slow drift back into a lethargic semi-barbarism. The task rested upon the king alone. No other power—no spontaneous movement—arose in England to do the work. The events which soon after followed showed the problem in a clear and dramatic form.

III

The point at which started the process destined to transform the system of government in England was represented by the episode of the abbess of Leominster. Swein, Godwin's son, on his return from an expedition to Wales, abducted the abbess of Leominster, kept her as long as he wished, and dismissed her again.

A taste for abbesses is rare ; and those men who possess it are of a particular and highly objectionable type. Swein must have known that the scandal would be far too serious to be passed over ; and that he chose to defy the consequences is sufficient evidence that power was passing into the hands of a new and dangerous kind of man. He was outlawed, together with the king's constable, Osgod Clapa. Godwin could not easily raise any objection ; and to do him justice there are no signs that he wished to do so. Swein took refuge at Bruges with Count Baldwin of Flanders—then the natural resort of all disreputable persons.

In the old days, Swein could have made himself a dangerous enemy ; but with the changes that were almost insensibly coming over Europe his opportunities in this respect were now somewhat limited. This very year of his exile, King Swein of Denmark sent urgent appeals to England, asking for fifty ships to help him against Magnus of Norway. They were refused. The bad seasons still continued ; England was in no position to bear the expense ; and to involve her in possible hostilities with Magnus of Norway seemed unwise. These were reasons good enough to save English statesmen from the need of asking themselves whether they wished to admit any liability to help Denmark, or any responsibility for her safety. King Swein was driven from his kingdom, and in the strange reverses of fortune the world beheld the realm of Knut the Great fall into the hands of the son of Olaf the Holy. But fortune was content with the gesture, and had other intentions in the sphere of practical politics. Magnus died before the year was out, and King Swein returned.

The successor of Magnus was one of the most formidable personalities of the age—Harald Hardcounsel, the ex-captain of the Varangian Guard at Constantinople, the lover of the empress Zoe ; a man who would have left a far greater repute behind him had his objectives been as steady and as well-founded as his methods were courageous and deft. He sent friendly messages to England. Swein again asked for English help, and was

T

again refused. Harald sent Lothin and Erling with an unofficial fleet, to see that England was kept engaged on its own affairs. They plundered the Isle of Wight, Sandwich, and the Essex ports : which brought the king's fleet out in pursuit. They disposed of the plunder in Bruges. Earl Swein went to Denmark ; but the Danish king did not care to hazard his chances of English help and English friendship by an alliance so doubtful, and the earl returned empty-handed.

Not only so, but Bruges itself became none too safe. The emperor had decided that the cup of the misdeeds of Baldwin was now full, and set his hosts into motion. Edward was requested to watch the sea-exits ; and accordingly the English fleet lay off Sandwich. Earl Swein came across to see the king, and to make, if he could, some attempt to get his sentence reversed. The opposition came from his own brothers, Harold and Biorn, who are not likely to have been prejudiced against him. Unless they surrendered the lands of Swein, which had been regranted to them, even a reversal of his sentence would have been useless to him. He went on to Bosham to wait.

IV

As soon as the fleet, its purpose accomplished, was dismissed, Godwin and Biorn sailed with forty-two ships to Pevensey.[1] Hither earl Swein came to meet them, and a conference took place. Swein seemed particularly anxious to secure the intercession of Biorn with the king, and at length Biorn consented to go to Sandwich, but apparently without undertaking any definite action on Swein's behalf. From the consequences as they later on

---

[1] Possibly this part of the fleet was booked to disperse at Hastings, a very old and important naval station. Pevensey is a walk from Hastings. Bosham as a port has, of course, long given way to Portsmouth.

revealed themselves, it is clear that Godwin also had been unable to make any promises. It would appear that Godwin returned home by road ; at any rate, Biorn accompanied Swein to Bosham, intending to go with him to Sandwich by sea.

Before he went on board, Biorn's suspicions were aroused. He declined to go. He was abducted by force. Instead of sailing to Sandwich, earl Swein coasted westward to Exmouth. There Biorn was murdered and buried. The Thingmen, as soon as they heard of Biorn's abduction, had followed from London. They were too late to save him, and could only search for his grave and bear back the body for solemn interment at Winchester, where Knut, the dead man's uncle, lay.

This second crime caused the hasty dispersal of Swein's fleet. No one was anxious to claim a share in the deed. Swein was outlawed afresh ; whereupon he returned to Bruges.

Other and separate considerations began to add their weight to the case of Swein. A council was held at London during the year, and it was decided to reduce the Thingmen. Nine crews were dismissed. For Godwin to oppose such a measure was difficult. The Danegeld, the permanent tax by which the Thingmen were supported, was the most hated of all taxes : and in view of the scandal connected with Swein, Godwin had lost some degree of influence. But the measure was a blow at his power.

Matters were not yet at a crisis, but they were rapidly drifting towards it. The next year marked a further stage in the struggle. Archbishop Eadsine of Canterbury died, whereupon Edward appointed Robert, bishop of London, to the vacancy, and sent him promptly to Rome to receive his pall. Sparhafoc, the abbot of Abingdon, one of the contrary party, was promoted to London : but naturally his consecration was obliged to wait until

Robert's return. The king then reversed the sentence of outlawry on earl Swein. The measure which constituted the price was the disbandment of the Thingmen and the complete abolition of the Danegeld.

V

Edward had been wonderfully adroit in the successive steps he had taken ; but Godwin was not a man likely to submit to defeat. Public opinion is, in all ages, the controlling factor in political action. Godwin could not take any step against the king's policy until a sufficient reason could be shown. So far, the occasion had been wanting. It was soon to arrive.

Archbishop Robert returned from Rome with his pall in June 1051. Sparhafoc lost little time in waiting upon him with the king's writ of appointment to the bishopric of London. Robert flatly refused to consecrate Sparhafoc, and maintained his refusal on the ground that the Pope had forbidden it. Unable to compel him, Sparhafoc returned to London and continued to hold the see without consecration. Robert's conduct plainly showed that the king's party felt themselves able to take a strong line. It probably did not pass unnoticed by the astute Godwin.

Somewhat later, Count Eustace of Boulogne arrived in England on a visit to Edward, whose sister he had married. Some obscurity rests over the facts concerning Eustace—an obscurity which accurately reflects the confusion which surrounded them at the time, and the partisan use made of them. Edward had in all likelihood granted to his guest, during his temporary stay in England, some of the royal rights of purveyance : the ready and simple means of entertaining him. The rights of purveyance were never popular in England ; and foreigners as a rule have been less popular still. The hated rights of purveyance, exercised by a detested alien, formed a combination almost sure to lead to trouble. On his journey back to Dover Eustace seems to have resolved to enforce his legal rights, and to take lodging in a place which suited him. The result was a really serious affray —practically a battle—in which twenty of the townsmen were wounded, and nineteen of the Frenchmen. Eustace hurried back to the king to explain and justify himself.

From the king's point of view, a serious infringement of his ancient prerogatives had occurred—an act of contempt for the royal dignity which could not be passed over. He required Godwin, as earl of Kent, to punish the offenders. The earl's opportunity had come !

A question such as that of Eustace, involving English domestic prejudices, could never be argued coldly and rationally. It afforded all the necessary means of appealing to unreasoning passion and of obscuring the facts. Godwin declined to proceed against the citizens of Dover. He did more than decline. Patriotism may be the last refuge of a scoundrel, but it is often the first resort of a traitor. Sure now that he had sufficient backing, he summoned a secret conference of his sons at Beverstone.

The conference was betrayed by some neighbouring Welshmen who were on the wrong side of the law, and who jumped at the chance of ingratiating themselves with the king. The nature and intention of the meeting were made plain. Edward, warned in time, sent to the northern earls for help.

They were, of course, unaware of what was happening, and they set out with their ordinary retinues. Before they arrived, the true state of affairs was disclosed. Godwin was in revolt. They sent back word for a general levy. It was perilously late in arriving, but it came in time.

VI

Godwin and his sons arrived at Langtree in Gloucester-shire with a great host. They sent the king an ultimatum demanding the surrender of Eustace and all the Frenchmen. Their demand was practically that Edward should abandon his policy, and the men, trained in continental schools, who were its instruments. Before the king was driven to any definite consent or refusal (the result of which would have been much the same in either case) earl Leofric, earl Siward, and earl Ralph were at hand with the levy of the north, only too eager to come to grips with the Wessex host. Had the Thingmen still surrounded Edward, Godwin could have seduced them. He could not seduce the northern earls ; and the king knew it.

Edward's chief task was to restrain them. A civil war was of no advantage to England. He was old enough and wise enough to know that nothing was to be gained by the mutual destruction of the best men in the kingdom ; nor had he any interest in destroying one party in order to hand over supremacy to the other. It was finally agreed to discuss the matter at a General Council of the Realm in London.

There was prudence in this. Godwin was playing upon emotions very liable to cool. By the time he arrived at Southwark, his army had dwindled. He demanded hostages for his safety before he entered the Council. They were refused, and with good reason. Godwin had no right to stipulate for provisions which would anticipate and render null any decision adverse to himself. He clearly foresaw that he had no chance of gaining a favourable decision, and he left by night. The following morning the Council went into session. Godwin's whole family was outlawed. He took ship at Bosham with Swein, Tosti, and Gyrth, and went to Bruges, while Harold

and Leofwin fled to Bristol. The king issued orders for
the pursuit and arrest of Harold, but without effect. He
and Leofwin made good their escape to Ireland.

Godwin's partisans were involved in his fall. Edward
dismissed the queen, putting her into the custody of his
sister at Wherwell. Abbot Sparhafoc was removed from
the see of London, which was given to William, the king's
chaplain. The earldom of Wessex was broken up. Odda
was invested with Devon, Cornwall, Somerset, and
Dorset, while Harold's earldom of East Anglia went to
Alfgar, the son of earl Leofric.

VII

And now the *deus ex machina* appeared : for promptly
upon these events Duke William of Normandy crossed the
sea and paid Edward a visit of state. There were very
many reasons for his visit : Godwin was out of the way,
and William had something to speak of which he preferred
to discuss in person.

The weakness of Edward's position was that he had
not sufficient force at his command to defend the creative
elements in England from the destructive. Persuasion
alone was insufficient to carry out the policy he had set
himself to follow. William, who was in sympathy with
the policy, was both able and ready to use force for his
own purposes ; but he could not create the necessary
temperament in Edward, nor spin for him the requisite
web of personal influence. The Norman duke must have
had many thoughts. There would come a time when
Edward would be dead ; and what would then be the
fate of this country, so obstinately sectional, so less and
less likely, with every year that passed, to act vigorously
as one undivided whole ? Edward, whatsoever his faults,
was the link that held it together. When he died, the link

would disappear. And a strong and vigorous man, with thoroughly up-to-date ideas, might seize the control of a prize that was unable to unite in resistance.

The question was perhaps only whether Godwin or William would be the man. But while Godwin never showed any sign of intelligence, William possessed the mind of a jurist and a statesman, able to see things from every side and to judge their value. And William cannot possibly have been unconscious that he wielded a power which as a political organization was of higher rank than any controlled by Godwin. A feudal aristocracy, such as William was prepared to table, could fight and govern England not only better, but more cheaply than a comitatus : and the cheapness was a very important factor in the case.

VIII

Meanwhile, the comitatus was active and vigorous. It must have been now that Harold founded his House-men,[1] those famous successors to the Thingmen, organized on the same model, and not impossibly composed of the same men. In tradition, in tactics, and in excellence the Housemen were identical with their predecessors.

Godwin left Bruges next spring, and prospected along the narrow seas, where earl Odda and earl Ralph were on the watch. Bad weather drove Godwin back to Bruges ; and the king's fleet presently ran out of its term of service. Although it was supposed to be promptly replaced by a fresh instalment of the levy, none arrived, so that the ships at Sandwich dispersed, leaving the seas unguarded. Godwin set sail again, and steered for the Isle of Wight.

---

[1] The Irish ports were very convenient places for the discharged Thingmen to wait ; and Harold's dash for Ireland may not have been purposeless. Edward was anxious to prevent his arrival there.

His course was not accidental. Harold was leaving Ireland at the same time, and, after touching at Porlock, doubled Land's End and came up to Portland. Father and son joined forces there, and got into touch with their supporters. The combined fleets moved eastward, everywhere seizing all ships found in the harbours, and persuading or terrorising men, until they came to the Thames mouth. The king sent for aid : but he was now dealing with a fleet, not with the local agricultural militia of inland counties. Its movements were swift and skilled.

Godwin reached London. He entered into negotiations with the citizens, who gave way. The king's ships were surrounded. The king himself was very unwilling to fight. Stegan came forward as intermediary, arranged the exchange of guarantees, and conducted the negotiations.

The Frenchmen were under no illusions. Archbishop Robert and bishop Ulf lost no time in making a bid for safety. They cut their way out of Aldgate, galloped for the Essex coast, and took the first ship they could get. Some fled one way, some another. They were wise. Godwin had returned to more than his old supremacy. No effective resistance was offered. At the Council which soon after assembled, he cleared himself formally from all charges, his outlawry was reversed, the queen was received back by Edward, and all Frenchmen were put beyond the pale of the law. Neither Siward nor Leofric had time to act.

Godwin's period of supremacy was short. He was already a sick man. At Winchester, the following Easter, he was dining at the king's table when he was seized with a stroke, and fell against the foot-rail. He was carried into the king's room, and it was thought that he would recover. But he died on the Thursday after Easter, never having spoken nor moved again.

IX

The death of Godwin at this particular juncture was a master-stroke on the part of Providence. It made certain that he should never need to demand from the northern earls the return of Harold's earldom of East Anglia ; it averted the civil war which would have torn England in consequence, and it secured all the conditions and limitations necessary to the battle of Hastings and its results.

Godwin's power had not been purely a personal power ; he had been a party leader rather than a man of exceptional individuality. His eldest son, Harold, at once stepped into his place. Harold was a far abler man than Godwin, though neither so prudent nor so successful. Part of the contrast between the two men lies in the different functions they appropriated to themselves. Godwin was a forerunner ; one of those men, fairly common in every age, who devote themselves to the task of paving the way for a successor—never themselves reaping where they have sown, nor expecting to do so ; perhaps not even wishing to do so. Harold was the man for whom Godwin's work had been accomplished ; and Harold's task was to reap.

As a man who actually wore the crown of England, and swayed her destinies, Harold has a claim upon our attention. Our means of penetrating the secret of his character are few ; for most of our knowledge of it we have to depend upon inference from his actions. But as far as we can carry this method of interpretation, certain broad outlines seem to be clear and assured, even though the details can never be filled in. He was an active, energetic, ambitious man, self-confident and conscious of his strength : he seems to have been brought up to feel himself the destined heir to England. We never see in him any signs of doubt or hesitation. In this connection it is well to remember that his ancestry was an unusually distinguished one, though on the Danish, not on the English side. He was the grandson of King Swein Forkbeard, and the great-grandson equally of King Harald Bluetooth and King Burislaf of Wendland. On the other hand he was not a man of original ideas or of intellectual force. The battle of Hastings has such an appearance of being an extraordinary accident that it is difficult to divest ourselves of the expectation that Harold, if he had lived, would have been a great king. But there is no evidence of any sort whatsoever to justify this expectation. His energy was that of a man who knew nothing beyond the provincial politics of his day. He ranks with King Stephen and Richard III rather than with the great Normans or Plantagenets. He was a first-rate captain of Janissaries, and a good party chief.

This was the man who now succeeded to Godwin's earldom of Wessex. From the first he followed a policy of conciliation. The powerful Mercian interest was placated by the confirmation of Harold's former earldom of East Anglia to Leofric's son Alfgar. Stegan, Knut's chaplain and Emma's, took the archbishopric of Canterbury. From this time forward, King Edward was a figure-head—a king without power.

X

The death of Godwin seemed to be the signal for great changes, as if the time had come for a general clearing of the stage against the great events that were to follow. Earl Siward led his expedition into Scotland against Macbeth, in which his losses were severe. Both his son Osbern and his nephew Siward the Younger fell. The earl did not long survive these catastrophes.

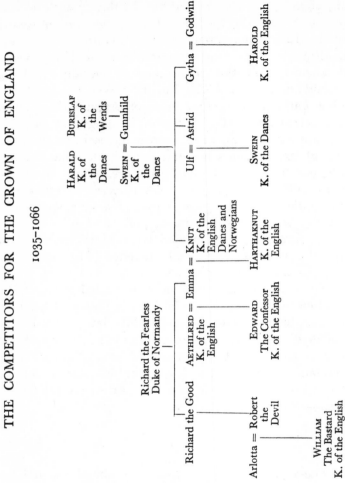

THE COMPETITORS FOR THE CROWN OF ENGLAND
1035–1066

He died at York the next year. His exit, and the circumstances attending it, considerably affected the balance of power in England. Leofric now confronted Harold without the help of the powerful Northumbrian.

Harold's activity showed that he had far-reaching plans for the future. His first step was to secure the

Northumbrian earldom for Tosti : while Alfgar was charged with treason, and outlawed. Alfgar promptly fled to Wales, organized an army, and called upon the Irish wickings for help. Harold was compelled to give way and restore him : at least, for the time being. The ecclesiastical appointments fell more and more into the hands of Harold—whose preferences were not Cluniac. His own chaplain, Leofgar, who got Hereford, was a typical fighting priest, far more a secular baron than a cleric ; and Leofgar found his rightful end when he was slain in a Welsh war, soon after his appointment. Men were dying off. Earl Odda ended his days in the retreat of a monastery. Edward Aethiling, returning from Hungary, died, and was buried in London. Leofric died. Earl Ralph died. Bishop Heca died : and Aethilric got his see. The struggle with Alfgar continued. He was again put out of the law ; and again the Welsh brought him back. Stegan at last, after long delay, received his pall from Rome, and became in full form archbishop of Canterbury.

Harold turned his attention to the Welsh problem, which so continually troubled him. Wales was invaded, and King Griffin slain. From this, however, had to be deducted the fact that Tosti was turned out of Northumberland by a general revolt. Harold was unable to reconcile the quarrel. Morker, Alfgar's son, was given the earldom, and Tosti went to Bruges. As the year waned, last of all King Edward died. His last act was the consecration of the new abbey of Westminster. Harold was accepted as king.

XI

As if the death of Edward had broken a spell, the waiting forces were unleashed, and England became the centre of a fierce struggle for his crown. Harold had it safely upon his head ; but it became clear that he would need to fight for it. Edward left no heir. The young Edgar, the grandson of Edmund Ironside, was a child incapable of taking part in the contest. It was fought out by three fierce and formidable men—Harold, Knut's nephew ; Harald Hardcounsel, king of Norway ; and William the Bastard, duke of Normandy. They were all of them ready. Before the year was half over, two were dead and the third sat triumphant on the throne of England.

XII

We are too apt to think vaguely of these ancient times as if the men who lived then had no means of acquiring accurate information. They possessed it as much as we do. Peasants were then what peasants are now, and statesmen and soldiers were much the same as they are to-day. The pace was slower, but that was all.

It was clear enough that the man who played his card last would be the likeliest to take the trick. Harold Godwin's son, to be victorious, would need to fight at least two great battles, and win them both. It was possible that he might do so. He was no Aethilred. His Housemen were trained professional fighting-men, modelled carefully on the pattern of Knut's Thingmen, whose direct successors they were. He himself was half a Dane by blood ; and in training, tradition, and temper wholly Danish. Harald Hardcounsel knew what he had to deal with. He lay in Scottish ports, resting and re-fitting—and waiting.

Harold Godwin's son followed the Danish strategy. He assembled his fleet at the Isle of Wight, ready for all events. William lay close : he did not intend to risk a fight at sea with what was to all intents a Danish fleet. At last the season wore so late—it was already autumn—that Harold could no longer keep the levy in being. It had to be let go home to harvest ; and the equinoctial storms were at hand. In fact, the fleet lost many ships on its way to Sandwich.

The pressure that forced Harold from his position similarly forced one of his opponents. Harald Hard-counsel now sailed south and entered the Humber. Three hundred ships came up the Ouse towards York. The earls Edwin and Morker raised the northern levies. Instead of waiting for the king and his Housemen they elected to fight a pitched battle on their own account in defence of the city. How little the two earls were fitted to direct the fate of nations became visible when they faced one of the great contemporary soldiers of continental Europe. Two miles from York, at Fulford, Harald took ground with the Ouse on his left and a dyke on his right, beyond which lay deep fen. He took the left wing, near the Ouse, for his own station, and concentrated his main force there.

The Northumbrians, when they advanced, found it easy to drive in the weak Norse right that lay along the dyke, and this they proceeded to do. As soon as Harald judged them to be sufficiently far forward, he ordered the charge to be blown and his banner advanced. Swinging half round to his right, his assault, delivered with all his force, cut the army of the earls in two. By this oblique thrust, moreover, both halves of the Northumbrian army were penned, one against the river, and the other against the dyke. The dead in the latter place lay so thick, that it was possible to cross the dyke dry-shod.

By this one blow, Harald had Northumbria utterly at his feet. York was his, and all the north with it. He demanded hostages, and let it be known that there was nothing to fear from him if Northumbrians would march

south in his company. He took up his quarters at
Stamford Bridge, until the hostages should be delivered.

This was Wednesday. Swift as he had been, a still
swifter blow was struck at him. Harold Godwin's son
had the news almost instantly, and was on the road.
Marching night and day, he was at Tadcaster by Sunday,
and on Monday he was at York. It was one of those
rapid mounted-infantry marches which Hingwar had
first taught his countrymen to make. Harold came to
Stamford Bridge ahead of all news of his approach. It was
a warm sunny day—the 25th of September—and Harald
Hardcounsel, starting out early for the meeting at York,
at which the hostages were to be placed in his hands,
had passed the word that defensive armour need not be
worn. He had proceeded just far enough to be out of
reach of his fleet, when dust clouds began to rise ahead,
and through them came the glitter of arms. Hasty
conferences failed to elicit any explanation of the presence
of this strange army. The Norwegian king divined the
fatal and incredible truth—Harold Godwin's son was
at hand.

This was the biter bit indeed ; for renowned though
Harald Hardcounsel might be for his towering height
and his adventurous daring, he was still more renowned
for the astuteness which had brought him safely through
a hundred difficulties in the past. Here he was, beaten
at his own game and caught in his shirt ! What followed
is a very famous scene in the drama of English history.
A group of splendidly armed men rode up to the Northmen.

Said their spokesman : " Is earl Tosti in this army ? "

Tosti answered : " You will find him here."

The spokesman said : " Harold your brother sends
greeting, and adds that you shall have pardon, and the
earldom of Northumbria, if you will come back to him ;

and if that is not enough, he will give you the third part
of his realm to rule over jointly with himself."

We must remember that Tosti, like Harold, was a
grandson of Knut, an heir of Denmark and England,
and a possible candidate for the crown. It was highly
necessary to get him away from Harald, or alternatively,
to create suspicion between them. The good faith of
this offer was thus not absolutely beyond doubt.

" Things might have been different if that had been
said before," answered Tosti. " But if I accept, what
will he give King Harald ? "

The spokesman answered in the immortal words :
" Seven feet of England, or as much more as so long-
limbed a man may need."

" Go back," said Tosti, " and bid King Harold get
ready for battle. It shall never be said that I came
here with King Harald Hardcounsel and left him in the
lurch."

The horsemen rode back. Presently Harald Hardcounsel said to Tosti : " Who was that man ? "

" King Harold Godwin's son," answered Tosti.

Harald said : " That was concealed from me. If I
had known it, he would not have lived to tell the story
of our death."

" He was imprudent," answered Tosti, " but he
came in outward kindness to me ; and I would rather
he were my slayer, than I his."

Harald turned to his men. The remark about his
length of limb seems to have rankled. " A little fellow,
that," he said, " but sits up straight.' '

And in all this we have the character of Harold
Godwin's son neatly portrayed. He never quite opened
his hand ; he never fully convinced ; he never absolutely satisfied. He neither perfectly prevented beforehand nor completely cured afterward.

U

XIII

On the day of Stamford Bridge the Danish tradition had no opportunity of proving itself a mightier thing than the Varangian, but it certainly proved that it possessed a much greater gift for getting its blow in first. A deadly blow it was. All day long the Housemen rode round the bristling ranks of Norwegian spearmen, never closing, but shooting them down one by one, and cutting off stragglers. Unarmoured, and on foot, they could make no reply. Harald Hardcounsel, beaten in craft, saw that unless he could succeed by some other means they must all perish. He himself headed, sword in hand, the onslaught that attempted to get to close quarters with the Housemen. It was in vain. He was shot down, together with most of those who shared the venture. Abandoned, by his death, to their own re-sources, the Northmen defended a gradually shrinking circle until help could reach them. It came at last—mailed men from the ships who could grapple hand to hand with the Housemen. It came too late ; and so fast had the rescuers hurried that they were exhausted before they arrived. Their attack was beaten off, and the Housemen continued to ride round the contracting circle. Many of the defenders died of exhaustion and suffocation. At last it was every man for himself. We may place during the evening flight to Stamford Bridge the famous episode of the Northman who held the bridge against all comers. He could not be shot down. At last he was slain by a spear-thrust from below the bridge. Only darkness ended the battle.

Harold Godwin's son used his victory with modera-tion. He exacted oaths of good faith, and let the son of the Norwegian king depart with twenty-four ships. He had no time to waste—for now the second blow fell.

XIV

Two days after the battle of Stamford Bridge William had seized his opportunity and had ferried his army across the Channel. On the morning of September 28 the Norman fleet and transports safely assembled off Pevensey. The design was curiously irregular in conception. To land at Pevensey is a plan conforming to no recognized rules. But William had done something daringly new—he had transported the trained cavalry horses necessary for feudal knights of the continental model : and he required a little time while they recuperated after the voyage. Nervous he doubtless was. Tradition had it that William—always a heavy and clumsy man—missed his footing and fell on his hands and knees as he stepped off the gang-plank on to the beach. The Normans had no time to worry over the evil omen, for as he scrambled to his feet one of his men remarked : " Well, duke, you already have some of England in your hands ! " [1]—and the incident passed off satisfactorily.

Harold had the news not earlier than the first day of October, and returned south as rapidly as he could. By October 6 he was back in London. So fast he moved, that only mounted men could keep up with him : but after the disaster of Fulford he could hardly expect help from the north, and he was no doubt counting on the levy of southern England for all the extra support he would need. The main work, as before, would fall on the Housemen. For nearly a week he remained in London, resting the Housemen and waiting for the levy. On the 12th he advanced to find William. He pitched camp about seven miles from Hastings.

[1] This is William of Malmesbury's version of the famous episode. Sir James Ramsay considers it probably the earlier form.

For two days neither he nor William made any movement. Harold was strongly advised to retreat upon
London, devastating the country behind him, and to
make his stand in the London neighbourhood. He declined this perhaps prudent, but certainly expensive
advice. There were advantages, as well as disadvantages,
in the position he occupied. The Housemen had made
two tremendous forced marches, and the general levy
was not present in anything like full strength to support
them. But they had all the prestige of recent triumph to
steel their hearts. If the Normans were fresh, they were
also to some extent untested. They represented a new
military system which had yet to establish its unquestionable superiority to the Danish methods. Harold was not
likely to be frightened by mere novelty : and in all
probability he was confident that he had more than a
merely reasonable chance of success, especially if he could
rely upon fighting a defensive battle. The Normans were
living upon the country. In a very short time, lack of
supplies would force them to fight upon Harold's terms.
No advantages that could be secured by retreat upon
London outweighed these.

One by one his calculations began to prove true. Two
days after his arrival, William left Hastings early in the
morning with the whole Norman force. The battle was
at hand ; and it would be, for Harold, a defensive action
on a position especially chosen and prepared to his design.

XV

The ground which Harold had chosen [1] was carefully
selected for a variety of reasons. He had two main

[1] The following description of the battle of Hastings is based mainly
upon the Hon. Francis Baring's careful study (with map) in *Domesday
Tables*, together with Mr. Fowke's *Bayeux Tapestry*, and Mr. J. H. Round's
Feudal England, p. 359 *et seq.*

objects : one was to break the charge of the Norman knights ; the other was to prevent the battle from slipping round the English flanks. The position was therefore so chosen, that the Normans were guided straight upon a prepared front. The habit of field-fortification had been a Danish tradition ever since the days of Hingwar. Too strong a front might have given William the inconvenient idea of not fighting at all. Harold wished the Normans to fight ; and since they would fight mounted, he wished them to arrive at the top of the hill with the sting of their speed drawn, and to be stayed there for the fraction of a moment. He therefore had a light field-work made across the whole English position [1] sufficient to produce such a momentary pause. Behind this were ranged, along the whole length, the Housemen. At Stamford Bridge the battle had been won before it was fought. This time the fighting would be in earnest, and the Housemen would use the tactics to which they were trained.

The battle of Hastings, the last great battle fought by the old type of comitatus, is also the only one which has been plentifully illustrated for us by nearly contemporary hands. We are not left to grope wholly in the dark. In the Bayeux tapestry the brilliant sunset of a historical age suddenly reveals to our astonished eyes a glimpse of the actual men whose story we have been following. As they stood on the battlefield on the morning of October 14 we see the Housemen—those towering, slender, clean-shaven young men, with the tapering fingers and exquisite feet—in their loose combinations of ring mail, their conical helms and general well-tailored turn-out. They numbered between two and three thousand.

[1] Dr. Hodgkin and Sir Charles Oman, experienced judges, agree in accepting the idea that some kind of light field-work covered the English front. The presumption that it existed is very strong. Archer, *Eng. Hist. Rev.*, ix, pp. 22–25. Gen. E. Renouard James, *Royal Engineers' Journal*, vol. v, No. 1, p. 26 (Jan. 1907).

Behind the entrenchment they were drawn up, probably in four lines. The first line was armed with the single-bladed battle-axe, with a haft five feet long. This axe was one of the most formidable weapons ever invented by human ingenuity, and it was the speciality of the fighting men trained on the model of the Jomsborg guild. It was wielded left-handed—so that no shield was of much service against it. Used by a trained man, it could hew down nearly anything on two legs or four. As the axe needed room for its swing, the front rank cannot have been spaced closer than some six feet apart. Each man, like a goal-keeper, had charge of a certain space through which he was to let nothing pass. Some paces behind, the three supporting ranks stood shoulder to shoulder, covered with their great kite-shaped shields, and armed with stabbing spears—very much like King Teia the Ostrogoth, centuries before, at the battle of Vesuvius. Behind these, again, were the masses of the general levy, the English thanes of the old-fashioned type ; a somewhat various and—by the newer standards—not fully trained body of men. Packed close, with spear and sword, they may have formed some eleven or twelve ranks, the whole army totalling perhaps a little over ten thousand men.

The task of the axemen of the front rank was to bring down everything that came against them. To wield the axe with effect, they needed both hands, and therefore carried no shield. The task of the supporting ranks of Housemen was to relieve and replace the axemen when necessary, and to finish off all that fell or got past. The rest of the English were prepared to facilitate the work by gathering, passing forward and delivering every kind of missile that was likely to embarrass a Norman. The attention of the axemen was wholly concentrated upon the charging horsemen. They did not attend to anything upon the ground.

This was the defensive formation on which Harold
Godwin's son staked the crown of England. The Normans
had no illusions about its strength.

XVI

In the early morning of October 14, the Normans,
having risen by the light of a moon five days past the
full, set out at six o'clock from Hastings, taking the
road along the ridge where the road to Battle now runs.
At half-past six the sun rose. William halted at Heche-
land, two miles from Battle Hill, in order to inspect his
men by daylight. Proceeding on, they deployed at the foot
of Battle Hill, the Bretons and Normans wheeling left off
the road, the Franks wheeling right. They were arranged
in a roughly geographical order, so that neighbours were
more or less together : and they numbered some eight or
ten thousand men.

Here William, excited and nervous, struggled into his
own armour. It turned out that he had got it on back
to front ; but he only laughed, and said that all his luck
was good luck. This being satisfactorily settled, business
was proceeded with.

It was about nine o'clock in the morning when the
deployment began. The Normans formed two lines, of
archers followed by mailed knights working with them.
Later ages would have considered these knights light or
medium cavalry.

When William at length gave the word, and the
trumpets blew, the Norman archers began to ascend the
hill. They were commissioned to annoy the English front
and tempt it to break its order, so that the knights could
charge it : but from the first their shooting was drowned
by the cloud of missiles hurled by the English. Darts,
throwing-axes, and hurling hammers drove them back.

The knights instantly advanced to their support, and since they were equipped only for hand-to-hand fighting, they closed upon the unbroken English front.

For six hours, on that October day, the mailed and

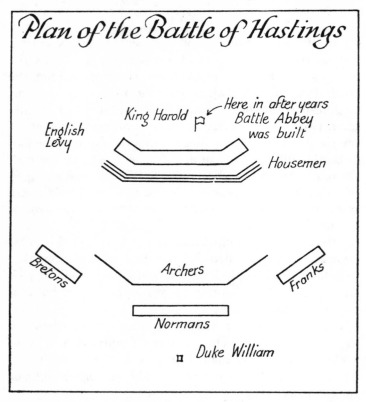

mounted continental knights rode again and again upon the ranks of the Housemen ; again and again they were beaten off by the five-foot axe and the spears and darts of the massed supporting ranks. As the morning wore, the axemen warmed to the work, and hewed down everything they touched. Although earl Gyrth and earl Leofwin fell in the early struggle, the Bretons were the first to feel the strain. Losing their nerve, they were seized with panic at the growing energy of the axemen, and bolted down the hill in disgraceful flight. The panic spread. The Normans themselves recoiled. The whole line gave back. The death of Gyrth and Leofwin meant that the English control was now becoming disorganized ; for after the fugitives, in defiance of Harold's strict injunctions, came a rush of pursuing English ; and the rout rolled to the foot of the hill.

The battle of Hastings was all but a hair's breadth won by Harold in those moments when the stream of fugitives poured down, some of them crying that the duke was dead. It was the supreme crisis of William's life, and he rose to meet it. Charging forward into the mass of falling men and somersaulting horses, he lifted his helmet so that his face could be seen, and thundered : " Look at me, all of you ! I am yet alive, and by the help of God will win this battle." If ever the daemonic energy of a single man held and turned the minds of others, it probably did so then. The rout was checked, stopped, and rallied. The reaction of feeling brought the Normans back into the fight fiercer than ever. William himself led the counter-attack that now fell upon the English pursuit. The pursuers were surrounded and destroyed to the last man.

XVII

The Housemen closed their ranks, until no sign remained of the loss which had befallen the defenders, and the struggle began afresh : but it now began to turn slowly to the advantage of the attack. The force of the Norman onslaught was met with an unbroken front, but by degrees the wear and tear revealed itself. The line of the Housemen was successfully breached ; and though it was at once repaired, the duke could see that he was making headway. He ordered the Franks on the right wing to do with intention what the Bretons on the left had done without intention. A feigned flight by the Franks twice succeeded (again in defiance of Harold's orders) in attracting large English pursuits. Both were surrounded and destroyed. The Housemen continued steady. All attack was concentrated upon them. Still they impregnably held their own.

At length William resorted to the old Norwegian tactics. He massed his bowmen afresh and ordered them to shoot high. The axe-hurlers and spear-throwers of the English were now shrunk in numbers, and had perhaps run out of supplies ; for they could no longer interfere with the Norman archers. The falling arrows were a decisive factor. Harold fell mortally wounded. The axemen, fighting unshielded, were slain or driven back into the ranks. Once the axemen were got out of the way, breaches were driven into the line of the Housemen ; through one of which a party of Normans penetrated as far as the standard, and slew the wounded Harold. The Housemen, knowing that all was lost, fought on. Dusk began to descend. A stream of English fugitives, on horseback or on foot, set north-westward. The defenders were melting. Still the Housemen fought, one by one toppling and falling where they stood. Night came down ; and Duke William could definitely ascertain that he was the victor. A false alarm arose up at Malfosse ; but on the open hillside the Housemen were lying, as by the long tradition every comitatus should, round their dead king. There is no record that any of them ran. Few battles in English history were more ferociously contested, or won by a margin more narrow and doubtful. The comitatus did not decay. It perished at Hastings in the height of its power and pride. It was destroyed by an institution stronger than itself.

When, that evening, Duke William knelt among his knights and barons to return solemn thanks for his victory, one age of English history had passed irrevocably away, and a new one had begun. English thane and Danish Thingman, all the old world that they represented, were gone, never to return ; and in their place had arisen the baron and the knight. The Middle Ages had arrived.

INDEX